To Lorraine
I wish you all success on y
journey
Enjoy

BUSINESS SKILLS?

DON'T BE DAFT I AM A LAWYER!

BUSINESS SKILLS? DON'T BE DAFT I AM A LAWYER!

What you need and why you need it

Ann Page

This book is not intended to provide personalised legal, regulatory, financial or professional ethics advice. The Author specifically disclaims liability, loss or risk which is incurred as a consequence (directly or indirectly) of the use and application of the content of this book.

Cover design and typesetting by Ashdown Creative.

ISBN 978-1-9162992-0-7

This book is dedicated to all those lawyers
who are forging their own path, or thinking of doing so
whether in Yorkshire or elsewhere.

ACKNOWLEDGEMENTS

All those Yorkshire Stars who gave their valuable time to be interviewed for my book.

Rosemary Heslop, my sister for all her support both personal and business. In particular, she has provided valuable insights and assistance on the contents of this book. As well, I as a good sister, agreed with her title suggestion and so my book was named.

Emma Pearmaine President of Leeds Law Society and Managing Partner of Ridley Hall Solicitors for agreeing to read an early version and provide a Foreword to this book.

Jake Fox Managing Director – Professional Risks at J M Glendenning (Insurance Brokers) Limited for his appreciated contribution to Section 4 Chapter 1.

The team at **Ashdown Creative** for all their hard work in making this book come alive.

Andy Pickering, my blog copywriter for proof reading and his input to the resilience portion in Section 4 Chapter 4.2.

Tiffany Kay, my coach for her feedback on an early version of this book and general business support.

Lee Jackson Professional Speaker for his advice and support on the self-publishing route for this book.

Jon Whittle LexisNexis for all his valuable reports and permission to quote from the contents in this book. Aiming to explore and investigate the issues facing the legal market, the **LexisNexis Bellwether report** series conducts ground-breaking market research in order to advise, guide, and offer insights to independent law firms and contribute to the discourse on their future. To read the reports in full visit – www.lexisnexis.co.uk/businessoflaw

Sonia Kellar, law student for transcribing most of the interviews when the transcription software couldn't cope.

CONTENTS

SECTION 5: **WHAT DOES THE FUTURE HOLD?**

SECTION 6: **THE YORKSHIRE LEGAL STARS WHO HAVE FORGED THEIR OWN PATH**

APPENDIX A: **RESOURCES TO ENABLE YOU TO MASTER YOUR BUSINESS SKILLS TO SERVE MORE CLIENTS PROFITABLY**

FOREWORD

As Managing Director of Ridley and Hall, a Yorkshire Law Firm delivering direct to consumers legal services locally and nationally, I am always interested to gain an insight into others approach to the business of law and opportunities which could present to us inside and outside of the legal profession. I speak to Managing Partners/ Directors of law firms regularly in my role as President of Leeds Law Society and I am consistently impressed and enthused by their innovative visions, strategies and business plans.

The Stars in Ann's book are 'real' and that makes all the difference. It is off putting when presented with perfection which few of us can aspire to and Ann's stars give a very 'real' insight into their motivation, method and experiences in business, which are truly relatable and inspiring.

Ann has taken a practical approach to helping her reader to understand clients, how to develop products and services, consider pricing, business planning and the importance of leadership. There is something for every reader to take away.

By Emma Pearmaine
President of Leeds Law Society
Managing Partner Ridley Hall

INTRODUCTION

Whilst I have been teaching and coaching lawyers on business skills since 2003, I have noticed since 2013 there has been a significant growth in lawyers leaving mainstream firms to start up their own business and/ or become a consultant solicitor.

This also coincides with my own business journey as around that time, I would move from predominantly being a 'freelancer' (for large legal training companies both here and internationally) and focus on building my own business in my beautiful home county of Yorkshire. So www.yorkshirecoursesforlawyers.co.uk was born.

This book is about business skills for lawyers who run their own practice or would like to. I was originally only going to interview ten people and add their stories. In fact nearly 50 lawyers who were doing amazing things were contacted with 29 interviews being conducted including my own. These interviews took place predominately between July and October 2018 with two more in 2019. Therefore this book contains all our business journeys as we navigate the changing legal landscape or move out of law altogether.

Interviewees have ranged from a complete 2018 start up, **Simon**, right through those who have been managing their firms for years such as **Peter**. I have also included some lawyers who used their legal expertise and experience to move into different fields within Yorkshire, for example: **Cathy** who now runs her own electrical and property business – to give you a flavour of what is possible.

You might notice that even though there are so many lawyers who have spread their wings to realise their vision and dreams in the UK, I have only interviewed those locally based in my beautiful county of Yorkshire.

Given that nearly all the interviews took place in 2018, the interviewees have developed their businesses significantly since then. **As there is always a gap between when they talked to me and when my book gets published to land in your hands –be aware they have not let the grass grow under their feet and neither should you!**

OVERVIEW OF THE YORKSHIRE LEGAL STARS WHO HAVE FORGED THEIR OWN PATH

As mentioned 29 out of the 50 contacted completed the interviews. 14 were legal business owners with a team, plus four more were using the consultant model. Of the fourteen Legal business owners with teams, two are owned by a husband-and-wife team who are both solicitors. Six Sole Practitioners have been interviewed who in the main operate on their own (not including any support staff they may employ), one of who is a husband-and-wife team (the latter being a different professional). Four Yorkshire Stars run a consultancy model business delivering legal services, and five have left the law to start up a different type of business.

22 of the Yorkshire Stars were niche (including the non-legal businesses) and six offered several different legal services.

Legal sectors covered include:

- Business sales and purchases including commercial property: **Noreen**
- Commercial Property: **Claire**
- Construction and Commercial Property: **Bill**
- Employment: **Jodie**, **Samira** and **Simon**
- Family: **James** and **Jill**
- Family and Employment: **Laura**
- Inheritance Disputes only: **Martin**
- Intellectual Property (contentious and non-contentious): **Liz**
- Litigation, Commercial and Risk Business Solutions including an educational and law-tech approach: **Gary**
- Litigation and insolvency: **John**
- Mixed Legal Services: **Andrew**, **Ian** & **Matt**, **Peter**, **Richard** and **Thomas** – dental sector niche
- Residential Property – Conveyancing: **Jade** and Disputes – **Geoff**)
- Wills and Powers of Attorney: **Jane**
- Wills, Powers of Attorney and Probate: **Rachel**.

The business areas covered in the book outside legal practice are **Andrea** (coach focused on freeing your innate potential) **Ann** (author, motivational business trainer and coach), **Cathy** (electrical business) **Kate** (supporting non–legal professionals working in the family justice sector) **Kirstie** (providing part-time legal directors for business) and **Miguel** (in-house legal recruitment). Whilst not interviewed for this book, one of my clients has left the profession to become a Business Analyst and is really enjoying it. So the sky really is the limit! I am aware of other stars outside Yorkshire but had to draw a line somewhere!

These Stars have shared their inspiring business journeys including the 'highs' and the 'lows, their challenges and their success in a rapidly shifting business environment. **The Stars have not let that stop them from creating their own destinies.**

Business and the law do not stay still so change continues to be a major factor for any business. This being the case, I have avoided including any statistics about this sector or any focus on tech law as this will depend on when you start and what field you wish to run a business in.

Section 6 contains their stories of how these business owners are realising and managing their vision and business during this uncertain times at the time of the interviews (2018). **Again I reiterate that Section 6: Chapter 6.1 documenting their journeys is a 'snapshot' in time.**

WHO IS THIS BOOK AIMED AT?

This book's primary aim is to point 'you' in the right direction to seek your appropriate path for your legal expertise; and to give you tips, techniques and real life experience of being able to spread your wings and realise your dreams, wherever you practise law and/or move into another business area.

I have included all these stories of those who have **forged their own path** to motivate you on your working journey wherever it takes you, even if this is out of the law.

Having said that, there are many synergies with other professionals who might want to set up and run their own professional business or even a different business.

It is also for those that serve the legal profession to have a bird's eye view of what it is like to run a legal business and the challenges and success that these Stars experienced in doing so.

Lastly this book is useful for historians when they look back at how some lawyers are tackling the changing face of their profession and how they deliver their legal services to clients. This is because there is so much 'noise' and information about LegalTech and how it is going to impact on legal practices. I have shown in **Section 6 Chapter 6.1** how some of our Yorkshire Legal Stars are tackling this now or how they propose to tackle this in the future or not in 2018.

HOW TO USE THIS BOOK

This is a 'how-to' book which is intended to provide you with knowledge that you were not normally given in training to become a lawyer nor in your legal career – **legal business skills**. Therefore it contains practical exercises for you to work through. Please keep this vital question in mind, when completing the exercises or reading the Star's personal stories: **Will it work for me?**

Section One focuses on what are your 'drivers and dreams' for your working life. This is a crucial segment and is extremely important so don't skimp this 'Why?' section.

You can use the **second and third sections** to examine your dreams by testing some of the viability of what you want to do. So these sections centre on knowing your market from your products/services to your 'ideal' clients.

Section Four provides an overview of the mechanics (but not the financial or regulatory elements) of running a business. Use this section as a prompt to become as professional in running a business as you are in delivering the legal services.

Given the changes that are happening in our Society at large and the legal sector, **Section Five** is about the short-term future as seen by our Stars. These views are focused on where their part of the legal or the other sector they are involved in is headed as they concentrate on how they want to grow their businesses.

All of the earlier sections include excerpts from the personal stories of our Yorkshire Legal Stars to provide you with encouragement to start your own legal or non-legal business.

Enjoy!

SECTION 1

TURNING YOUR PASSION AND EXPERTISE INTO A BUSINESS

THE PURPOSE OF THIS SECTION

Is forging your own path for you, and do you have what you need to start? Therefore this section starts with the 'Why?' drivers and gives you an opportunity to review your own.

CHAPTER 1.1
WHY PRACTISE YOUR LEGAL EXPERTISE AS A BUSINESS?

What drove our Stars to run their own businesses?

Our Stars set up their own businesses for lots of different reasons. Some felt driven to start something because they wanted to change their situation, whereas others had the real drive to start a new type of organisation or move out of law completely. Below is a summary of the reasons they gave.

So whether you:

- Were frustrated by your last firm or in the wrong firm or department: **Cathy**, **Gary**, **Laura**, **Miguel**, and **Thomas**.
- Found that your current job was making you ill: **Andrea**, **Jodie** and **Simon**.
- Were fed up with the politics: **Ann**, **Martin**, and **Simon**.
- Didn't have enough flexibility in your current firm: **Andrew**.
- Have been made redundant: **Claire**, **Jade**, and **Kate**.
- Felt it evolved: **Claire**, **Rachel** and **Richard**.
- Are feeling too old or different to be employed: **Gary**, **Martin** and **Richard**.
- Tried the consultant solicitor or freelancer route first: **Ann**, **Ian**, **Jodie**, **Kate** and **John**.

Or you:

- Have a great idea to do something different and/or make a difference: **Ann**, **Andrew**, **Cathy**, **Gary**, **Ian** & **Matt**, **James**, **Jodie**, **Martin** and **Noreen**.
- Wanted control and freedom over your destiny: **Bill**, **Cathy**, **Geoff**, **Jade**, **Jane**, **Jill**, **Jodie**, **John**, **Laura**, **Liz**, **Martin**, and **Miguel**.
- Had an opportunity come your own way: **Jade**, **Peter**, **Simon**, and **Thomas**.
- Wanted to deliver a more personal legal service your way: **Bill**, **Jane**, **Gary**, **James**, **Jodie**, **John**, **Liz**, **Noreen**, **Samira**, and **Simon**.
- Want to be at the forefront of change: **Gary**, **Laura**, **James**, **Martin** and **Rachel**.
- Wanted more flexibility to spend with your family: **Andrea**, **Andrew**, **John**, and **Geoff**.

- Felt the time was right to strike out on your own: **Andrew**, **Rachel**.
- Wanted to control the ethics and ethos of your practice: **Jill**.
- Are a serial entrepreneur or love the business of law: **Andrew**, **Gary**, **Matt**, **Kirstie**, **Liz**, and **Miguel**.

You just need to understand what is driving you and what is not.

As **Miguel** said *'it is always a combination of factors'.* Indeed you can see a variety of factors in the bullet points above, and that both positive and negative drivers were present for some of those interviewed.

ANN'S STORY: In my case, when politics drove me out of my last in-house post, I turned to my second love after the law - leadership and management training. I was passionate about these topics and about creating interactive motivational learning experiences that were practical.'

I was also looking for interesting work, which I could do whilst taking lots of time out with my husband (who was fully retired at this stage) to travel the world. I wanted to take my own leadership and management training and experience from the corporate world into the legal profession. The first time I did this was when I was Chair of the Law Society Commerce and Industry Group. Whilst there, I initiated six firsts for the Group including Corporate Governance Guidelines for In-house lawyers. I started by freelancing for the major legal training companies. I was in fact approached to work for one of the companies to set up their leadership and management programme for lawyers, which I did.

It was not till the death of my mother and husband in the same year, that I took time out to decide what I wanted to do, given all my plans had been changed. This led me to return to my home county of Yorkshire and to undertake specific training on setting up and running a business including marketing. I explored a number of ways to set up and develop businesses both in and out of the law. I realised that actually I loved working with my profession on the teaching and coaching side. Following the business skills training I decided to add these skills to my products (e.g. The Business Brilliance Blueprint Programme) and coaching services.

I did not want to be wedded to any one particular system so I offer a customised holistic approach to lawyers to address their challenges. This in turn has led me to deliver a number of mini workshops on a number of current challenges for lawyers. Mindfulness and Stress Management is just one example. I continue to deliver themed workshops alongside my business coaching and training as set out in the Appendix A.

What keeps me going - my 'Why'? It is making a difference to the lawyers that I work with or meet on my public leadership and confidence courses for MBL Seminars. The crucial factor for me is the human interaction and the amazing feedback I receive from both my training and coaching. I just love working with people who want to improve their business and interpersonal skills. It is a real privilege to watch my clients grow as leaders, business owners and lawyers.

YOUR TURN

Identifying your 'Why?' drivers

The model I am using here is called the 4MAT Framework. 4MAT is a highly validated and world-renowned learning and communication tool. It is based on essential human differences regarding how we perceive, process, understand and pass on information. It can be used for a number of purposes, particularly for presentations. In fact this is one of the ways I was taught to approach the crafting of my workshops and seminars.

It always starts with the 'Why?' question as that is normally what drives us. This is then followed sequentially by 'What?' by 'How?' and 'What else?' starting on the right side of the table. In my strategy session with my clients I always start with this exercise varied to their circumstances.

Here you can adapt this simple version to your current circumstances to establish your reasons for turning your passion into a business and forging your own path. Start filling in the table at number one.

4. What else can I do with my expertise/passion?	1. Why am I doing this?
3. How am I doing 'it'?	**2. What am I doing?**

The dangers of chasing perfection - *the Imposter Syndrome*

'Release the perfectionist driver – be self-motivated.' **Andrew**. In fact business is messy and full of learning.

Nowadays when I am teaching business and leadership skills there is an emphasis on 'being real'. You will also see this pressure on lawyers particularly on social media too. Anyone who tries to come across as perfect just pushes people away and is not believed.

To demonstrate our humanness, I asked everyone for his or her best and worst business habits to show you what I mean. See table below. For identifying your best, what do you enjoy or what do you do that flows easily and effortlessly? For your worst, think about the issues you regularly experience and what might be underpinning them. Once you have come up with them, why not check them out with one of your peers and see if they concur. Sometimes our best (or worst) habits go unnoticed because they are so automatic to us.

	Name	Best	Worst
1	Andrea	I love following my intuition. I love following what feels right, connecting with people and coming up with a unique way of doing things.	Magpie - we can do this or we can do that. Hurtling one direction after another - do have to rein it.
2	Andrew	Being a serial entrepreneur with lots of ideas.	Not being able to switch off from work and lack of focus.
3	Ann	Passion for all my business subjects and clients. I love the face-to-face training, coaching and mentoring to inspire and support my clients.	Bad diary management and sometimes a lack of focus, like Andrea, I can be a bit of a magpie.
4	Bill	I love the work I do.	Working too much.
5	Cathy	My best business habit is probably being willing to take on a new type of job and learn how to do it rather than be frightened of it.	My worst I think is falling soft on clients when it comes to charging them for odd jobs or odd bits here and there, they soon add up!
6	Claire	Part of my USP - personal delivery of service.	Workaholic and perfectionist.

	Name	Best	Worst
7	Gary	Stubbornness to make sure you don't quit and you see things through. Resilience and learning new stuff - I keep a journal.	Stubbornness can be a dual-edged sword.
8	Geoff	Flexibility and how I work.	Flexibility and how I work.
9	Ian	Ability to recognise where we are and where we are going.	Inability to delegate.
10	Jade	A good mentor in leadership and training.	Sucked into fee earning and difficulty in stepping back.
11	James	Social media/marketing strategy.	
12	Jane	Building rapport and client relations.	Untidy desk.
13	Jill	I love organising and structuring my matters and business processes	Not being able to switch off from work.
14	Jodie	Willingness to try anything.	Spreading myself too thin.
15	John	Work best under pressure.	Not as efficient as I should be.
16	Kate	Not afraid of trying new things.	Lazy - not following up emails.
17	Kirstie	Understanding priorities.	Not delegating or saying no enough.
18	Laura	Not scared of change and never complacent.	Relinquishing control.
19	Liz	Keeping a close eye on figures.	Keeping a close eye on figures can lead to impatience when looking at long-term investment.
20	Martin	Vision, great ideas and belief.	Getting the focus right.
21	Matt	Good at delegating.	Inability to switch off.
22	Miguel	I can be very analytical to weigh up all the options before making a decision.	Perfectionism where it holds me back and I find delegation hard.
23	Noreen	Seeing a task through to the end.	Procrastination by doing the easiest job first.

	Name	Best	Worst
24	Peter	Optimism, my continual striving to achieve better, do better, continue to grow the practice, try new things, try new ways of marketing the business, trying things that perhaps others haven't done so, treading into territories that others have decided is not for them.	Optimism in underestimating what came with becoming a business owner – being responsible for my employees, finance, marketing and the rest, in how much time these take.
25	Rachel	Doing one thing at a time.	Getting distracted by emails.
26	Richard	Chasing work and being proactive.	Non fee-earning work goes on the back-burner.
27	Samira	My mindset of that you can achieve anything as long as you put your heart and mind to it, and sending quotes out quickly.	Not making enough time to be working on my business.
28	Simon	Quick and responsive communication.	Spending disproportionate time on LinkedIn even though I get business from it.
29	Thomas	Very straight and honest in dealing with people – staff and clients.	Don't devote enough time to being a managing director.
30	So now over to you...		

CHAPTER 1.2
WHAT SKILLS AND QUALITIES DO YOU NEED TO START?

Learning the hard way

There is inevitable learning on-the-job when setting up on your own business of any kind. So the question becomes do you want to start with or without any type of business training?

Nearly all of the interviewees started with no or little formal training and some found that really challenging. **What is more telling is that none of them recommend this as a sound strategy for you.** Whilst I recognise the Stars' choices this is not how I wanted to build a business when I returned to Leeds. As this might be useful to you I have set out an overview of my own steps to equip myself to run my business.

ANN'S STORY: When I moved from being a senior in-house lawyer to being a trainer and coach, I decided to learn the craft of coaching and training. I began with studying coaching with The Coaching Academy. I then studied Neuro Linguistic Programming (NLP). The NLP training was focused on how adults learn because I realised it was not enough to share my knowledge and experience. I wanted to craft motivational learning workshops and courses specifically tailored to the delegate needs.

I started by working as a freelancer for the major training companies. This is a similar route to being a consultant solicitor before becoming a legal business owner such as **Jodie** and **Simon** took. I tried to learn the 'business' of training from these large companies but their whole approach to marketing and in particular pricing meant it was not a model I could or wanted to follow once I branched out. For a start, I would not have the database these companies had or their marketing resources nor did I want to only compete on price as they did. Once you focus on the latter the only way is down. So even if you have had business training, which is unlikely, in your large firm it may not serve you when you spread your wings.

My experience with the different training companies (2003-2013) enabled me to embed great motivational training techniques and taught me how to cope with those 'awkward things' that happen in class.

In terms of my topics and content, I gained valuable insight and training of business, leadership, management and interpersonal skills during my 28 years as an In-house Solicitor for several organisations and in various roles. I am also a member of the Professional Speaking Association (PSA) and there have been numerous members who have inspired and informed my journey including Joy Marsden and Eilidh Milnes. These amazing ladies are sadly no longer with us. I would like to particularly thank Lee Jackson and John Howtoka from the PSA for their continual support, wisdom and guidance. I continue to read extensively and to incorporate all and any learning from delivering my services so I can continue to develop and improve.

In 2013 to 2016 I started to study business skills from various sources and covering all the main topics that I teach and coach. I love learning. The decision I made following this substantive training and coaching was that I did not want to run a business outside of the legal profession. I wanted to continue to deliver motivational training and coaching using business skills translated into the legal profession.

How much training/coaching do you actually need?

This is a loaded question as many lawyers are not sure and each of those Stars interviewed had a different take on this. From the interviews and sometimes reading between the lines I found:

- Six had some form of business training before starting up.
- 11 relied on their experience working for others either at partner level or in a senior role.
- Another two, whilst having considerable experience also have continued with business training or coaching.
- Six started some form of business training or coaching once they had begun to forge their own path.
- Four continue to learn 'on-the-job' as they go forward in building their businesses.

The LexisNexis Bellwether 'The Good Solicitor Skills Set' Report (2019) by Jon Whittle, posed the question: *Are the human, legal, and business skills solicitors recognised as the most important ones, in fact, the most lacking in the profession?*

He consulted 176 solicitors and found that:

- 61% agree strongly that 'human' skills are increasingly important with 21% slightly agreeing.
- 60% strongly agreed that having good business skills is increasingly important to succeed in law whilst 9% disagreed.
- Although only 35% stated that entrepreneurial skills were important, 48% recognised the ability to generate business was important.

There are 22 attributes identified by this report.[1] Here are a few: entrepreneurial skills, service industry mentality, smart user of digital technology, good at generating business, empathy, ability to build relationships and also create trust, good understanding of finance including cash flow management, efficient case management, good negotiation skills, common sense.

If you see yourself as a managing partner or a business owner then you will need to change your mindset and your knowledge and skills in these areas. **This report is worth reading in full.**

I would recommend that you take stock of who and where you are now, and where you want to go with your career or business, to decide what type of business training and/or coaching is appropriate for you using the exercises in this book.

YOUR TURN

A simple assessment exercise to establish what you need

This will become your corner stone for your learning process and understanding your 'Personal Brand and Qualities' from a business perspective so keep a copy in your success and learning Logs.

Where you have a low score for any of those attributes you have identified from the list above that you think you will need. Then the first step is to acquire knowledge. The most obvious way is with training. This can be supplemented by reading books, podcasts, videos and webinars. If you have the knowledge but are experiencing difficulty in 'doing' then having a coach and/or a mentor should be the most effective solution.

What business skills or attributes do I have now?	Score out of 5 and why
What business skills or knowledge do I need?	**Score out of 5 and why**
So how do I want to acquire them?	**Coaching/training/other**

How do you know if you need coaching or training?

Training's role is primarily to provide you with the knowledge, insights and skills that you will need or will make life easier for you at work or in business. Coaching is about embedding these new skills into effective habits and changing your life to capitalise on the training taken.

Here are just four reasons why my clients sought my coaching expertise and may resonate with you:

1. They found that there was lot of difference between classroom learning and dealing effectively with real life leadership, management and business tasks. 1-1 coaching puts the focus directly on what enables them to have personal useful techniques embedded to deal with those real life challenges. For example: if your communication is not having the desired impact. Then this is a safe place for you to craft specific influencing sentences and practise these. You can then return to the situation having the confidence to influence your staff or your clients. This provides both the skills and confidence to tackle your communication challenges.

2. The evolving nature of the business and legal worlds means lawyers and business owners are continually moving into uncharted territory in respect of their legal or other businesses. For example, how much time do they devote to exploring the leading edge of technology? And is it still a worthwhile use of time if the newest technology is not related to their Unique Selling Proposition (USP) or their clients? Everyone is on social media – should they be on all channels? Having a sounding board with a coaching guru with industry expertise offers a safe place to reflect and decide on these difficult decisions.

3. For some leaders and managers, dealing with uncertainty led to a micro management approach –characterised by phrases like 'I am a control freak' and/or 'my biggest weakness is I can't delegate'. So when the pressure intensifies they returned to what they know best – their legal expertise, which often included interfering with how their colleagues/staff were working and their billing targets! Without clear leadership, the firm's continued success is threatened. Therefore a change in mindset was required to enable them and others to move forward successfully. A coach can be a source of help, assisting a leader/business owner to stay on track with both their individual and business objectives. This includes being able to let go but not abdicate responsibility.

4. Most of us are adverse to uncertainty, which in turn increases stress levels. Sometimes it can be lonely at the top and some business owners found it very difficult to admit they needed help. With no outlet, that stress can be expressed inappropriately in their team. Stress spreads like wild fire from partner to colleagues and team members. Having the support of an external coach give the opportunity to work through those stresses in a healthy way, without impacting on those around you.

YOUR TURN

Why do you want or need coaching or mentoring support?

List your reasons below. Knowing what you want from coaching will make it more worthwhile and value for money.

So I can't set up my business until I have self-confidence?

Yes and No!

It would be very easy not to 'fly' until you were totally confident about everything. That is not going to happen! You can see from the interviews that this is not necessary and indeed you cannot foresee where the journey will take you – **you just have to take a leap of faith.**

Some had/have a Plan B such as **Thomas**, but most did not. They took that leap of faith. **Self**-confidence is more about belief in your abilities and in yourself to handle the challenges without the drive to be perfect. This means self-confidence includes a positive belief that in future you can generally accomplish what you wish to do or achieve. Not that you have all the answers from the get-go and you are prepared to ask for help.

We all have an 'Inner Critic' including me. I know this is a shock! Your 'Inner Critic" is actually there to support you by keeping you within your comfort zone and therefore safe. For example it can say: **'You took a step and failed – don't do that again.'** One tip to changing your 'Inner Critic' to 'Inner Cool' is to use the experience to learn what worked and what did not so you can prevent the same mistake happening. Further if we frequently avoid such challenges then we miss the chance to train our subconscious and/or our 'Inner Critic' that it is ok to try new things. Indeed your confidence will grow in trying new things even when this takes time.

If you want to run your own legal business then you need to find solutions for tackling these types of negative thoughts, as there will be ups and downs on your journey. *'Get rid of the beliefs you don't need or these will stop you'* said **Andrea** and **Ann** endorses this. In fact **Jodie** has posted on social media about her anxiety attacks and how she manages these as well as running a successful legal practice.

A lot of the things in business just don't work out the way anyone planned. One of the greatest sources of despair is the **belief that things should have been easier than they turned out to be.**

Professionals give up, not because events are difficult but **because we expected them not to be.** This is because of the belief that you won't meet any obstacles is a belief that sabotages the formation of new habits. It is important to recognise that **difficulties are an inescapable part of any worthwhile contribution.** This will help you therefore interpret your worries, reversals, troubles as unavoidable landmarks not aberrations or fateful warnings.

For example, in writing this book, I came face-to-face with an unrealistic belief that as I had written two previous books so this one should be so easy!! Well that was an unrealistic expectation! I had not conducted and recorded interviews before; and I can fill a book with the learning I got from this exercise. Suffice to say for my next book, I am totally rethinking this part.

You can also see from all the interviews that the Stars are as 'flawed' as you and do not consider themselves to be perfect. They are uncertain, anxious and have an 'Inner Critic' like you from time to time – they do not let this stop them. **Peter** reframes a Churchill quote which I think is very apt for business – *'There is no failure – just degrees of success!' 'Success is not a destination; failure is not fatal. It's the courage to carry on that's the inspiration.'*

> 'WHEN IT IS OBVIOUS THAT THE GOAL CANNOT BE REACHED; DON'T ADJUST THE GOAL, ADJUST THE ACTION STEPS.'
> **CONFUCIUS**

Who do you need to support you on your business journey?

Without fail all the Stars said spouses/partners/family were the most supportive and without which their business journey may have been impossible. In particular this is an excellent piece of advice: *'Don't do it if your partner is not 100% on board with your decision.'* **Kirstie**

The second most important collection was friends and peer group members. What was very interesting is that very few of these were legal business owners, although some did have a network of local legal business owners. For those that are no longer delivering legal services, they all had strong network connections to their relevant peer groups.

Clearly where they had business partners then this was their first port of call: **Bill** (Trish), **Ian & Matt**, **Jade** (Rodney), **James** (Frank), **Laura** (Marie), **Richard** (Robina), **Simon** (Juliet), **Thomas** (Sarah and two non-lawyers).

Some have business coaches including yours truly, either on a regular basis or at certain times during their journey.

Most but not all read widely. This included non-legal books/podcasts on self-development, business management and philosophy. Examples of **support** networks:

- **Ann** and **Liz** are members of formal 'master mind' business groups to support them as business owners.
- Leadership groups – **Peter** (Yorkshire Lawyer Leadership Group) and **Gary** (Elite programme with the London Stock Exchange).
- The family lawyers, **James**, **Jill** and **Laura**, were members of Resolution (an association of family law professionals) and a few were members of their local law societies.
- Law societies: **Ann**, **Claire**, **Geoff**, **Jill**, and **Rachel** were members of the Yorkshire Sole Practitioners Group and **Ann**, **Bill** (a past president) and **Gary** are members of Leeds Law Society whilst **Andrew** is a member of Harrogate Law Society (in fact he is a past President too).
- A couple of the Stars have experience of BNI (their focus is helping their members increase their business sales through referrals) such as **Andrew**, **Bill** and **Cathy**.

For other networking groups see **Section 1 chapter 1.3** and **Section 3 Chapter 3.2**. Find the one that works for you.

YOUR TURN

Who and what will support you?

Write down who and what will support you in forging your own path and revisit this table from time to time as things change.

Partner - personal and/or business	Family members with or without business experience	Friends with or without business experience	Books/ podcasts	Formal training and/or coaching

CHAPTER 1.3
ADVICE FROM OUR STARS

Overview

Lets get this one out in the open – *'I don't think being an entrepreneur or a law entrepreneur is for everybody'* **Andrew** and I endorse this, which is why **Section 1 Chapter 1.1** concentrated on your 'Why?' drivers, even before we got to your vision. A vision without motivation to make it happen is an aspirational dream not a vision.

Below you will see excerpts from our Stars on four key themes and in **Section 5. Chapter 5.6** their advice to you is set out in full.

Getting the timing right

There were different views on timing.

'Just do it!' Was the recommendation from **Andrea, Jodie**, **Noreen** and **Samira**.

Bill thought that when you are in your *'40's is a good time – and with someone you trust'*

'The best time is now when you make the decision' **Gary**.

'When is the best time to start up a business? Its never the best time' **Ian**.

An alternative view given by **Matt** to a young lawyer was *'to stick it out a bit longer if you are getting decent experience and hopefully get a bit of a following.'* Although he did go on to say *'you can only make a judgement about your experiences in your rear view mirror.'*

Having the right mental attitude

Attitudes are important and these are a settled way of thinking or feeling about something. Our Yorkshire Stars are really strong on attitude – *'Attitude – I happen to love the work that I do'* **Bill**.

This is what others had to say on attitude:

'If anyone else can do it then you can do it! I sometimes get worried or nervous about new things but the thing that helps my confidence most is just thinking about all the other guys who have managed this, if they can do it I can do it!' **Cathy**

'Just keep going. It often feels like it is comparable to being in a really dense forest and having a knife to hack away and get though it.' **Kate. Rachel's** advice was similar and she suggested that *'you keep in mind why you are doing this'. 'You're going to be ok. Whatever course you take you're going to be ok. Different things happen. I've never yet had a door close where another one hasn't opened.'* **Martin**

'Well, don't be afraid. I didn't think I could do it. I was a bit scared. I was a lot scared. I was very naïve. I've made some humungous mistakes. But I've had some great successes. I've had an amazing journey so far. Would I do it again? In a heartbeat! And every time you get knocked back, pull yourself up, dust yourself down and get on it and do it again because business is a journey and you're not travelling to a destination.' **Peter**. *'I think you got to be a little bit brave in terms of having a go or having the confidence to do it. It is doable'.* **Noreen**. *'I think a lot people will try and talk you out of it. I think that you need to have the confidence to believe in yourself and you can do it.'* **Simon**. *'But actually if you just have to stick with it I promise you won't regret it.'* **Laura**

Preparation

'Do a lot of research and spend a lot of time working out what your competition is, who's out there doing that in a particular way and go all in.' **James**. *'Start out with a proper business plan and I would say that anybody who started a business without a proper business plan is looking to fail.'* **Liz** and **Jade** also recommended this and doing it properly. *'Have systems in place. Be very systematic when you are setting up, e.g. letter templates.'* **Jane**.

Having a network

'I would say develop a network as early as you can, because as you grow in experience in the level of cases that you deal with, they will grow with you in those organisations. If you are looking after their best interests then it is a good basis to build relationships that last.' **John**. **Peter** also specifically mentioned this: *'I think this is probably one piece of advice, if you can call it advice that I would offer to anybody, is make sure you've got a network around you, if you are planning to set off on a journey where you are going to be solely responsible for a business. It doesn't matter how big or small that business is, be it a one-man band making cupcakes for a farmers' market or you're growing a business that's supplying dozens and dozens of people and operating from a variety of locations. Having a really good network of people that you trust and that can give you the support that you need. Having sounding boards is really useful. Being able to talk to people in the same industry.'*

See also **Section 1 Chapter 1.2** and **Section 3 Chapter 3.2**.

YOUR TURN

Where are you?

Use these four key areas to help you get all your *'ducks in a row'* before you launch. However don't use them as an excuse not to forge your own path.

Getting the timing right	Having the right mental attitude
Preparation	**Having a network**

YOUR TURN

Yearly success log

Keep a year-on-year success log for continuous improvement tracking and more importantly **celebrating your achievements**. It is so easy to forget these in our day-to-day lives. These are the stepping-stones to building your future; and when you write your story you won't have to hunt for this valuable information! It can be work or personal and it does not have to be three. The table below is an example of a simple success log you can complete showing at least three monthly successes.

January	February	March
1. 2. 3.	1. 2. 3.	1. 2. 3.
April	**May**	**June**
1. 2. 3.	1. 2. 3.	1. 2. 3.
July	**August**	**September**
1. 2. 3.	1. 2. 3.	1. 2. 3.
October	**November**	**December**
1. 2. 3.	1. 2. 3.	1. 2. 3.

CHAPTER 1.4
WHAT ARE YOUR DREAMS FOR YOUR BUSINESS? (VISIONS AND BUSINESS PLANS - DO THEY HELP?)

Introduction

Visions are short inspirational statements, which communicate effectively that you, and/or the firm know where it is going, and what kind of experience your clients can look forward to when they engage you.

One of the reasons it's called a vision is that the owners/leaders/managers should have a mental picture of what their vision would look like if it were reached. A vision implies that the firm is moving forward in a cohesive direction with everyone working towards this vision. The client/employees can then see easily if there is a match.

Powerful visions focus on the clients that they serve. A vision should be unique to the firm AND important to their clients. Most law firms use generic words such as best, successful, largest and this may or may not be affixed to areas such as best in their region or sector or services. Visions, brands and straplines can be synonymous in the public eye.

How did our Stars approach their dreams?

You will note from the interviews that:

- Ten had a vision and it remained steady at the time of interview – **Andrew**, **Bill**, **Gary**, **Geoff**, **Kirstie**, **Jade**, **James**, **Jane**, **John**, **Samira**, and **Thomas**.
- 12 had a vision or a vision of sorts which evolved or is evolving over time* – **Ann**, **Andrea**, **Claire**, **Gary**, **Jodie**, **Ian** and **Matt**, **Kate**, **Laura**, **Liz**, **Miguel**, **Peter**, **Rachel**, **Richard**, and **Simon**.
- And **Noreen** did not have a specific vision at the time of set up just a childhood one and a desire to develop her legal and business skills together with a 'a get up and go' attitude to see how far she could go.

*Some of these might be timing issues. **Peter** has been in business since 2006 whereas **Simon** is a very recent start up who commenced trading in 2018. Some of the business owners focused on the business plans rather than the vision in the interview; and some of the visions encompassed personal as well as business ones.

Below I have set out five examples of visions with the remainder set out in **Section 6 Chapter 6.1**.

1. **Steady vision: James** *'I want to create a successful legal practice that impacts on our industry. We didn't want to just be a family law practice we want to make waves. We hit the fixed fee idea because nobody was doing fixed fees [at that time] and we saw an opportunity and the demand from clients because it's all about clients and what they want from their lawyer.'*

2. **Evolving early vision: Jodie** *'it was more about creating the right environment for me to work in and then attract like-minded people to share those values. So the key thing for me is to create a brand that reflected me and I think I've done that now which is really good but then attracting the right people that's a massive challenge in itself. The idea for me is then to grow the business to a point where it is says is obviously sustainable but also can run without me or with very minimal input from me so that I can then develop other areas of the business whether that's to do with training or well-being or everyday behaviour. I'd like to have go off and have a baby at some point so this needs to be factored in, in terms of my personal vision.'*

3. **Steady vision being put into action: Gary** *'I suppose I did, yes. And the vision was purely I could see how we could make it better. I think that two decades or more inside law meant I knew how to break it and reconstruct it. Technology and the Legal Services Act 2007 came together. Technology gave me the means to scale it in an educational Hub Empowering a complete new platform for the business and the Legal Services Act allowed the de-regulation so I could embrace a completely new model.'* **Martin** *'we want to be the best. Mine's not measured in terms of size and turnover. We want to be the most compassionate and well-respected practice in the country and in fact I don't have any visions to go beyond the six members of the team. I want to be able to have a personal approach to each client's problem, each family problem because we deal with distressed families post-death. That's why we come at it in quite a unique way. The second part is IDR Technologies to produce innovative tech products.'*

4. **A non-legal example of an evolving vision: Kate** *'in the last six months this vision has really started to crystallise. I just want to deliver training but there has to be a better way of delivering it. So I realised everything was moving digitally so I launched The Safeguarding Academy.'*

5. **A legal example of an evolving vision: Peter** *'I wouldn't say that I started out with a vision. I knew what I wanted the firm to feel like*

in terms of being a supportive, cooperative culture in terms of being supportive to staff and encouraging them and helping them progress their careers. I knew I wanted my business to be part of the communities in which it operated rather than being at a distance from the community. So it was more a case of how I wanted it to feel rather than having a vision. It's easy isn't it in hindsight to say we have a great vision of being able to launch this practice and grow it and it hasn't happened like that. It didn't happen like that. It would be rewriting history to say that I started with the lovely grand plan about what it was finally going to look like because it is a journey and there is never a final day that you've achieved it all. Well, perhaps there is the day you sell your practice.'

A 'mission' statement expands the 'strapline' approach to the vision by providing more detailed information that is normally measurable. Therefore it addresses the following questions:

- Who?
- What?
- Where?
- When?
- How?

These questions provide the 'how' you are going to achieve your vision and the 'Why' exercise in in **Section 1 chapter 1.1** should have helped you to answers these. You will note from the recorded interviews set out in **Section 6 Chapter 6.1** that often the 'how' is attached to their description of their vision.

YOUR TURN

What is your vision or dream of your working life?

As you can see above these change over time so you may wish to segment this into time periods – e.g. next 12 months or next 12 years?

Personal vision

Business vision

Working life vision

Are business plans useful?

Yes for many reasons, apart from the regulatory and/or seeking finance ones.

Ann *'Over the years I have had many different types of plans some were more useful than others and it is a question of finding what works for you. I combine my strategic and business goals in one document on a yearly basis. My strategic business plan covers my purpose and values (normally three words I am going to focus on for the next 12 months). This year's three words are: Joy, Creativity and Connection. The financial information contains potential income streams required from different services with detailed plans re marketing and course planning but no specific monthly targets.'*

Of course the Stars needed business plans for compliance and insurance purposes and to get their thoughts down in detail about their business in the early stages. Therefore I asked the question 'what worked and what didn't?' This is important, as plans need to change to reflect reality.

Nearly all of our Stars found business plans useful in achieving their goal and in particular they liked:

- **Jade:** seeing the figures in black and white.
- **Liz, Martin, Noreen Richard:** tracking the key financial performance indicators (particularly cash flow), controlling overheads, forecasting and tracking business intelligence data.
- **Kate:** *'I think it is quite useful to have a 'check in' once every six months to see where you want to be and give yourself some points to measure along the way including marking off items as you're moving through to see if you have completely gone off the kilter or if you are on the right trajectory.'*
- **James:** at the beginning focused on getting the right software package identified as needed by their business plan.
- **Laura, Rachel, Thomas:** seeing their achievements being realised.
- **Kirstie:** for a new Chairman and to keep their growth plans on track going forward.
- **Rachel:** finds it useful to include market place analysis, services overview and technology assessment.

Then there are those who prefer to work the visionary plans rather than a detailed business ones. **Andrea, Jane**, and **Kate**. For a couple of the Stars it was too early to say at the time of the interview sessions what was working and what was not – **Jodie** and **Simon**, and **Cathy** was now focusing on producing this to support her vision.

Please turn to **Section 4 Chapter 4.1** for a checklist of items to be considered for your business plan, especially at the start.

SECTION 2

KNOW YOUR MARKET - SERVICES AND PRODUCTS

THE PURPOSE OF THIS SECTION

Given the increasing commoditisation of legal services, before you set up or even if you have, it is a good idea to understand what part of your legal expertise is a service and what is a commodity. Please see **Section 5 Chapter 5.2** Strategic Tools to help you do this. **Technology will always be changing** and so this will form a continual theme of your strategy going forward. So the aim of this section is to prompt you to start assessing **what** you want to deliver and **how** to deliver your legal expertise.

CHAPTER 2.1
YOUR CORE LEGAL SERVICE(S)

Introduction

What is the distinction between legal services and products? The main difference between **services** and **products** for the purpose of this book is that products are bought normally online without legal input therefore services include your expert support in some way. This is the 'value' you add to their experience not just providing the documentation but the human touch as well.

The main consistency for legal service is **guidance**. Your experience will be invaluable here – however long that is. This means that you have 'trodden the path' your client is now starting down and therefore you can save the client time and money they would have spent treading this path on their own. Your client is seeking you because you have specialist and/or sector experience of using your legal knowledge on behalf of clients not because you can produce legal documents per se. They require comfort from you that you have dealt with these types of issues and/or transactions many times and that you totally understand their situation; and in some cases their emotional turmoil. Here the legal services and solutions delivered will depend on a number of factors. These include the amount the client is willing or able to pay.

There are many 'gurus' who have analysed what lawyers are 'selling' or delivering including David Maister, Professors Stephen Mayson and Richard Susskind. I would recommend all three.

These are the 11 categories I found when examining the approach by my clients and contacts interviewed for this book. I have listed these in alphabetical order.

1. **Client Sector Emphasis** – such as the healthcare/dental profession. **Thomas.**

2. **Custom-made solutions** – here an example is **Claire** with bespoke property solutions for her clients (which is also her strapline).

3. **Campaigns** – **Jodie's** reputation is not only about her employment expertise but also about her campaign for Mental Health First Aiders and her work in the mental health field, which is a fundamental part of her brand.

4. **Geographical advantages** – **Peter's** firm with its offices spread throughout Yorkshire and Teesside serving the local communities.

5. **Legal Services** to clients alongside online products. **Gary**, **Martin** and **Rachel**.

6. **Passion for changing the face of law – Gary** with his vision of changing the perception of law and lawyers.

7. **Rare niche** – new build dispute specialist services to homeowners. **Geoff**.

8. **Simplifying complex standardised ways of working.** For example using your experience of assignment of a lease to produce a flowchart of the assignment process in a way that engages the client as well as guiding them through the process. **Noreen** is a great example here. Another approach is used by **Rachel** to produce short guide booklets explaining wills and probate. This type of work lends itself to standard fees.

9. **Specialised knowledge and/or expertise** Many of our Stars operate in this category. They use their own prior years of experience of practising their expertise. This normally goes hand-in-hand with the contacts they have grown and which are invaluable where you are a young firm or have just set up on your own and/or have yet to establish your firm. For example **Martin** and **Simon**.

10. **Specialised knowledge and/or expertise for a fixed fee.** Service is an important component based on extensive experience of their specialism. **James** is example where the Stars see themselves as *'holding the hand'* of their family clients who go through this legal process at a time of great emotional turmoil.

11. **Specialist reputation** of the '**firm**' and/or **person(s)** over the last decade and more. Thus the importance of your brand to maintain your pre-eminence as an expert. This will be supported by testimonials, recognition within your peers, formal awards, and inclusion in the various directories to stand out from the crowd. Your vision of being the best and a strategy to achieve this is essential. An example is **Liz.** A sector example is **Miguel**, who focuses on the in-house recruitment market and has built his reputation over a significant period of time.

Competitive advantage *or doing something different*!

Currently nearly all our Stars have taken their own expertise and experience to market, which is one strategy. The other strategy is to identify a gap in the market and plug that gap: **Gary, James, Jodie**, **Liz** and **Martin**.

Innovation can include incremental/continuous improvements as well as transformational approaches to your particular service. It is also about implementing your innovation ideas. **See Section 5 Chapters 1 – 3** and **Chapter 5.5**.

In this changing legal landscape, all law firms have to be 'forward thinking' in some respects, see **Section 5 Chapter 5.2** for some tools to support you on your innovation journey. You can use these strategic tools to spot gaps in your markets – both on and offline. Don't forget to include your clients in this process, and where you ask for feedback, use this to continually improve your client's 'customer experience'. For those with business clients, then understanding their business strategy and plans for the future is a great way to know how they view business and legal risk. This is a valuable base on which to become a 'Trusted Adviser'.

Any competitive change you want to introduce in your business, will be in addition to running your business so have realistic time frames for this. **Section 5: Chapter 5. 2** contains the best principles to manage change because innovation is not only about 'light bulb' moments but also about hard work sustained during the time to get your ideas into practical format. Implementation will also include trial and error parts as you move into the new system/approach to ensure that you stand out from the crowd.

Here are some seven examples from our Stars to inspire you.

1 **Finding your niche.** Jon Whittle's LexisNexis Bellwether Reports in 2014 (Brave New World) and 2019 (The Changing Face of Law) reviewed niche practices. Sole practitioners or sole directors run 28% of all legal practices in England and Wales, many of whom are specialists in their chosen field.

His 2014 report found a new breed of lawyers who are '*networked, innovative, often niche specialists who've set up their business to compete directly with major industry players*'. These lawyers become the 'go-to' professional trusted advisers.

The example I am using of the route to become a 'go-to' professional trusted adviser is **Martin**. He has:

- Contacts built up over time. He has 4500 LinkedIn contacts, which is impressive and unusual for lawyers.
- *'Business intelligence of ten years'* to build some LegalTech products.
- Qualified in 1995 and has deep experience of his expertise to lead his field – *'Most proud of IDR Law, my competitor is Irwin Mitchell, size wise my firm is only three people.'*

Jon Whittle found that clients are increasingly looking for real expertise, which is recognised by your credibility in your niche. This is also attractive to your referrers to recommend you to others in their network or even their own clients, if you are the 'go-to' person. 'Go-to' professionals continue to deepen and broaden their expertise on a yearly basis.

Another advantage is that it is generally easier to build a brand for a specific niche, which should assist in target marketing your organisation and your expertise.

From a recruitment perspective, you can find that the potential candidates and consultants you want to help you grow your business are seeking out your organisation. The downside identified by the 2019 report mentioned above, is that these are likely to be more junior staff (solicitors/trainees/paralegals), which require a heavy investment of your time in training and may pose a flight risk once trained. **Laura**, **Liz**, **Jodie** and **Noreen** have experienced this, to name four.

Niche practices normally don't have massive overheads either. These all save time and money. See also **Section 2 Chapter 2.3**, and **Section 4 Chapter 4.1**.

2 **Finding your passion and turning it into a campaign.** Another way to stand out – is to stand up for your values and promote change. Two examples here from two different fields of law:

- **Jodie** is a campaigner for Mental Health First Aiders to be compulsory for the workplace and has set up Thriving Minds, which organises mental health events and provides free resources and information. '*We have a very strong presence in the mental health sector. We are not afraid to give an opinion on what we believe is the right way to do things and to put our own stamp on things*'.

- **Rachel** *'I get involved in and campaign for change. The associations I am involved with include, SFE, STEP, Alzheimer's Society and*

Dementia Friends, Dementia Action Alliance, The Diana Award, HM Hubbard Law Scholarship and The Parliamentary Review.'

3 **No one else is doing this.** Innovation is about something entirely different in the service/products or how you deliver these services and products compared to the current market place propositions.

Examples from our Stars:

1. Totally different educational and tech approach combing these with delivering business legal services with 'joined up' thinking. **Gary**.
2. A Safeguarding Academy for those non-legal professionals working within the Family Justice Sector. **Kate**.
3. An electrical business that is predominantly female. **Cathy**.
4. A legal industry focused business training and coaching service for Yorkshire, by a solicitor (non-practising) who spent 28 years as an in-house solicitor. **Ann**

4 **A specific sector focus.** Choose a specific sector that you have experience in. For example this is what **Thomas** did *'when the recession happened I found myself acting for dentists, lending to the healthcare sector, particularly dentists remained a green light for the banks. I ended up, not by choice, specialising in that strange niche which I found myself in. As time went on I exclusively did that and moved to a firm where they had a dentist niche specialism. Throughout that time you meet various people, met brokers, I headed up teams and became a partner at a regional firm at five years qualified'* Then he became Managing Partner of FTA law in 2016'. *'I wouldn't say we are number one but FTA Law are in the top three or four.'*

This does not mean that you can't expand into complementary services such as wills for your clients as well as business services for dentists **Thomas**. To be successful you need to choose a sector, which has enough clients to keep you going. This is because being reliant on any one business or professional sector means that you and your firm have to be able to weather any storms from economic trends and market forces affecting that sector.

The danger here is not to decrease your 'go-to' reputation for a specific sector by starting to become a full service firm for anyone by default. If using a sector as a springboard into a full service firm is part of your vision, then that is fine.

5 **Full service in a unique geographical area:** Coles is a full service firm serving a specific geographical area with great links to the community. **Peter** is even a parliamentary candidate for an area that his firm serves.

Andrew being Harrogate-based uses his authenticity about his values to stand out in the home crowd. These are being flexible and discretionary, focusing on personal service and knowledge of matters, and putting the client first which is underlined by his Quaker Philosophy. If you are going to use your own USP then you need to factor this into the building and marketing of your practice.

6 **Single or holistic service?** I often talk to clients and contacts that describe themselves as niche in one sentence and then say they are going to offer another 'legal' service, which may or may not be relevant to what they are currently offering. They see this as a way of expanding.

I take them back to their vision. So in your vision exercise you may want to start with the end in mind. That does not mean you can't change your vision, I would just recommend that you do it thoughtfully and not ad hoc. Expanding because you can see a potential income stream but it's totally unrelated to your niche may give the wrong signal to the marketplace and dilute your original brand.

An example is if you have a particular sector such as the dental trade, then offering wills and LPA's alongside buying and selling dental practices moves your service into the holistic realm **Thomas.** This can make the perfect sense for your client base to offer them a 'one-stop' shop approach.

Another approach is planning to do this incrementally. For example, for employment start-ups you may start with a focus on employment law services, and then you want to add training on this topic. This is often done as a route to market rather than as an income stream as clients are used to seeing this type of training for free. So looking at paying services to move into a more holistic offering, adds HR services, health and safety services – **Samira** is an example here. Depending your client base you may move into different offerings that are attractive to them such as corporate, commercial and/or litigation work. Offering private client services has to be relevant to them. So if you were to add family legal services only to your business services would be odd and could take you away from your core strategy.

Alternatively you could create or join a network whereby you can refer your clients for that particular service. **Laura** likes to show

how she can provide these services to other law firms either direct through her network or via the professional body such as Resolution for mediation services. Further you can do this with 'alliance' partners – **Andrew** and Blacks (immigration services). Obviously you could bring in the relevant expertise to your organisation via consultants and/or employees.

Ann *'I have been an advocate of tiering product and service offerings, and I use this in my business skills coaching offering. For example identify what would be your Platinum, Gold, Silver and Bronze approach to services and then this can be reflected in your pricing strategy.'*

7 **Other:** Some of the Stars see themselves differently from their competitors by **creating an environment for lawyers to thrive and be happy**. That includes flexible working, being and able to rise on merit not seniority – **James, Jodie, John, Liz, Martin** and **Samira**.

Otherwise your competitive advantage is **you and your team** and how you deliver and as the pressure increases on pricing, these will become more important. This is why you should understand your USP and how you are different from your competition.

Summary

As you can see from all the different approaches there is plenty of scope for you to choose what route(s) would work for you. I would strongly recommend that you examine the technology route going forward as this is where the biggest change is going to impact on the competitive ability of any business. It can be very exciting start to forging your own path, particularly, in legal services. **Gary** and **Martin**. To do this you should also explore alliances with those who are already involved in technology or with like-minded business 'partners'.

The following quote by Tom Peters is so apt and relevant in today's fast-paced moving competitive environment and is a favourite of mine. Business skills are lifelong learning.

> 'THE ONLY COMPETITIVE ADVANTAGE
> IS TO LEARN FASTER THAN ANYONE ELSE'
> **TOM PETERS**

YOUR TURN

What are you passionate about?
Or what turns you on?

What do I love about my legal or other expertise?
What challenges and/or frustrations have I overcome which would prompt me to want to deliver legal services my way?
What gaps in the market have I spotted for my expertise or passion? prompt me to want to deliver legal services my way?
Other

CHAPTER 2.2
YOUR MAIN LEGAL PRODUCTS

Overview

Whilst you may start out with services in mind, it is likely at some time in the future, that all or part of your services will or could be turned into products. There is much debated and written about this and so I am flagging this up for you to be aware of this flow from services to products.

By products I mean these have little or no input from you. Your clients here want efficiency – fast and cheap. So this covers online products and documents that they can complete themselves because if you add the personal service then it will increase costs and move this into the service category. If completely online, the good news is that you can earn money while you sleep! And given you have taken yourself out of the equation then you will have time to sleep!

Often these types of products can provide a high profit margin as they are heavily dependent on software because it removes the 'high expert people' cost from the service. In the legaltech sector this has meant employing paralegals or legal assistants instead of solicitors to keep costs low. I always recommend to young lawyers to learn business skills so that they do not become just very expensive technicians, who can be replaced

General features, which are often seen in product offerings:

- Many suppliers in the marketplace all competing with each other.
- Market reputation in the sector and/or with consumer groups.
- IT dependent particularly using mobile devices.
- Ease of use to access and download or follow the product instructions.
- Market price sensitive and continual pressure on cost reduction.
- Heavy use of paralegals and/or legal assistants.
- Fast response times built into the process.
- No or very little competitive advantage.
- Tracking of the utilisation of social media and website for profile and engagement.
- Marketing and selling to attract clients to use these products is also required.

Online Products introduced by our Stars so far

Setting up online products to support your legal services or stand-alone products might be something you are passionate about. **Gary**, **Rachel** and **Martin**. Whilst it is true our Stars here have learnt so much and are ahead of their competitors, do not underestimate the time and cost of doing so. You may want to link with other players in the marketplace like **Martin** has or go it alone with an outsourced supplier to deliver your online product like **Rachel** or to start something totally different like **Gary** to become a game changer. Each one of these approached the development of LegalTech products differently.

Training and coaching can be done remotely **Kate**, or delivered by a social platform such as Facebook, **Andrea**. Thereby making it more affordable to their clients. Whilst I fully appreciate the benefits in forging my own path I have chosen deliberately not to produce any online training courses or remote group coaching on any platform.

Whilst not exactly an online product, under **#UKBusinessHour James** provides an online service. Another approach is online access or information on the website in the employment or litigation fields about relevant insurance products to cover legal costs. **Jodie** and **Samira** – employment insurance products. **Liz** provides information about finance that their clients can access to fund intellectual property litigation.

What about AI?

It would seem that AI is about to take over the delivery of legal services as it is constantly in the legal press. It would seem that we could hardly move before hearing that a law firm announces a new innovation committee or sets up AI or tech hubs. There does seem to be an obsession with this direction with lots of publicity and hyperbole.

There is no denying that there is an evolution of legal services going on and the services and products it delivers. It is recommended that you evaluate AI's impact on your particular service in a more thoughtful and logical fashion. Going into denial that it will not affect your sector or specialism will not help you in the long term even if in the short term there is no discernable impact. The more junior you are in the legal profession or any business venture the more you need to track these developments.

Further when you have developed your online offering or are using new platforms to engage your clients, a period will be required for you (and your team's) training. This needs to be built into your timeline for maximising the rewards from using this new system. Technology alone will not transform your services or products. How you lead and manage change is going to be crucial here as change is messy, inconsistent and does not happen in a straight and logical line. Please see **Section 5 Chapter 5.1**.

Another test for AI systems is the amount of data it needs to be effective; therefore data security is going to be another challenge. For the smaller firms it is recommended that you track the AI developments and evaluate these using the strategic tools in **Section 5 Chapter 5.2**, to help you decide how your clients want their services.

The next stage is how you position, promote and sell these products either ahead of your competitors or in what may become a crowded market place.

You will need to be extremely passionate, like Gary, to even start down this route.He is a prime example of the drive to find ways to disrupt the current delivery mechanisms of legal knowledge and services in the business world. You might also want to include this in your vision, as Gary did, to set you on the right track from the beginning.

CHAPTER 2.3
PRICING AND PROFITABILITY

Introduction

Pricing legal services has always been a hot topic, particularly since the recession. There is not an intrinsic price for services and it can be trial and error finding out which one wins you most business. This is also true in the training and coaching field. Business owners and lawyers can sweat daily over how they can 'price to win' and keep work *profitable*.

LexisNexis Bellwether Report (2019) on 'The Changing Face of Law' by Jon Whittle found that *'33% of solicitors believe that a significant portion of their business is won purely on price rather than expertise'* except where they were small niche practices. This is good news for our favourite Yorkshire niche practices. Again the full report is worth reading.

Whilst pricing is not the only area of disconnect between solicitors and clients, it is the focus of this Chapter.

Most law firms still price by charging on a strict time spent basis, with invoices detailing work done by each fee earner and the rates applicable. Clients generally consider the average hourly rates expensive, for example these can range from an employment paralegal at £125.00 up to £225.00 for a family law solicitor, and beyond. Therefore there is a drive for firms to provide services on a fixed fee basis. Eight of our Yorkshire Stars did fixed pricing for all products; four charged by the hour and 17 did both.

Since December 2018, the SRA Price Publication Rules state that on certain private client work, fees have to be published on appropriate websites. This includes any hourly rates charged, or estimates. This does at least afford the client some certainty around potential costs. It also enables law firms to benchmark their fees in the marketplace too.

The training and coaching marketplace, except for the large training companies, do not post prices on their websites; and some use webinars as a 'loss leader'. **Ann** *'I experienced this with my own webinars. As as they were filmed in 2015 and this is not an area in which I want to take my business, I took these down last year.'* **Cathy** *'In the electrical industry it is easier to find what the competition is charging and then the question becomes what prices are you comfortable with charging to your customers. This is because what you normally find is a range of prices attached to different work types with some overlap. So self-esteem and your perception of the value of* *your service or product affect what you charge too. More importantly is the client's perception of value for the price they are paying.'*

Visible fee structures

A quick check of our Stars' websites after the introduction of the new regulations, and these are the ones who show information about costs calculation and/or any fixed fees or hourly rates charged:

1. **Claire** – commercial property.
2. **Ian & Matt** – debt recovery, employment, licensing, residential property.
3. **Jade** – residential property.
4. **James** – family law.
5. **Jodie**, **Samira** – employment.
6. **John** – debt recovery and litigation.
7. **Kate** – fees for joining the Safeguarding Academy.
8. **Kirstie** – legal director fixed fees and hourly rates.
9. **Laura** – family and employment.
10. **Noreen** – commercial leases and buying and selling businesses.
11. **Rachel** – wills, lasting power of attorney, probate and administration services.
12. **Richard** – debt recovery and employment.

The freebie revolution

In connection with legal services, a 2013 YouGov poll found 57% of adults say they expect to receive free advice or information about their legal issues, compared to 29% who did not expect any free consultation from their solicitors.

This should be a business decision that supports your commercial or community goals. Two examples: **John** *'charity donations for free advice'.* **Ann** *'delivering a free presentation on self-confidence to the Junior Law Division Conference on a Saturday is giving back to my profession.'*

When a general networking organisation asks you to deliver 'free' presentations here are some factors to consider in deciding if it is worth your time and effort.

Is your presentation are about:

- General profile raising for you and your business,
- Practising your presentation skills,
- Trying out new material,

- Adding value to the audience without giving away everything you know,
- An opportunity to be in front of the 'decision-makers' in your target market so you can 'strut your stuff' so to speak?

As these networking events are invariable pitched as marketing opportunities, then you should have a follow up method to continue the 'dialogue' and build the relationships. This should then provide you with information about who is ready to buy your products and services.

If you decide to offer other 'freebies', be clear as to what these are going to be and why are you doing this?

What freebies are you offering?

- Are you going to offer free consultations like these Stars, **Andrea**, **Andrew**, **Ann**, **Jill**, **John Laura** and **Richard**, The latter uses this as part of his client sifting approach given the nature of his expertise.
- Are you going to package your expertise into free resources such as precedents, informative blogs, flow charts and/or webinars on your websites? The following Stars have used a variety of these – **Andrea**, **Ann**, **Andrew**, **James**, **Jodie**, **Kate**, **Noreen**, **Peter**, **Rachel**, and **Samira**.

Why are you using 'freebies'?

- Social media purposes, to increase awareness of you and to establish your credibility?
- Promoting your profile within your referral network and/or clients?
- Demonstrating your expertise credibility in your field and/or sector?
- Providing valuable resources to clients to entice them to instruct you?
- As part of your marketing and sales funnel, including measuring the effectiveness of this route to market?

The main caveat is: be careful that you don't fall into the trap of being very busy 'going out' of business because you are giving away too much expertise. Especially where you do not have an appropriate follow-up process to gain new business. You have to decide for yourself how much time you can either give away or use these presentations as a route to market. You can use software to track this, which might be in your case management system or a specific client relationship management program. This can be a great tool to learn what is working and what is not in terms of 'freebies'.

Value versus price

According to the Jon Whittle's **LexisNexis Bellwether 'A Question of Value'** (2016) Report found 30% of lawyers say they offer 'excellent' value for money, but only 8% of their clients agree. What's behind this discrepancy?

For one thing, lawyers and clients seem to have different ideas about what 'value for money' actually means. Lawyers tend to equate 'value' with 'price'. Like most of the professional services industry, they have been under immense pressure to lower their fees. Having done so, they now feel they are offering their clients excellent value based on that alone.

Clients, on the other hand, felt those fees were too high to begin with. So even though fees have come down, they still don't feel as though they are getting value for money.

Similarly, lawyers also tend to rate the quality of their own service significantly higher than their clients do. There are many different factors, which constitute quality in the eyes of your clients, and you need to ascertain what these are. The clients have put caring, communication (including accessibility and listening) and successful outcomes high up on their 'value' list.

Jon Whittle's **LexisNexis Bellwether 'The Riddle of Perception' Report** (2016) found 80% of lawyers rated their own firm's service 'above average' or 'well above average' – versus 42% of their clients. Some of this may be due to the fact that 77% of lawyers don't recognise that they are operating in a service industry stated this report.

Although legal professionals are becoming more focused on the communication process and recognising that, speed and achieving outcomes are vital parts of the value equation to their clients, there is still a long way to go to achieve parity of perspective with clients, even though three years has passed from that report.

But is that what clients want?

A 2015 YouGov survey of 2,097 adults found that 75% see cost as an influencing factor when choosing a legal representative, a rise of 6% from the last survey done in December 2013.

This means that cost now surpasses experience and reputation as a factor when choosing a lawyer, with 74% saying those factors influenced their decision. *'Costs of services and fee charged now play a much bigger role for most adults using legal services,'* James McCoy, Research Director at YouGov Reports, said. *'There has also been an increase in the proportion of consumers who now receive legal advice – whether expected or not – suggesting that legal representatives are becoming more open to the idea of providing free consultations,'* he added.

Overall, 62% had used a law firm or solicitor at some point in their lifetime, unchanged since 2013.

Profitability

Clearly when setting your prices you will be mindful of market rates where appropriate. Where you are operating virtually or from home, then it is up to you whether you pass any overhead savings onto your clients. You may even have a different rate for 'steady' volumes from other law firm's clients when they have been referred to you. The price for your products will be different from your services and are generally expected to provide significant cost savings for clients to buy products online.

Whatever your charging structures you really need to understand the difference between turnover and profitability. This includes knowing your most profitable service and/or products as well as being aware of the efficiencies that can be introduced or utilised within your office to increase your profitability.

From an operational perspective, all businesses with a team should have a clear and uniform policy on pricing. This pricing structure should be aligned with productivity rates. The capacity of the team, when you have one, is another factor to ensure the firm's activities are profitable.

Another factor to be taken into account when setting your pricing structure is a clear understanding of the strengths of your brand and services. Geographical factors also come into play – the fees paid in Yorkshire are significantly cheaper than London. There are many ways to measure a firm's market performance, but the main one is 'file openings', as the average rate per case equates to future fees. This is why you must have a write off policy, as it will affect your forecasting.

An example, when I delivered a business development workshop for Liz in 2017– the first thing we did was establish who the ideal profitable clients were and a strategy for connecting with them. Her team developed a multifaceted strategy aimed at the different client types they identified at that time.

YOUR TURN

Pointers to help you price your 'offerings':

1. There is not a one-size-fits-all approach. So think about different prices for different categories of clients or services.
2. Have a strategy for pricing different products or parts of your service and understand the impact on profitability.
3. Think about offering different types of services (Platinum/Gold/Silver/Bronze) you must articulate the difference in a way that the client understands.
4. Think about price options for packages of services available to check profitability of these.
5. Price and market position disconnect – most legal practices do not understand that price is a powerful proxy for quality. Do you as a business owner have a handle on quality and value of your services? Alternatively you do not want to price your services and products too cheaply as this can undermine the quality message.
6. When you first start out you might be underpricing and if that is the case then you need to have a strategy about when you increase your prices.
7. Pricing analytics and tracking documentation can be anything from a spreadsheet to sophisticated software. There are so many packages these days that will provide you with this information and more – so why would you even consider using a spreadsheet?
8. How do fixed fees, contingent or conditional fee arrangements contribute to your turnover and profit?
9. What 'value' you are delivering and how to capture that so that the clients understand and will pay for it.
10. Use pricing templates and pricing precedents to achieve consistency and pricing integrity. Otherwise you could forget what you have offered to one client versus another. Further, these might be easier to change and insert with any client care letters or other client communication documents.

To continue to remain profitable have a really good a 12-month review of what's worked and what hasn't in terms of your pricing strategies. And in particular where you may need external assistance to make changes to these or your costs.

Self-confidence in costs conversation

Claire states strongly that you have *'Got to be on top of the fee situation so there is no earthly point in setting up your own business if you're unable to have conversations about fees, chase up fees, manage cash flow and be quite hard.'*

It is one thing to set your price and another to be able to discuss these appropriately with your potential or actual clients. Negotiation skills are key here and just stressing your expertise is missing the client's perspective on costs. See earlier sub-sections in this chapter.

Confidence is absolutely critical to good pricing communication. In order to be confident you need:

- A broad range of price negotiation skills, including knowing what is negotiable and what is not in terms of your price structure.
- An awareness or understanding of the many pricing strategies and tactics available for your particular product and/or service.
- An understanding of what your clients are comparing your prices to, as most people use a comparison approach to prices and knowing what their options are. There is a great story/myth about the Americans spending millions of dollars to produce a pen that would work in space and the Russians took a pencil.
- Knowledge of what is your most profitable service or part of your service.
- What part of your fees is set in stone and what part can be flexed?
- Negotiate from a mindset that knows the value you provide to the client not from a perspective of fear. Whilst a fear of losing the client and/or fear of losing the business or a particular transaction is normal in these situations, it can make for non-profitable pricing.
- To avoid using the word 'discount' as this can lead to requests for more and more discounts. Or if it is appropriate spell out clearly the reason for this discount and when it is available. Much better to use a special price label rather than discount.
- To have cost conversations that includes value and outcomes as well as beliefs around your worth and the worth of your services to the client.

Where there is more than one business owner and/or a team a shared and consistently implemented approach to pricing is fundamental. There needs to be a clear understanding of what is negotiable and what is not.

SECTION 3

KNOW YOUR MARKET – WHO ARE YOUR CLIENTS?

THE PURPOSE OF THIS SECTION

This section is to assist you to identify whom do you want to serve? Which clients do you get excited about helping? In marketing speak – what is your 'ideal client' and your 'target market'. The more you have clarity about this the more focused your marketing and networking can be, thus saving you time and money.

CHAPTER 3.1
WHO ARE YOUR CLIENTS AND ARE THERE ENOUGH OF THEM?

The truth is that you cannot serve everyone

What research have you done? Have you actually sat down and analysed who your 'ideal' target clients are?

I know the glib answer is **'Anyone who pays!'** When setting up your own legal or other business, it is wise to do as much research as you can about the marketplace you want to serve. This may be based on your experience from where you are currently working, seeing an opportunity that no one has spotted, or researching through Google or a third party researcher about your potential market. Or you can just start up and hope for the best!

In 2015 The Legal Ombudsman published a survey, based on profiling from survey company YouGov of 32,000 people who had used a legal service in the past two years. According to the research, two-thirds of service users are classed as ABC1 – middle to upper class – with a gross income of £35,000 or more. Indeed, around a quarter of legal services users earn more than £70,000. Almost two-thirds are married or living with a partner and 43% are aged over 55. These statistics could be useful for legal business owners in terms of positioning for those involved in family law matters or services to the senior population.

The survey goes on to say that one-third of consumers read a redtop newspaper, with 19% not reading any. The most watched television shows are news programmes, with Coronation Street and Strictly Come Dancing the most popular entertainment ones.

As the legal services market is fragmenting and commoditising, it is important to understand not only how your clients want the service delivered but also what specific parts of your service suit them, especially if you are going to be involved in developing online products. Please see **Section 5: What does the future hold?**

Following the exercises in **Sections 1 and 2** you will have a clearer idea of what your products and services mean to clients, and also how your USP and personal brand connect with clients.

The following questions and exercises are aimed to enable you to have a place to start from or review your current strategy.

Let's start with some critical questions:

There are three main sets of critical questions – basic, result based and value.

Basic:

1. **Who?** Can you describe your ideal or target client? **Ann** *'When I set up YCFL I found out that 9000+ solicitors are based in Yorkshire. Further examination found that there were predominately based in large and medium law firms. There were less than 800 Sole Practitioners and small firms (4 partners/directors or less). Some of these employed small teams and some large. This meant that different training and coaching programmes were required for where the lawyers worked. In order to develop these different offerings then I had to examine their challenges. Some of the challenges are the same wherever you work – stress management for example and some were different. For example having an internal networking plan to get to know key players and your colleagues is not necessary when there is only four of you working in the same office.'*

2. **What are their challenges?** Once you have identified your ideal client(s) then you can then list their challenges. This latter will inform your language on your website and social media platforms so that it speaks direct to those that you want to attract. This will also assist you in identifying the benefits not the features of your service or product.

3. **How they like to access legal services/products** (or parts of the your service) to answer their challenges can inform your delivery systems.

4. **Where and how** do they want the service to be delivered? Online? By telephone or in person? And how much do they want to pay for each part?

5. **Why?** Do they want it from you? What is your credibility in the market place and the USP of your firm? The questions to be answered here is: What do my clients gain by working with me?

Turn to the following exercise to start to answer these for your business.

YOUR TURN

Where do you start?

When completing the table be as specific as possible. For example don't just say buying and selling businesses but what do they need to achieve this. Do they need an Assignment of a Lease or a Purchase of Commercial Property, Asset or Share Purchase Agreement and so on? What else might they need, for example tax or business advice and how are you going to cover that?

Who are my ideal or target clients?
Why do your clients want your type of legal services?
What need does your product/service fill? And/or what are their challenges? And/or what is it that they require?

What is the risk of losing 'work' and what is the potential for growing 'work'?

How do they want my services delivered? Online or in person?

What else might they want from me?

Result-based questions approach

Often we are concerned with the activities we do on behalf of clients not the impact. Here are three result-based questions for you to answer from your client's perspective.

1. What do my clients SAVE by working with me?
2. What do I IMPROVE for my clients?
3. What do my clients GAIN by working with me?

Let me share with you how I have used this:

1. What do my clients SAVE by working with me?

1. Time, as this is my 'day' job I can share customised techniques, tips and shortcuts with them on their business challenges including leadership and management.
2. Money – same as above
3. 'Wear and tear' on themselves by reducing stress and by increasing their knowledge and skills in these areas
4. Travel time and costs as training is locally provided, often at their office.

2. What do I IMPROVE for my clients?

1. Understanding of the 'business' of law
2. Managing their clients' expectations more effectively
3. Their communications skills such as active listening and influencing techniques to engage their clients more effectively
4. Their leadership and management skills and techniques to motivate their teams more powerfully
5. Dealing with difficult behaviour of colleagues, clients and bosses
6. Strategy for their career or business or clients
7. Their networking, business development and social media skills.

3. What do my clients GAIN by working with me?

1. Inspiration and motivation to change even though it can be uncomfortable and challenging from time to time
2. Practical knowledge and techniques of legal business skills including leadership and management
3. My own knowledge and experience of running my own business

4. The ability to practise these skills in a safe environment – training or coaching
5. Some one who has their 'back' and supports them in their endeavours
6. Introductions to relevant business people and clients.

The above is a starter for ten. You can then use the answers to describe your services. I have expanded the following to include 'added value' and other relevant questions for you to consider.

YOUR TURN

Results-based and additional questions

When considering these questions, have in mind the generic benefits of saving your clients – money/emotional turmoil/time/information/contacts.

1. What do my clients SAVE by working with me?

2. What do I IMPROVE for my clients?

3. So what do my clients GAIN by working with me?

ADDITIONAL QUESTIONS
Have you identified areas you should emphasise that are likely to create value for your clients? What are they?
Have you sought outside assistance or a fresh perspective on possible ways of increasing value for specific clients or sectors?

Why did the client buy? Have those reasons changed in the light of experience?

Who else does the client buy from?

Is there brand loyalty or is the relationship based solely on economic criteria or individual personalities?

Do your clients want different levels of service/products? As mentioned earlier an example is **Ann** *'I have three 'business' themed coaching packages (Gold, Silver and Bronze) as my clients are often at different stages of their business journey.'* This approach to services provides your clients with different price choices too.

CHAPTER 3.2
REACHING OUT TO YOUR 'IDEAL' CLIENTS

There are currently two routes to market for you – online and offline. You should have a strategy for both, incorporating any synergies of both, for your business.

Online – What is a digital strategy?

Put simply, a digital strategy is the process that you undertake to determine that your vision, goals, opportunities and initiatives benefit from what the digital world has to offer to your business.

Developing a digital strategy is about:

- Identifying opportunities and/or challenges where 'digital assets' can provide possible solutions e.g. online packages.
- Identifying the needs of your ideal clients that are closely related to those opportunities – e. g. accessing their documents and/or files.
- An understanding of how digital assets and marketing will meet and fulfill your clients' needs.
- Developing a digital plan which can deliver the vision and that you enjoy or you can outsource to a social media expert to deliver this for you.

A well-managed digital marketing strategy will:

- Increase your market exposure to those ideal clients who use or prefer digital delivery.
- Increase general awareness and specific clients' knowledge of the firm's products and services.
- Save money through a reduction in traditional marketing spend by involving time (not money) and potentially making sales cycles shorter.
- Reduce process costs e.g. using Mail chimp. Though it should be noted that a lot of business email systems would stop bulk emails using this type of system through their security or spam filters.
- Add value to the firm's brand online.

These should be aligned and contribute to your growth, client acquisition and client retention objectives.

It is very easy to get up-to-date statistics about all the Social Media channels so I have not included them here. What is not so easy is to find statistics about legal services and social Media.

The 2015 Legal Ombudsman survey found almost half of consumers visit Facebook at least once a day, with 14% on Twitter and 4% on Instagram and Tumblr. Of those on Twitter, 45% follow Stephen Fry and 24% follow Jonathan Ross so you have to examine how useful Twitter is for you.

Two-fifths of people had used price comparison site MoneySupermarket.com.

Some of our Stars are more active than others as you will see from the table below. Most have a strategy for social media either in place or waiting to be developed. Your social medial strategy should focus on those channels where your clients 'hangout'.

Social media channels preferred by our Stars at time of interview to reach out to their ideal clients

Name	LinkedIn	Facebook	Twitter	Other	Comment
Andrea	Y	Y		N	
Andrew	Y	Y	Y	Google	Very interested in SM
Ann	Y	N	Y	N	Outsourced help
Bill	Y	N	N	YouTube	
Cathy	N	Y	N	N	Most of work comes from Facebook and reviews are shown here
Claire	N	N	Ad hoc	N	
Gary	Y	N (hates FB)	Y	Tech savvy products in pipeline	Has teams dedicated to producing virtual content

Name	LinkedIn	Facebook	Twitter	Other	Comment
Geoff	N	N	N	N	
Ian & Matt	Ad hoc	N	N	N	
Jade	N	N	N	N	
James	Y	Y	Twitter hour	N	Successful Twitter focus
Jane	N	N	N	N	
Jill					
Jodie	Y	Y	Y	Instagram	Has SM employee within the firm
John	N	N	N	N	
Kate	Y	Y	Safeguarding hour	YouTube	Has 6000+ twitter followers
Kirstie	Y	N	N	YouTube	Outsourced marketing
Laura	Y	Y	Y	N	
Liz	Y	Y	Y	Link TV Google	SM employee within the firm
Martin	Ad hoc	N	N	N	
Miguel	Y	N	N	N	
Noreen	Y	N	N	Google	Outsourced assistance
Peter	Y	N	N	N	
Rachel	Y	Y	Y	Instagram	
Richard	N	N	N	N	
Samira	Y	Y	Y		Has SM/marketing employee
Simon	Y	N	N	N	
Thomas	Y	N	Y	N	Business Partner 1500 followers

YOUR TURN

What social media channels do you wish to use?

Here is a table for you to identify and map your strategy for each of the channels that will enable you to access your ideal clients and/or convert your contacts into clients. I suggest you work through in order.

1. Define your *virtual* networking goals for this channel.	**2. Marketing: Identify your clients/ contacts and the messages/ information flow for them.**
3. Set out your conversion activities to your contacts and clients on this platform.	**4. What measurement process will you use to track effectiveness?**

Offline – What is your marketing/networking strategy?

Strategy

In order to maximise your time and money, it is worth having a specific strategy to target your ideal profitable clients first. Your strategy should also be realistic about your time and money available to physically connect with contacts and clients. The old adage – know, like and trust – takes time.

Evaluate your strategy on a regular basis looking for gaps. For example **Jade** reaching out to clients direct where previously they had predominately relied on introducers.

The main two used by our stars are:

1 **Networking**. In **Section 1 Chapter 1.2** there is a list of *support* networks and **Section 1 Chapter 1.3** shows the importance of networks as identified by **John** and **Peter**.

Networking is one of the primary marketing offline routes used by all professionals and business people. So if this is a challenge for you, then I would definitely recommend training and coaching to provide skills and confidence to build the 'know-like-trust' in these groups. Then you need to join one! My recommendation is not to join too many and stretch yourself too thin; and to give each one at least six months before you decide whether this is for you or not. Building relationships takes time. The more time you spend networking the more opportunity you have to practise your 'elevator speech' and small talk.

If you want to build links with your networking groups in your home city, just Google as there are too many to list here in this book. An example by two of our Stars is York Breakfast Club. **James** and **Rachel**. **Andrew** found his local BNI 'mind blowing' when he first joined because he came face-to-face with lots of different business perspectives. **Bill** is another fan of BNI.

There are gender based which are open to all sexes. Three examples are Women In Business Network: **Ann**, **Cathy**, **Jane** and **Noreen**, Women in the Law **Ann** and **Jodie**.

One of our Stars actually started two of her own networking groups – Thriving Minds and Thrive Women: **Jodie**.

There are many different ones for you to choose from finding the one where your target market attends or provides support to you and your business is worthwhile. Be ready to move on when it no longer serves you.

2 **Presentations/Conferences:** Some of our Stars use presentations to promote awareness to clients – legal colleagues – referrers and/or 'trade' associations: **Ann**, **Jane**, **Jodie**, **Laura**, **Rachel** and **Thomas.** Two of which have had training from me to make best use of presentations to engage their audience both during and after the presentation.

Others stated that they attend relevant professional conferences and seminars: **Ann**, **Bill**, **John**, **Laura** and **Thomas**.

Given their longevity in the profession some of our stars have built up a considerable network of referrers and professional contacts: **Martin**, **Miguel** and **Richard** to name three.

YOUR TURN

Which clients do you wish to focus on in the next 6-12 months?

For example what online or offline activities do I wish to do in connection with the following areas to support my new strategy and/or client acquisition or business growth plan?

New or potential clients or referrers

Existing clients or referrers

Communities

Business Sectors

Other

A key question is how do I not lose focus and avoid being distracted but at the same time take advantage of opportunities? Short answer you check to see if it is in alignment with your vision or whether you need the cash!

Don't forget to record in your success log what worked so that you can do more of the activities that work and that you enjoy.

CHAPTER 3.3
HOW DOES YOUR PERSONAL BRAND HELP YOU IN YOUR MARKETPLACE?

Overview

There is a lot of mythology about brand. Most business owners including legal ones start with a logo led normally by some marketing people. The next stage most businesses seem look at is a strapline without understanding that these are the result of *who and what you and what your business stands for*. I would strongly recommend that you look at your values and visions first as this will really infuse your logo and strapline.

Social media has most young lawyers wanting to show a personality, beyond their legal function e.g. **Jodie** and **Laura**, which then becomes a vital part of their brand.

An example this type of brand is **Jodie**. She is a campaigner for Mental Health First Aiders in the workplace and is passionate about everyone *thriving* in the workplace. So the name of her firm is Thrivelaw with a strapline of *'Achieving more together'*. This supports a holistic offering of services and products around employment to enable clients to thrive. Strong social media coverage about her and her team is a dynamic component of her brand too.

In fact I would strongly recommend that you start with your personal brand and see how that fits with your business model.

Therefore you need to start with vision (see **Section 1.Chapter 1.4**) for your legal or other business now and in the future to be able to choose the right logo/strapline and all the other visual representations of your Brand.

Prerequisite to creating or understanding a your own 'brand' is considering:

1. Your personal qualities as a lawyer;
2. Knowing how you are currently perceived, and how accurate is the current perception;
3. Clients (or potential clients) perception of legal services, and lawyers – solicitors – barristers generally;

4. Your firm's attributes that make you different and better than your competitors, and;
5. How to capture your brand positioning statement (strapline) and/or logo to demonstrate this.

Qualities of our Stars – which forms the bedrock of their brand and business

Where do your personal qualities fit with your brand? Some of these may resonate with you but if you are not sure or would like to get a more detailed picture of your qualities then try the following exercise in the next section. Also please note that these may change over time and as they are reduced to three, these are not all of their qualities.

Name	Top three qualities
Andrea	1. Unwavering belief in my clients 2. Naturally positive person 3. Nice to work with
Ann	1. Enthusiasm for teaching and coaching 2. Passionate about maintaining and developing my own expertise 3. Generous with my time and expertise
Andrew	1. Truth (so important it ended up in the name of his firm) 2. Being a Quaker 3. Helping people
Bill	1. Resilience 2. Passionate 3. Proactive
Cathy	1. Reliable 2. Honesty 3. Thorough
Claire	1. Personable 2. Professional 3. Proactivity and accountability
Gary	1. Stubbornness 2. Persistence 3. Problem solving
Geoff	1. Persistence 2. Compassion for my clients who are often in a distressed state 3. Constantly looking for quicker ways to achieve objectives
Ian	1. Incessant Optimism 2. Resilience 3. Creativity

Name	Top three qualities
Matt	1. Stoic 2. Resilience 3. Straightforwardness
Jade	1. Efficient 2. Personable and approachable 3. Our personalities
James	1. Tenacious 2. Calm and collected under pressure 3. Entrepreneurial spirit
Jane	1. Professionalism 2. Energy 3. Approachability
Jill	1. Genuinely care 2. Identify the true problems and obstacles 3. Stand up where they might not be able to
Jodie	1. Collaboration with others 2. Authentically passionate about what we do 3. Transparency - fixed fees
John	1. Care about the client and the outcome 2. Able to put myself in client's shoes 3. Client perspective - I help take away their stress
Kate	1. Openness 2. Being approachable 3. Trustworthy and reliant
Kirstie	1. Commercially focused 2. Openness 3. Passionate
Laura	1. My legal expertise as I only focus on one area 2. Pragmatic 3. Approachable
Liz	1. Tenacity 2. Imaginative 3. Good Lawyer
Martin	1. Clear direction - take worry and fear to a linear path and turn it into a goal 2. Visionary 3. Empathy
Miguel	1. Starting with end in mind 2. Seeking first to understand another person before seeking to be understood 3. Focus on combing the ingredients to make a long lasting placement

Name	Top three qualities
Noreen	1. Straightforward 2. Transparency - Fixed fees 3. Personal service
Peter	1. Optimism 2. Hard work 3. Just being friendly to people
Rachel	1. Approachability - clients and professionals 2. Efficient 3. Client's perspective - Not just legal experts but give practical advice in emotional situations
Richard	1. Persistent 2. Hard working 3. Very driven
Samira	1. Forward thinking - use technology quite a bit 2. Affordable and flexible 3. Lawyers with personality is our USP
Simon	1. Bold 2. Brash 3. Responsive and problem solving
Thomas	1. Reasonably humble 2. Approachable 3. Not thinking like a typical lawyer - more commercial

How do others perceive you, your services and products?

The perception of what you offer and your 'firm' are linked.

Above I talk about *'perception of added value'* and I would like to expand on this before moving to an exercise that brings 1–3 identified above together. So *'Brand' occupies 'space' in the perception of the client*, and is what results from the *totality of what the client takes into consideration before making a decision* about whether to instruct you or not. So lets bring these together.

Here is a testimonial example of mine and how I deconstructed it: A delegate on my Management Stage 2 course said: *'Ann was an excellent presenter. Extremely knowledgeable and approachable. I got a lot more from the course than I expected and will definitely recommend the course and Ann to my peers.'*

So the 'space' in my clients mind I occupy is from that one testimonial is:

- Excellent presenter
- Extremely knowledgeable
- Extremely approachable
- They get a lot from my courses – it exceeds expectations
- Clients will recommend me

This means when describing my training I can say '*that my delegates find me extremely knowledgeable and approachable so that they come away with real value from my courses. In fact as I exceed their expectations they will recommend me.*'

YOUR TURN

Reviewing yourself through your client's eyes.

List five of nicest things/testimonials anyone has ever said about you not your services (character assessment):

Testimonial	How can you describe yourself using their language?
1.	
2.	
3.	
4.	
5.	

Where does your 'name' sit within your brand?

Once you have decided on your vision and personal brand then you set about naming your business vehicle. This is not as simple as it sounds. You can see the challenges that this posed for our Stars below. Where possible you need to be aware of the future direction or sale of your business as name changing can be a painful and expensive.

11 key elements to consider in naming your business vehicle:

1 **Is the name going to be yours?** It can be tricky to sell your business based solely on your name when you have decided to move on without a rebranding for the new owners. An example is **Andrea** (see point seven). If you use solicitor in your name such **Bailoran Solicitors**, then to continue to use the word solicitor it would need to be 'sold' to owners, which included a solicitor. See point four below.

2 You could choose **Legal** as part of your name. Here are a few examples:

a. **Roche Legal** – *'That is my surname, and legal to make sure people know what it is from the title – important to convey we are a legal firm.'* **Rachel**.

b. Use your full name – **Claire Murphy Legal**.

c. Choose 'Legal' with a brand name such as **Virtuoso Legal**. *'I wanted a brand name that wasn't just me! I thought "Elizabeth Ward and Co" or whatever just wouldn't cut it in this day and age. Virtuoso indicated a brilliant skill level – which we have, and it also wasn't just about me. If you want to build a brand and a team then in my view you need a word that evokes your service and not one person.'* **Liz**.

d. How about something that you are passionate about added to legal? **Front Row Legal**. *'There is a plan to change the name – idea is to rebrand it, a new website but I have fallen behind with that task. So bear in mind that whatever name you choose you can and indeed may need to change this as your business grows.'*

e. What you stand for added to legal? Two examples – **Truth Legal** – Truth is a fundamental Quaker Value. *'We chose the name "Consilia" which means working together in Latin. We believe Consilia represents who we are and our relationship with our clients.'* **Laura**.

f. *'My wife is Italian so when you walk around Italy you see 'Studio Legale' everywhere"* – **Matt** and so Legal Studios was born.

g. **The Legal Director** – *'it is exactly what we do, we find part time Legal Directors for SMEs'* – **Kirstie**.

3 Are you going to choose both **owners**' names, such as: **Lester Campbell**, **Robinson Ralph** as your branded name? This means you are starting with a 'virgin' brand that needs to be built.

4 Do you want to add **'Solicitors'** in your chosen name to demonstrate that you are regulated professionals? For example, attaching it to your initials **SCE Solicitors** like Samira, or to a name of your choice **Kaiser Solicitors.** In the latter case, this was the name of **Noreen's** father.

5 You can choose the **service** you provide as part of your firm name using an **acronym** such as IDR *'I was thinking of all sorts of names – keen to not want to put my name in it – make sure people knew it was my business but without my name. I had it in mind succession – makes it easier. I wanted to make sure it did what it said – IDR = Inheritance Dispute Resolution.'* – **Martin** Another way is to use the name of the product *'I was aware that if I wanted to go into any directory, A would be at the top, my surname begins with a W so that would also be right at the bottom.'* **Jane – Adel Wills**. Do you want your name to have the advantage of being 'A' at the front of the alphabet?

6 An unusual choice is to **tie your name up with that of an external organisation**, which provides an 'instant' brand to your start up 'firm'. This could be particularly appealing to ABS entities. *'The FTA is interesting actually, we thought about whether to call ourselves that or not because FTA as a brand in the dental industry is quite well known. A dentist knows them as brokers and finance brokers and that kind of thing. And we thought as well: do we advertise the fact that this new legal entity is linked?"* **Thomas**.

7 If you have moved **outside legal services** then using your own name might be the best approach, such as **Andrea Morrison** and this can make it easier to choose domain names for your website. This does not stop you setting up other websites such as the Safeguarding Association, **Kate** if you want one that reflects more your services than you.

8 Are you buying a business and is there a good reason to **keep the name**? **Coles**. *'So the very first firm we acquired in 2006 was called David J Cole & Company Solicitors founded by David Cole in North Allerton in 1965. It had a good reputation in the town. It had been there for over 40 years. I found it a little frustrating listening to people on the phone introducing that name as it was quite long but equally I wanted to respect and reflect our*

heritage and the history of where we came from. We're very much firmly rooted in North Allerton – that's where our head office is. That's our history and heritage and respecting David's name. David's son still works for the firm and is still part of that. We have a relationship as a firm with David's widow, etc, so it's a matter of respecting the past but transforming the name to something a little bit more easier on the tongue, a little bit quicker to be said on the telephone and it's little bit higher up the alphabet as well.' **Peter**.

9 Choose something entirely **different or unusual** such as **Rradar** *'I did not want anything that was like a normal law firm name. I wanted to build something about a regulation radar, a responsibility radar, a risk and reward radar, it was about navigation and radar. Earlier I also used to do CPD teaching and things like that and lectures to the profession about criminal law to build my brand and network and opportunity for business. I used to talk about RRA and the double R advantage – rules and regulations and how you cannot avoid them – if you don't want to get caught offside in football, then learn the damn rule, then you can play the way you want to play. The laws are there as we as humans cannot be trusted to do the right thing all the time – so we keep on having to manage behaviour. 'This is where it's great, some people in the firm would be shocked and say you can't do that with a brand name but that's where you need a sense of humour in life'* **Gary**. Where the name is radical or different then you may need a fast acting PR campaign to get your message across as to what you stand for in your early days. Does **Paradigm law** provide your clients with knowledge that you are delivering legal services to them that is radically different from other law firms e. g. fixed fees to provide certainty in an uncertain time? **James** *'well we hope that everybody knows that we are the fixed fee firm of family lawyers. Can't say more than that – it's all over the website'.* The challenge **James** found is that it is often misspelt and searching on Google shows a lot of judges who use the word – paradigm in their judgment was totally unexpected.

10 Focus on the **feelings** conjured by your brand. What will your clients or potential clients feel when they say the name of your entity? If you've conducted adequate market research, no one knows your audience better than you – then choosing the perfect firm name is your chance to demonstrate that fact. Your name should fit snugly into your brand strategy, making your entire plan one cohesive system. **Jodie** wanted **Thrive law** as this conjured feelings about 'thriving' and fit with her campaigns and expertise.

11 **Brand Evolution. Ann**: *'Beyond the Brief was set up in 2003 as a training company aimed at lawyers in private practice. In 2013–4 I returned to my roots, the In-house lawyers section. As I had already written*

a book in 2007 called Managing External Legal Resources, this seemed the perfect name and brand for my website aimed at this market. What it meant was that I had to set up a new website to support the brand and keep it totally separate from Beyond the Brief which was aimed at private practice. I then wrote another book for this sector with my co-author Richard Tapp called The In-house Lawyers Toolkit.

Following an illness and two knee operations, I decided to set up Yorkshire Courses for Lawyers as staying with my in-house clients, would have meant working more and more in London. As my old Beyond the Brief website was set up in 2003 and was not Word Press I have now taken down Beyond the Brief as a live site. This will now take you direct to Yorkshire Courses for Lawyers.'

Some further suggestions for consideration:

- **Your name should be simple to recall.** Branding is all about creating experiences that go hand-in-hand with the brand name and logo, making positive, associative memories as a means to revenue building. When brand names are easy to remember (and hard to forget), the sales funnel is shortened. A brand name that's difficult to pronounce, spell, or remember is unlikely to surface in crucial conversations – the ones where word-of-mouth marketing happens. Also a small practical tip is that it must be easily pronounced on the telephone. Having said that, as you saw from the Stars, some of them 'broke' these rules. When you are forging your own path, this is your choice.

- **Respect copyright laws.** This will require some research, but is well worth the effort to avoid copyright infringement lawsuits. You should also register your own brand name's copyright (internationally) to protect it.

- **Consider available domain names.** It is advantageous for your brand name to double as your website URL – for Internet search reasons as well as for brand consistency. A search for available domain names may help you to settle on a brand name. The same applies to any limited company you may set up too.

- **Is there a chance your brand name will go global?** Whether this is your goal or you simply don't want to rule out enormous success, beware of the cultural implications that some brand names may carry. Something that is adored in one country or culture may break social convention in another, eliminating chances of your brand even being considered in a global market.

Why are we doing this?

It is helpful to identify from day one, or at other significant points in your business journey, your USP and your alignment to your brand, especially as you and your business will grow over time.

This raises the question 'can you now condense your USP qualities into a single statement that is relatable to your clients? My current example is *'enabling lawyers to release their business brilliance so that they can serve more clients profitably'*. **Ann**.

From our Stars these are generally about service, for example *'legal experts that work for you'* **Noreen**, *'Proudly serving you from Yorkshire and the Tees Valley* **Peter**, *'Achieving more together'* **Jodie**, *'lawyers for business, for healthcare, for you'* **Thomas**.

Another reason for reviewing your brand and website is to keep them up-to-date, as your business evolves. During your first 12 months it is likely that your website will change as you get to know what is or isn't working or it may be that you can now spend more time and money on it.

Summary

Once you have as much clarity as you can, then I recommend that you look at Branding in **three** areas; and it is important to have these aligned.

1. **You (and your staff if you have one whether they are employed or consultants).**
2. **Legal and/or non-legal services or products.**
3. **Your Organisation or business** – see visions **Section 1 Chapter 1.4.**

The first one concerning your **personal brand is key** as it is the core of your business especially where you are a sole practitioner. As the saying goes *'people buy from people'*. Even when you expand you will probably want to include others within your team with similar values and brands to support yours.

SECTION 4

BE A PROFESSIONAL NOT AN AMATEUR IN BUSINESS

THE PURPOSE OF THIS SECTION

Here is an overview of the business mindset and mechanics required to move from employed to business owner.

CHAPTER 4.1
MOVING YOUR RISK TOLERANCE FROM LEGAL RISK TO BUSINESS RISK

Introduction

One of the major differences is that if you get legal risk wrong you can lose your practising certificate, which stops your career in law. If you get your business risk wrong then it may be possible to practise law for another depending on how the business folded. Having said that, do not underestimate the financial implications (e.g. losing your house) of not understanding and managing this risk, particularly cash flow nor the adverse emotional turmoil. See **Section 4 Chapter 4.2**.

Another difference is that business risk is an art and a willingness to try different things. In doing so, business development has to be tracked to ensure that you can move quickly to grasp an opportunity or minimise risk.

There are five choices to deal with risk and you must assess your risks and decide which you are going to do:

1. **Accept** these as part and parcel of running a business. Everyone's risk appetite is different. Consider those that you can and will take personal responsibility for versus those that you want to transfer to or share with someone else.

2. **Eliminate** these by choosing not to do a certain kind of work. For example, transactional work such as conveyancing is definitely higher risk than other work types. It also carries the need to have a client account, so consider carefully what work types you will choose to offer.

3. **Manage** these, for example, within your office manual have a social media policy to ensure you and your staff stay within the ethics of the profession as well as the law; have back up systems in case of hacking, to name two.

4. **Insure** (see insurance section below)

5. **Transfer** to another*

*In order to minimise the risk of setting up as a sole practitioner, you can form a partnership either with a spouse **Bill** and **Thomas** or with someone more experienced who you trust and that can and is willing to help you **Jade** with Rodney, or who you can share your vision and values, **Ian & Matt** or **Simon** with Juliet.

There are now quite a few different legal organisational structures for minimising the risk such as setting up a limited company or limited liability partnerships as well as forming an ABS. When you are ready to start your business, then you will need to think what is the right vehicle for you including the tax implications of each one as well as the right one to grow your business.

Risk identification process

Make a list of risks integral to your business from the following areas:

- Strategic including competition risk.
- Operational.
- Reputational.
- Financial (profitability).
- Technology risks.
- Communication risks with clients including mistakes handling.
- Regulatory risks – see below.
- Knowledge management.
- Compliance – see below.

You could use a 'traffic light' process to assess the seriousness of these and which to tackle first and what measurement systems you will need. Our Stars who are legal business owners tend to do this with their compliance managers, insurance brokers and their accountants.

Stay regulated or not?

There is now a choice of regulators depending on what area of law you practise.

Anyone can, in theory, offer any form of legal advice provided that the work is not:

- Reserved Activity (The Legal Services Act 2007) such as the right to conduct litigation and rights of audience (now includes Chartered Legal Executives); certain elements of the conveyancing and probate registrations procedures and witnessing certain documents.

- Immigration advice or assistance if you not registered with the Office of Immigration Services Commissioner.
- Work which is covered by the Compensation Act 2006.
- Legally aided work unless you were an approved provider in the legal aid scheme.

Even if your area of law is outside these categories, you may also want to be regulated by the SRA. It may be important to your clients that you have the SRA as your regulator. **Jane** decided to practise her legal services as a 'regulated' lawyer under the Institute of Professional Will Writers *(IPWW)* instead of a practising solicitor under the SRA. This is why she chose to do so: *'I had been a solicitor for a number of years and also worked with the Crown Prosecution Service. I had taken a break from the law so was coming back into the forum. I was looking for an alternative from the S.R.A., which was not attractive to me as a sole practitioner. I investigated various professional will writing institutions. The one I chose was the IPWW when I came off the roll of solicitors. I re-qualified. With the IPWW I still have a code of conduct to abide by, an insurance obligation (£2 million) and the bonus is that it is Trading Standards Approved'.*

There are many compliance managers who serve sole practitioners and small firms. They can assist you at the start and audit your processes to ensure you are compliant with the SRA rules. It is not the purpose of this book to recommend any specific ones. As **Simon** advises *'speak to people who are already doing it and see who helped them'* and this is why I suggest you reach out to your contacts and find one that suits you and your legal business. Don't underestimate the time and effort it will take. **Section 5 Chapter 5.1** is relevant here.

The SRA is continually updating the rules and regulations so these will need to be checked out when you are ready to set up and during the life of your regulated business. As I was nearing the end of writing this book, Professor Mayson published a paper re-thinking legal services regulation, so watch this space.

For those outside of law, regulations are tricky, as often there are no official regulators. For example: **Ann** is a member of The Professional Speaking Association and The Professional Speakers Academy, and **Kate** is a member of The Trainers Association. These are commercial organisations set up to aid and provide professional guidance to their members.

Do not cut corners on regulatory matters whoever you are regulated with

More solicitors are prosecuted for misconduct than ever before and the complexity of some of the cases is resulting in longer proceedings and larger bills. In November 2018 the Solicitors Disciplinary Tribunal requested an extra £300,000 for its operating budget, based on an estimated 35% rise in its workload. The SRA has projected it will need 406 sitting days in 2019, as opposed to 300 last year, while applications to prosecute will increase from around 136 to more than 200.

One of the known pending changes is that from 25th November 2019 solicitors will have even more freedom to choose how they want to offer legal services to their clients. There is now flexibility for solicitors to practise law away from the direct regulation of the SRA. That being said, any solicitor choosing to operate, as a freelancer should still respect that they have significant obligations from a risk and compliance perspective. Remember that irrespective of your regulation, your clients will still expect the highest standards and duty of care, and will still hold you to account if you let them down.

If you do choose to operate as a freelance solicitor you may no longer be obliged to purchase professional indemnity insurance, but it would certainly be advisable to still do so, to protect your clients and more importantly to protect yourself! When you choose to step away from operating in a regulated environment, only those freelance solicitors that can still demonstrate the right approach to risk management and compliance will actually be able to obtain affordable and appropriate insurance. Do not be tempted to use this new regime as an excuse to cut regulatory corners. It is recommended that you engage with the right professional advisors to ensure you are protecting yourself and your clients adequately.

The 'boring stuff' – business infrastructure reminders to reduce risk

There is so much information available on these topics that the purpose of this section is to remind you to think about what you need.

You also need to think what are you going to do yourself and what support do you want from 'outsourced' or virtual suppliers. A recommendation is that you focus on the parts that you enjoy. Whilst this is not the most exciting part of your business, the quicker you implement these support structures the better.

I have set out a checklist of areas for you to consider for your business plan in alphabetical order. This is not meant to be comprehensive.

Accounts

Clearly all of our interviewees have accountants, they just use them differently. **Rachel** has three and utilises the three for their different strengths. You can use one firm to assist your strategy and another for the operational accounting. **Richard. Jodie** has an external Finance Director to look at financial strategy on a monthly basis as well as an accountant for operational work.

From a pure business perspective all business owners need to monitor their cash flow and accounts on a regular basis and have regular meetings with their accountants. This is both a time and cost factor to be taken into consideration when assessing your time management capabilities. There are also banking and accounting apps – in fact, nearly everything is an app so it is worth checking out if this is your preferred way to have instant access to financial information.

All of the Stars involved in regulated legal practice, work hard to ensure compliance with the SRA Accounts Rules.

Back office automation to improve efficiency

Successful small firms understand that their very survival can depend on how they manage their costs. One way to do this is to utilise technology.

Do you want to be a paperless office? Are you going to be Cloud-based? **James, Jodie** and **Rachel** to name three who are.

What client-based templates, apart from your client care letters, do you require to be set up on whatever system you use?

What legal templates do you need to have set up to provide quick and efficient services to your clients? For example commercial/corporate agreements, employment agreements such as settlement agreements, commercial and residential property documentation.

If you have to use a range of documents for your transactions, then you may want to investigate software, which automate the production of these. For example Hotdocs claim to be able to reduce the time spent on creating your first drafts by up to 95%. Or you may have your own favourite or this ability to automate documents within your current case management system. Bear in mind that as soon as you have 'learnt' the system, there will be a software upgrade!

Another most important back office support is your accounts package. Quick Books/Xero seem to be the most popular amongst those interviewed? This should enable you to reduce expenditure on support from your accountants, but check how it feeds into your case management system.

Compliance support

This is relevant for each of our Stars and they all had their favourite external compliance manager to support them with compliance. A question you might want to consider is – do you want someone based in Yorkshire or does it not matter where they are located? Or do you want an ex-solicitor assisting you, as there are many who have moved into this market. It is worth chatting amongst your contacts for their recommendations like **Simon** did? Or do you want to be regulated by another regulator like **Jane**?

Case management software and software support

The most obvious is a case management system and most of the Stars who deliver legal services use either LEAP or Clio. It is worth checking in with your contacts to find out what they like and don't like about these systems.

Both of these systems should provide you with the management information for you to track the financial viability of your legal business as well as the legal services.

Client Relationship Management (CRM) software

There are many different types of software and it is worth reviewing what is out there at the time you want to buy this. The first decision is do you want to use a separate software product that is different to a case management system or even are you happy with a spreadsheet? For example two of us use Capsule, which is a dedicated database tracking contact, pipelines and sales. There is in fact The 'Link App', which was launched by a Solicitor now turned business owner called Lauren Riley; and had she lived in Yorkshire, I would have been able to include her inspirational story in my book! There are many attractive features including client portal, e-signing, and document sharing to name three. You could use a PESTLE or its equivalent to track the changes to your business and its CRM requirements.

Contingency plans

Lawyers are generally very good at looking at the worst-case scenarios and this should be translated to your business. Have you got a power of attorney in place to access your client files, business accounts and digital assets if you are a sole practitioner?

Do you have Key Man insurance cover for sickness and death or a policy to protect you should you not be able to drive? Take the example of Jake Fox, Managing Director – Professional Risks at J M Glendinning. He practises what he preaches and such a policy came in very handy when he recently broke a bone in his foot leaving him unable to drive for a period of time.

Exit Plans

Are you building a business that can be sold and/or attract others to succeed you? Do you have a time frame in mind on when to come out and is this built into your vision and business plans? **Ann** *'I don't have a time frame for coming out of my business because I am focusing on the work that I enjoy not building an asset to sell. That means it is a service delivered by me, and I do not plan to develop training products to sell online.'*

HR and/or office manager

Jodie and **John** have an outsourced office manager who spends time in their office providing assistance on things like office procedure manuals and appraisals whereas **Rachel** uses an outsourced HR manager. The important bit is not titles; it is ensuring this support is in place.

Insuring your risks

We have briefly touched on some insurance policies already. When setting up an SRA regulated firm you are obliged to purchase professional indemnity insurance (PII). Make sure you take this process seriously as without obtaining quotes for PII, you will not be allowed to set up your firm. Most insurers want to see a robust business plan as part of the application process. They will also need to understand your experience, not just in providing legal advice, but also on how you plan to run the business. If you are employing any staff you are also obliged to purchase Employers Liability Insurance and you may also need Public Liability Insurance if you will be meeting clients. You will also want to insurer the contents of your office.

Further don't ignore some of the newer insurance products, such as Management Liability Insurance, which insures you in your duties as a business owner, including any regulatory investigations. Cyber Liability insurance is also worth considering, particularly if you intend to have a client account and/or you will be maintaining client data.

Finally consider life insurance and critical illness cover to protect you and your dependents in the event that you suffer death or serious illness or injury. And to protect your business in the same circumstance, Key Man insurance really should be a must for all small businesses.

A good insurance broker that specialises in the legal sector should be able to help you with all of this and to explain the key covers you should be considering.

IT

IT support for all your different systems and Internet hosting is vital. There was too much variety between our Stars to provide any synopsis. One recommendation by **Liz** was to review whether you have outstripped your current provider and need to move to a larger organisation; or has your supplier grown with you? On the other hand *'I have just moved hosting companies because I wanted a local supplier not one in America; and it was relatively painless.'* **Ann**.

Marketing

Do you love marketing? If so what type of marketing? Networking? Emailing GDPR compliant lists? Having read and completed the sections earlier in the book you will have a clear idea about what type of marketing will appeal to your potential clients and what steps you want to do yourself or outsource to a marketing expert on professional services. There is plenty of opportunity to engage with a variety of specialists in this area from recommendations by your professional contacts.

To be effective marketing needs to be aligned to your strategy whether on or offline. It is strongly recommended that you are as clear as you can be in what you want the marketing initiatives to achieve for you, as well as tracking the cost of marketing against the benefits. Further there needs to be consistency of approach which builds trust in your name and service.

Social media

From **Section 3 Chapter 3.2** you can see which of our Stars loved using social media. Some of these did their own social media and some did not. **Jodie** has a social media apprentice working for her and **James** dedicates his time to a Twitter business hour, as social media is such an important marketing arm for both of these.

Website

You will need a website and I wish I had a pound for every legal website I have reviewed over the last 15 years. A lot of money can be spent on how it looks or not. The main driver here should be – does it represent you and what you do in a way that is useful to clients and not a vanity project or obviously a basic template.

One point about legal websites is that I feel strongly about is that it should show the people in the firm and not have 'invisible' workers. How can you build the 'know-like-trust' relationship, if they are seeing a 'faceless' website/ So I recommend that you use a good website developer who knows the legal market.

Websites can be more than a 'credibility' badge; it can have pop-up messages or contact boxes for clients to get in touch. It can be used to provide free resources such as blogs and factsheets. It can take payment online and lots more. How do you want your clients to access your services and interact with your website? Your website can provide you with a competitive edge if designed with the client's journey in mind.

Once your website is up and running – your job is done or not! I know that as trainers and coaches, **Andrea**, **Kate** and myself **(Ann)** are continually refining our websites on a yearly basis – even though it feels like a weekly basis. During the writing of this book, nearly all our Stars have updated/renewed/rebranded their websites. Again this will have to be factored into your running costs and time in running the business, as it will need to be continually refreshed. '*Very frustrating when people don't do the work I have paid them to do because I am then trying to find someone else – a lot of this comes from tech stuff. It has been a frustrating challenge over the last few years to get the systems and technologies in place*' **Rachel**.

You have to decide a budget to refresh your website that is appropriate to your legal business. If you are using a website just to show you exist then it is very unlikely to attract client enquires and that might be ok for you. **Jane's** website is a prime example as she meets the majority of her potential clients offline.

CHAPTER 4.2
MANAGING THE 'HIGHS & LOWS' OF RUNNING A BUSINESS

This is how our Stars manage 'Highs and Lows'

One Star **Geoff** did state that it depends on the type of 'low'. Was it due to financial or emotional reasons? You may have your own categories of these. I have set out below a selection of approaches being used by those interviewed.

Mental or mindset approach

Andrea's approach is to work on mindset from the beginning. In fact this is a very good starting point. Understanding how you view feast versus famine and having strategies to manage both is fundamental to a successful business.

Jane uses acceptance and flexibility. *'Accepting that business ebbs and flows. Having been in business before this I realised there is certain life cycle to work. I divide my day up into three – mornings, afternoons and evenings. If I am seeing clients or working in the evening then I will have part of the day off – I will not work a full day and the evening. The joy of working for yourself is you can choose what you do and when you do it.'*

Andrew uses philosophy to think like a Stoic. Again the purpose is to *'remain unfazed'* by it particularly if you practise litigation then you will see highs and lows here as well as your business.

Bill focuses on attitude: *'I happen to love the work I do, can't expect to love everyday. But I love my clients even the most challenging ones.'*

James emphasises positivity and flexibility: *'we try and try to see things in a positive light generally. I think it helps if there is that flexibility as well because if I don't feel like doing work.... I'll get off at lunch and maybe work a bit later in the evening.'*

Jodie uses a success record. *'Give yourself credit when you do something good. Because being a business owner you kind of get half the opportunity for somebody to appraise you and tell you that you've done really well. So you have to do that for yourself. So what I do is I actually reflect on a regular basis where I look at what I've done that way what my challenges what are my takeaways that week what were my wins and I have all of these different categories in a book that I write down. So those are really, really helpful. And* *then it also helps with the lows because when you look at the Low's you can then say: well actually did all these other amazing things this week. So it puts it into perspective rather than just dwelling on one or one issues.'*

John concentrates on problem solving, not taking things personally and surrounding himself with good people. *'Problem solving is part of the job. I think you have to not take it personally as you naturally instinctively do. You need to step back. If things have gone wrong you need to address it. Are you wrong instead of thinking instinctively you don't like the situation? Where can I lay the blame may be a natural reaction. Assess it – get someone else to look over. Scrutinise yourself a bit better. The lows can be pretty low because there is only you to deal with them and its your problem I think the other people around here are very aware of that. They are very supportive of both situations. So you work with a good set of people get that support anyway'*

Dealing with death of those close. **Samira** *'Again this was a difficult question – as a small business I have had a quite a few lows, one of which was the loss of my friend and senior associate last December. How I managed it was to keep going really. One of the first things I did was to get a mental health first aider certification in August. My clients still needed me at the end of the day – there is light at the end of the tunnel. In terms of the highs is to share it with the team – we try to have a quarterly night out and recently introduced end of month pizza just so that we can sit and get to talk to each other, nine out ten times we are in two different sites.'*

Family and connections that support you

Family life, particularly support from spouse and children was mentioned by **Gary**, **John**, **Martin**, **Richard**, and **Simon**. **Ann**, **Kate**, and **Peter** identified having a good support network. **Laura** and **John** said having both family and support networks was important.

Physical activities to combat stress

Exercise to de-stress with the gym being the most popular method, **Claire**, **Jade**, **Jodie** and **Noreen**. In my case, I don't like the gym so I have a personal trainer. Others have animals with walking the dog being the most popular, **Matt**, **Jodie**, and **Liz**. It is horses for **Jane**.

Other ways to support you as mentioned by the Stars

- Books on inspirational lawyers – **Gary**
- Holidays – **Ann**, **Jane**, **Jodie**, and **Miguel**
- Experience running your business – **Ann**, **Claire**, **Jay**, and **Liz**
- Reading and listening to professional self-help books **Ann**, **Gary** and **Jodie**.

- Meditation – **Ann, Jodie**, and **Miguel.**
- Mindfulness – **Ann** – *in fact I teach this and have written three blogs on this topic.*
- Sharing the highs with the team – I suspect that all do these but **Jodie** and **Samira** mentioned it.
- DJ-ing – **Miguel.**
- **Richard** – overcoming adversity in the past proves you are good at what you do – likes to use football analogies .
- **Thomas** perspective and fallback plan.

What is resilience and why do I need it?

Resilience is a person's mental ability to recover quickly from misfortune, illness or difficulties in general. Resilient people develop a mental capacity that allows them to adapt more easily during adversity, bending like bamboo instead of breaking.

As you can read, running a legal or any type of business has many positive sides, but it is rarely easy! Standing up to the challenges which legal business life throws at you is a key skill to a successful career, and a happy life in general. This takes **resilience**.

Resilience is **important** because it:

- Helps us to maintain balance during difficult or stressful periods in our lives;
- Enables us to develop protection mechanisms against experiences which could be overwhelming;
- Allows us to adapt to change and thrive in unsettled times;
- Supports us to bounce back from adversity;
- Protects us from a number of mental health problems.

How resilient are you?

To help you answer this question, here's another: have you ever had any bad days? I am certain you have! Everybody has; and this clearly shows how you also have a 100% success rate of surviving these.

However, 'surviving' a challenging or stressful situation may not be the issue, how you cope with adversity could be where the problems lie. What lasting effects do these experiences have on you? **Resilience helps you to do more than survive, it helps you to thrive.**

YOUR TURN

How to build up your resilience

As professionals, we use analytical skills *every day*, so let's put them to work identifying our resilience strengths and weaknesses. In this way, you can also recognise the current resilience/stress management strategies that you use to survive your 'bad days'.

These steps can help you in your analysis:

Step 1: Write out three situational factors, which test your resilience, the most. This will identify the main problems you are up against, so that you can plan your new resilience strategies accordingly.

Step 2: Review what you are currently doing to manage your stress and/or build your resilience. This will help you to see what is working, and what is not, in the situations you wrote out in Step 1. How do you act when these situations arise? Do you act at all?

For each situation, take a piece of paper and divide it into two columns headed 'What is working' and 'what is not working'.

In the first column, write down the positives that you feel work particularly well for you. Naturally, the second column should include behaviours which you feel do not help. For example it may be that you are eating well but not sleeping well, or it may be that you have a good intention to exercise– but you are not the doing the activity itself.

Step 3: Developing new resilience strategies, once you have analysed your current approach, you can develop new and improved strategies to help you. Different resilience strategies can:

- Prepare you;
- Enable you to be effective in the moment;
- Help you to make the best of things;
- Then assist with moving on afterwards.

Daily habits to build resilience

Choose **one** aspect to work on then work on it **every day** for the next **seven** days to ascertain if and when this makes a difference. It may be one from your 'working' list that you want to reinforce or something from the 'not working' list, which you may want to turnaround.

If you are stuck on choosing something from your lists, try this simple one: taking deep breaths waiting for your train or at traffic lights. You can start with three and move up to ten as a regular habit.

Good breathing habits will train your brain and body to relax more. Deep breathing acts as an instruction to your sympathetic nervous system and amygdala (in the Limbic area of your brain) to relax. The more you relax on a regular basis, the more the blood flow to your 'thinking' frontal cortex can get through, helping to keep you alert and resourceful.

If it's exercise that you want to increase – choose to walk up the stairs daily, rather than promise yourself you will go to the gym more if this is something you recognised as 'not working'.

If you prefer to learn from others then make use of those times when you are waiting (for whatever reason) to think of inspiring people who have shown resilience in the face of challenging times or adversity. You could daydream about having a conversation with this person as to what they thought, felt or did to enable them to be resilient. Perhaps this is something you could adopt for the next seven days?

It may also help you to stay off your mobile, as your focus will be shifted to building your resilience. If you are using apps to support this then that's great, but if you are using the phone as a distraction it will leave you very unsatisfied and stressed.

Making a lasting change

Whilst I have suggested doing something new for the next seven days – this is to get you started. It generally takes at least 21 days to embed a new habit. It is consistency, which is important to build resilience.

'WE ARE WHAT WE REPEATEDLY DO.
EXCELLENCE IS A HABIT NOT AN ACT.'
ARISTOTLE

SECTION 5

WHAT DOES THE FUTURE HOLD?

THE PURPOSE OF THIS SECTION

This section is to provide you with information in three areas. Firstly, provide you with information about what happens to you when you (and your team) are experiencing change. It includes strategic tools to track the changes for your business and to lead it, in the context of a rapidly changing legal and business world. Then this section shows how the Stars are future proofing their business and asks the critical question: Is running a business for you?

CHAPTER 5.1
MAKE CHANGE YOUR FRIEND

How do we react to change?

Change is one of the few certainties of business as well as taxes!

This chapter describes the normal process that happens when we experience change of any kind. **Fundamentally change can scare people on different levels even when they are expecting it!**

It is **not** possible to effect real change just simply by ordering people to do it. This approach will meet defensive resistance including covert or overt withdrawal from the change initiative, and ultimately the organisation.

The **function** of leadership is to lead change. As a leader of your business it can be useful to monitor where any of your people are on the significant issues or challenges being faced in the different stages of the change curve.

The change curve

Elizabeth Kubler Ross, a Swiss psychiatrist produced the original change curve from studying the impact of grief and bereavement and how people dealt with loss. This has been widely used and adapted by many organisations and change management consultants to explain what happens to us when we experience change of any kind. Clearly the intensity of experiencing the loss of a loved one can be different from losing your own office. Even though change is a near constant, team members and business owners are often resistant.

All will go through the five steps set out in this chapter.

1 **Sudden awareness and shock.** When you set up your dream business you can often have 'rose-coloured' glasses. There comes a stage early on in the change curve when you realise you did not have enough information to allow you to anticipate the **full** implications of this new venture, both on you and your life. New parents also express that being told about the changes brought by new offspring and experiencing these is two different things.

So when you set up or when experiencing the next growth of your business, you might find yourself thinking or saying:

'So that's what they meant when they said ...' – 'do I really have to wear all these different hats, just to have control over my own destiny?' – 'oh no – what happened to work/life balance.'

This is normal because any change, no matter how small, has the potential to generate conflict between existing values, beliefs, behaviours and anticipated altered ones. This is so even if the change is positive. For example a common **belief is that you won't be challenged or make mistakes.** You only have to read the stories set out in **Section 6 Chapter 6.1** to find all of our Stars underestimated the changes they experienced.

This is exactly the process that your team, where you have one, will also go through when you change a part of your business, add a new person or team to your firm (an example is **Laura**) or even promote someone. It is therefore important to know where they are and tailor your communication accordingly.

2 **Denial.** Denial is the easiest human response as it is aligned with a strong desire to return to what they previously understood not this new 'uncertainty'. People will need to act in a different manner and this will have an impact on both their self-perception and on how others externally see them.

You may see your team or even yourself use the following expressions to delude themselves that nothing has changed:

'This is really simple' – 'Nothing is different' – 'I've seen it before' – 'You're talking nonsense'.

The tactics you choose to influence someone at the 'Denial' stage should be different from those you would use if they were on 'Self-blame' part of the curve. Communication that educates is vital here to illuminate the differences between the old and the new; and covers any concerns as far as possible **Active listening is a really useful skill here**.

See reference to active listening on page 141.

3 **Anger and blame.** Once the reality of the change starts to be absorbed then the negative behaviour of anger and blame can occur. It springs from fear and an awareness of incompetence in the new order.

It can take two forms and here are some inner dialogues that may be present:

- **Blame others**

'It's their fault' – 'You are wrong' – 'You have always had a downer on me' – 'This firm is going downhill' – 'I don't need you' – I never liked working for you anyway'

- **Self-blame**

'I can't do it' – 'I will never change' – 'I will never get this 'business stuff' right – ''I'm rubbish at business – no one will employ me ever again'

Both types of blame are natural responses to the stress of change. Both or one may be experienced depending on your personality and stress levels at the time of experiencing the change. The same may be happening for any of your team members.

It is critical that any skills training is offered and/or taken to resource you and the team with proficiencies. Coaching is also useful for reframing negative beliefs and assisting you or your team in developing a plan to learn any new skills or move to acceptance of the new order.

4 **Immobilisation.** This occurs as a result of intense shock and overwhelm, creating a mismatch between your expectations and the reality of the situation. It may be that you are made redundant or don't get the promotion or business that you want or need. This can also occur with awareness that your values, beliefs and goals are incompatible with the change being experienced. For new business owners this may be a realisation of what is involved in bringing in business or even the day-to-day minutiae of running a business. For those that are expanding these are the challenges of leading and managing teams and sometimes the belief you don't need training to do this or are too busy to take it.

The pitfalls associated with this phase are that you or your employees become demotivated, unfocused and increasingly dissatisfied. This can lead to either a gradual or an abrupt withdrawal of their contribution. Either mentally (by just 'going through the motions', and doing the bare minimum, to actively undermining the change by criticising / complaining) or physically by resigning.

The inner critic script goes something like this:

I'm stuck' – 'I don't know which way to turn' – 'It's hopeless trying to be something I am not' – 'It unfair that I have to do everything in this firm/team/business'

Do not make important decisions at this juncture, as these will be of a poor quality due to the negative emotions or spiral you are moving through. Wait until you have been able to move through to the next stage.

5 **Acceptance.** The reason why this stage is quite challenging is that there is a 'letting go' of the 'old' ways of thinking or action before the new skills/action can be fully taken on board, and then integrated into your business habits.

There are three types of acceptance that may be useful for you to understand:

- **Acceptance of what is.** By that I mean you observe the change, such as the direction to marry legal services with AI, with neutrality by removing any emotional charge you have about it. Practising mindfulness especially detachment helps.
- **Acceptance of self.** Accepting all of you and your actions as you travel on your business (and life) journey no matter how you acted. After things have settled down look for the 'gift' as it is can be too hard during the intensity of the experience to ask – **what can I learn from this?**
- **Acceptance of others.** Accepting that your partners, clients, staff are all doing the best they can with what they know at this stage of their journey, learning their own lessons.

It is important to note that you cannot integrate what you don't accept. Internal and external communication here needs to focus on what the future looks like for you, any team members and your firm going forward. This can bring back your passion and enthusiasm for moving to the next stage.

The following thoughts may be present:

'So this is the situation – running a business has it highs and lows' – 'History cannot be changed' – 'here I am at this stage in the business cycle' ' I can be positive about it as I have a optimistic attitude'.

6 **Problem solving (and testing):** As business is an 'art' not a 'science' there will need to be some testing of any new process or thinking before embedding this innovative mindset or system and release what is not working. The challenge here is not to start this part of the process too early before allowing time for you and the team to assimilate the stages listed above. A positive attitude is invaluable here as well as a strong desire to learn.

Thus the following thoughts or communication is likely:

'Let's look at what is happening' – 'What exactly will be our goal?' – 'How can we work together?' – 'What other data is there?' – 'How do you feel about it?' – 'What are our roles?' – 'What other data is there?' – 'So what is working and what is not?' – 'What can we tweak or what needs a fundamental rethink?'

Summary

Whilst everyone goes through all of the stages, there are variances. Some of you or your team may get stuck in a particular phase. Also some people process change faster than others, so don't compare yourself with others. Part of the problem is that we do not recognise which element of the curve our team or we may be in. Further it is not a once-only experience during transition from the old to the new. There may be many times where people go through the change curve when experiencing altered circumstances.

For example for business owners – you may have initiated a new social media campaign and find that it takes up far more of your time than anticipated and you are falling behind in your legal work. This may trigger self-blame. If this happens review your stress support mechanisms to enable you to move along the change curve. Then as you move into more positive and resourceful emotions, the quality of your problem solving with be more thoughtful and objective. In this situation you can reflect on a number of solutions. This may include outsourcing or bringing on board a social media apprentice to do this or even bringing someone onboard to deliver legal services enabling you to devote more time might be the preferred option.

The goal of any leader is to help make the change transition as effective and painless as possible for their team. Your team will be watching how you cope with change and therefore being a role model on the behaviours you want to see is important. **Liz** and **Gary** are examples.

Also by providing education about the change curve then the leader can help people transition through the curve and emerge on the other side. It is advisable for you to have different communication approaches for each part of the curve.

Be aware that as you move through your change process, your levels of control over your lawyers and other team members should loosen and adjust as you empower them to build their skills, experience, and alignment to your vision. This will create space for innovation.

One of the dangers is that once you are caught up in the 'emotion of the change', you may miss the signs of threat, anxiety, etc. of any team members and ourselves. These may take the form of complaining, non-engagement, sabotaging or attempting to make things as they were prior to the change. This is where coaches and your support network have a vital part to play to be able to provide a sounding board and/or a different perspective, and help you and your team embed the changes needed.

CHAPTER 5.2
STRATEGIC TOOLS TO GET YOU STARTED AND KEEP YOU ON TRACK

Overview

A vital purpose of leadership is ensuring the continuing success of your business. See Section 5 Chapter 5.3 for more details. Therefore this chapter provides you with two strategic tools for you to assess and track the future trends and map these against your particular services and products.

The third tool is a high-level-tracking device that you can use with or without a team, to ensure momentum with the changes or vision you are looking to implement. It can also be used to assess your strategic and operational priorities.

PESTLE

The strategic tool to assess the challenges and opportunities is called a PESTLE. This can be used in a number of ways to ensure that you are not one of those that wonders what is happening but one who is making it happen. This is so, even if your career is within a large law firm.

P = Political factors including risk and change

Government policy affects the whole **economy**, and governments are responsible for enforcing and creating a **stable framework** in which business can be done. Only one of our Stars **Liz** said that Brexit was a threat.

Moving on from Brexit, the quality of government policy is important in providing:

- Physical infrastructure (e.g. transport such as the promised high speed train link to Yorkshire).
- Social infrastructure (education, a welfare safety net, legal aid, law enforcement, and the spending power of both consumers and businesses).
- Market infrastructure (enforceable contracts, competition policy, policing corruption).
- Regulation of businesses including opening up of markets or coming out of established ones, taxation regimes including import and export duties.

E = Economic factors

How does the state of the UK economy affect your services? **Cathy** was the only Star to mention that another recession could affect her business. This also includes your clients and their potential economic spending. If you operate in different jurisdictions like **Bill**, then each country will have to be examined. For **Kirstie**, then her in-house lawyers who are advising boards of SMEs could be involved in monitoring trends for their clients.

In this part you are keeping an eye on such items as:

- Overall growth or fall in inflation and interest rates.
- Levels of taxation affecting your business or clients.
- Local geographical economic trends e.g. North v South living standards and opportunities for jobs.
- Sector economic trends e.g. house prices rising or falling could affect conveyancing numbers.

S = Sociocultural factors

These would include areas such as:

- An aging population and their legal service needs such as power of attorneys, which could be good news for **Jane** and **Rachel**.
- Immigration from the global world including skilled workers to war refugees – this one may have an impact for **Andrew** as a supplier of legal services to non-UK based citizens.
- Changing ethnic origins of the population and where these are based. Currently **Andrew** has a large Polish client base, which could be effected by Brexit implications for those from the EU working here after the UK leaves, if it does.
- The types of household and family structures such as more people living alone and those needing social care, which is deemed currently lacking.
- Employment practices such as more core employees or zero hours contracts, and the implications of mental health. **Jodie** is campaigning for change to the law for Mental Health First Aiders to be compulsory for companies of a certain size.
- Some households have two incomes with two jobs and more are having 'golden' or 'sunset' businesses **Ann**.
- Wealth or not depending on the sector or social class of society you are in and which may impact on family disputes over assets.

Martin focuses on inheritance disputes. The family solicitors **James, Jill**, and **Laura** and those who work for **Peter** will be assisting in this area for those who are fighting over the family assets.

- The growth of consumerist behaviour such as they 'expect more for less' is continuing to impact professional service providers. They feel that they cannot deliver a quality service because due to this pressure. How is this affecting your business practices or service? Is it time to use technology more?

T = Technological factors

Technology is becoming a vital tool for competitive advantage and is beginning to be taken seriously by lawyers. Several law firms are setting up LegalTech hubs to develop this area.

Consider the following points:

- Does technology allow for products and services to be delivered more cheaply and to a better standard of quality for you and your business? **Gary**, **Martin** and **Rachel** have made significant progress in this area but it is always one to watch as new products are coming onto the market all the time.
- How does your organisation utilise the Internet, social media, new generation mobile telephones, to provide innovative services and/or reach out to clients and contacts? Does technology offer you a new way to communicate with consumers? The Link App by Lauren Riley has been mentioned as one example.

L = Legal factors

You might want to consider the following:

- Are there any pending law changes to the legal services you deliver? **Andrew** discusses the implications of these in his interview.
- What is the impact of the legal ramifications of Brexit for your organisation, if any? **Liz** and **Bill** raised this.
- Are there any pending legal changes to the way you deliver legal services or hold information on your clients such as GDPR?
- How do you manage the employment rights of your staff? The employment solicitors **Jodie**, **Samira** and **Simon** will be advising their clients on the various changes and case law as it arises, as well as taking changes on board that affect their own business.

E = Environmental factors

Whilst not normally an issue for professional practices you may want to consider how you want to contribute to your community? **John** has mentioned that he suggests contributions to charity for his 'free' advice in certain circumstances. Many of our Stars raise money for good causes, which may include environmental charities.

It is also recommended that you research trends that affect your business in its entirety so that you can track this using PESTLE.

YOUR TURN

What in the future do you know or suspect will affect your business?

Political	Economic
Sociocultural	**Technology**
Legal/Regulatory	**Environmental**

SWOT

Introduction

This is a really versatile strategic tool. You can use this exercise for your own career, team, for your firm, and/or your firm's competitors. The SWOT technique can also be used for specific areas of strategy such as IT and marketing.

SWOT Analysis is also known as a TOWS analysis because you can start in the bottom two boxes in the table below and once you understand the threats and opportunities you can match the strengths and weaknesses against those. The opportunities and threats might arise from the PESTLE and/or other competitive factors.

Strengths and weaknesses are internal to you or your business. Good examples of these are the team challenges experienced by our Stars. **Opportunities** and **threats** relate to external factors such as techlegal products.

Effective SWOT analysis does not simply require a categorisation of information; it also requires some **evaluation of the relative importance** of the various factors under consideration. This is because if your SWOT analysis just has a shopping list it can be overwhelming.

Once the internal and external analyses are complete and evaluated, the next task is to develop strategies to exploit strengths and opportunities, and to mitigate threats and weaknesses. These strategies equally need to be evaluated against your time and resources.

Below is a diagram that shows how the SWOT analysis can be used to guide your strategy formulation.

The first step is to **match strengths with market opportunities**. Strengths, which do not match any available opportunity, are of limited use in the short tern. Therefore the obvious benefit is giving you a clear picture so that you focus on your strengths that do. While opportunities, which do not have any matching strengths, are of little immediate value and can be left out until they do. Unless you want to change your strengths to ensure that they do. For example if you see a gap in the market place for providing wills in a specific target market but do not have this specialism then like **Thomas** you can recruit to do so and turn it into an opportunity matched to a strength.

The second step is **conversion**. This requires the development of

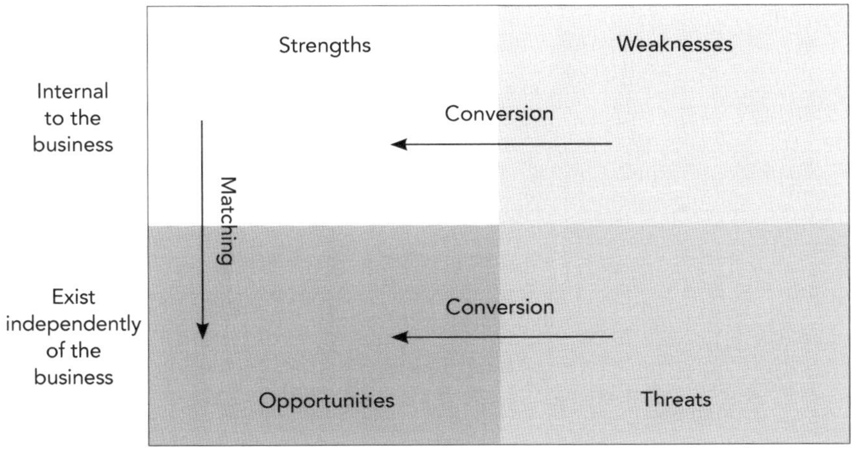

strategies, which will convert weaknesses into strengths in order to take advantage of some particular opportunity, or converting threats into opportunities, which can then be matched by existing strengths.

If you are having difficulty with identifying the strengths and weaknesses relevant to your situation, then try writing down a list of the characteristics you are analysing to enable you to consider whether these are a strength or not. Another good tip is when you have your list, to compare it, where appropriate, with your impression of the strengths and weaknesses of your competitors.

On examining opportunities and threats, you need to revisit your PESTLE to ensure that you are aware of trends affecting what you SWOT has acknowledged. As such, you may find that the PESTLE, analysis provides the context for this exercise. You can then examine those factors to explore what opportunities and/or threats exist. Again where appropriate, you should review what the competition is doing.

This is a good tool to examine the developments of AI in the legal sphere and how it will or won't impact on your business, and when to develop this as part of your business.

YOUR TURN

SWOT

Strengths	Weaknesses
Opportunities	**Threats**

A simple assessment and tracking questionnaire to start you off and keep you on track

If you have project documentation or software such as Trello to do this, then clearly these useful tools will be effective in supporting you in your change projects and business goals.

If you are a pen and paper person or want to have an overview before using more sophisticated tools then here is an abbreviated questionnaire that you may find useful. I have provided two suggestions under each category and left space for you to add your own.

In each of the sections, mark your impression as to where you and/or your team is in relation to the questions using the scoring system below.

Please mark up:

1. Not started
2. Some progress
3. Doing well
4. Fully achieved

1. Leadership	1	2	3	4
I have set down on paper my vision, values and strategy which reflects our current offering and/or future offering and growth				
I have a plan in place to build on my/our capabilities and reduce/remove limitations to achieve my vision, values and strategy.				
2. People and change management				
Each member of my team accepts responsibility for their current workload and future development by actively seeking out opportunities to grow their skills within the business.				
I, and my team have access to training/coaching/mentoring on how to handle change and the pace of change effectively.				

3. Client service	1	2	3	4
My business has targets (or some other measurement) for client satisfaction and these are tracked and circulated to the team.				
I, and my team, understand the charging structure for all of our services and can confidently discuss costs with clients.				
4. Communication				
I have created a culture and process of open communication for issues to be raised. (If you can, list the processes and then track their effectiveness)				
We have team meetings every week/fortnight/month (tick which is the one you consistently do)				
5. Process and measurement				
I have a case management process that I use to ensure quality and consistency of service for clients across the team.				
At our regular team meetings we share best practices to continuously improve the performance of our every member on a consistent basis.				
6. Innovation and change				
I maximise our internal use of technology to improve our service to clients. (List the systems you use and track their effectiveness.)				
I maximise the use of technology to drive innovation for our clients. (List these and track their effectiveness.)				

7. Risk management	1	2	3	4
I am committed to obtain appropriate credibility 'badges' relevant to my expertise and these are displayed on my website.				
There is a risk management system in place and my team knows and complies with this.				
Total				

Use the scoring to obtain priorities for your team/firm over next 12 months.

Summary

All these tools are meant to position you to be 'ahead of the game' by shaping your future business to accommodate changes and maximising strengths. These tools are useful in assessing and reviewing your business vision and goals to build a shared future with your team.

CHAPTER 5.3
WHY IS LEADERSHIP IMPORTANT FOR DEVELOPING YOUR BUSINESS?

Introduction

Without effective leadership – your success plans for your business have little chance of achievement. **There are three kinds of business owners:**

- Those that make things happen;
- Those that watch what happens; and
- Those that wonder what's happening.

So which kind are you?

Liz *'Well you don't work in this firm unless you embrace technology and you embrace change. And it's that growth mind-set that's really important to me. We all have a growth mind-set and embracing change and not fearing it. Not treating it in a way that it instils discomfort or fear. We know it's going to happen. Let's get on with it. Let's see how that change works for us. And you do that with a growth mindset.'*

Why is leadership important?

There are many, many books, webinars, podcasts and theories on leadership. From a practical point of view, for me, the purpose of leadership is to set a vision and convert that into action for the continued success of your business. This means being able to use the type of strategic tools set out in **Section 5 Chapter 5.2**. Using these for your business plan should enable you to set the appropriate vision to be as future proofed as possible.

As mentioned in this section the function of leadership includes leading and implementing change. Engaging your team or even motivating yourself to take the risk of the 'new' is constant. In my experience, both working in The Co-operative Bank and with lawyers, implementing change is the hardest part, and often is not sustained. See **Section 5 Chapter 5.1**.

Leadership starts with you

The first thing I would recommend is that you put the books down and go on some real leadership training. This should include some support – a coach and/or leadership support group that provides you with real life scenarios for you to understand and see how experts/ other business owners tackle these. Don't be stuck in 'Denial' or the myth that you can do it by reading books – leadership is about people not legal procedures; **so don't use the same learning approach.**

I am often asked if leaders are born or can be trained. Each individual has qualities and skills. Their qualities are what they bring to leadership such as integrity, authenticity, tenacity, confidence and enthusiasm and the skills are what they can learn to increase their effectiveness.

Whilst my leadership training goes into a far more depth, in this part I expand on two of the important qualities that are really significant in today's business world.

1 **Authentic Leadership** is an approach to leadership that emphasises the leader's ability to have 'honest' relationships and who is not seeking this role solely for their own benefit. Generally, authentic leaders are positive competent people with integrity who promote openness. Clearly this includes 'walking your talk'. Further this type of leader demonstrates that they value the input of their followers. This enables them to build trust with their team, clients and the business world as well as generating enthusiastic support for what they stand for.

There has been research, which shows that happy people are 12% more productive. David Maister who wrote *'Practice what you preach'* in the 90's reviewed 139 offices of 29 firms in 15 different countries in 15 different lines of business. He asked a simple question: *'are employee attitudes correlated with financial success?'* The answer he found was an unequivocal yes.

There is a greater demand for leaders of legal or any businesses to be more **than** about performance and profits; it is for them to be more **focused on people and ethics**. The SRA has set out in its competency framework the behaviours associated with ethics. The Co-operative Bank during my time there developed an Ethics in Action competency in 2000 as a result of introducing its ethical policies from its co-operative values in the 90's.

As a business owner your ethics should be visible and incorporated into your brand, value statements, culture including what behaviours are acceptable and what is not.

There are three aspects of an ethical behaviour to be taken into account:

- Knowing the right thing;
- Doing the right thing;
- Ensuring your actions and those that you lead or manage are taken for the right reasons.

2 **Resilience** is important for leaders because it helps you:

- Maintain balance during difficult or stressful periods of 'leadership' time.
- Adapt to change and thrive in unsettled times.
- Develop mechanisms for protection against experiences, which could be overwhelming.
- Bounce back from adversity.
- Be protected from the development of some mental health difficulties.

So I would like to ask you if you have had any bad days? **You have!** Then clearly you have 100% success rate of surviving those. So it is not about the fact that you survive that may be issue but how you cope with challenge, stress and adversity. Please see **Section 4 Chapter 4.2**.

Leadership Competency Behaviours

There are many views of leadership competency behaviours. Again most large businesses use these but they are not so popular with partners. I have included this here as a basis for one of the exercises in the following 'Your turn – Reviewing your leadership skill'.

Here is a generic example of one I have customised in the past:

- Create and convey a clear vision of success.
- Demonstrate commitment to your business's aims, values and strategy.
- Use oral, video and written influencing skills to motivate.
- Be inspirational with your enthusiasm and passion.
- Generate and encourage creative solutions to problems.
- Focus on results whilst not ignoring the means.
- Anticipate, facilitate and/or lead change.
- Deal flexibly and confidently with the unexpected.
- Adapt behaviour and style to the situation and competence of individuals whilst staying true to your values.

Be mindful that your skills in this area, are like your sporting or other skills, and take time to excel in. You will not become an expert overnight as it takes practice.

As leadership starts with you, your values and vision so the next exercises allow you to take stock.

YOUR TURN

Reviewing your leadership skills

There are **three** different exercises to try, so pick one that appeals and you can use to build and develop your leadership skills. See also how you can lead when not in charge, later in this chapter.

Part A – You could review your own skill set against the leadership competencies set out above. Using a scoring system of 1–5 for each part will enable you to ascertain where you should focus your leadership development and practice.

Part B – Set out below are some general questions, which will help you, understand your leadership approach.

What is my reputational capital - what am I known for NOW?
What kind of leader do you aspire to be - what do I want to be known for?

What leadership qualities do I have?
Authenticity: How do I lead from the front? How do I develop my team's values/standards using the power of example?
How do I establish trust in my business and me?
How do I show my resilience and establish resilience in my team?

What leadership skills do I need?
What leadership skills do I have in my current role that I can use in setting up my own business or department?
What do I need to do to be seen as an effective leader?

Part C Psychometric Assessment

The power of insight for a **leader** is extremely valuable. Have you tried a psychometric assessment or does it sound like a step too scary? There are many different types of these and all provide you with information that you can use to understand and strengthen your leadership skills.

I recommend the MiRo Assessment `Psychometric System as it has a specific leadership report. This report shows your leadership styles within the four categories of driving, energising, organising and analytical. These categories in turn have four sub-sections. MiRo shows which of the 16 leadership styles is your preference. This really allows greater customisation of the leadership training and coaching. This in turn speeds up the personal effectiveness of my clients as it allows them to focus on performing better using their strengths'.

Ann *'my leadership style is Instructor style in the Energising category (yellow)! So my natural style, amongst other things, is that I am an eloquent and outgoing leader. One of the struggles listed that I may encounter is holding self and others to overly high standards.'*

When you are a leader – what should you be doing?

These following suggestions are not meant to be comprehensive but are the ones most overlooked if you are already in a leadership position.

As mentioned values and beliefs propel you and your team into action. **It is essential to engage hearts and minds to produce effective change**. Do not underestimate the commitment and time required for this. Stephen Mayson in his book *Making Sense of Law Firms* states, *"The challenge is balancing client satisfaction, internal and external lawyer satisfaction while remaining true to everyone's values and beliefs."* A good opportunity to do this is in team meetings, partner and/or team away days which may include outside speakers on relevant topics.

Articulate your vision – don't just assume 'they' get it. The vision is your platform to lead others. Tell everyone what you want to achieve and what it looks like for them, including the criteria for success. Do it with passion. Two examples here are **Liz** and **Martin**.

Show the way by **"walking the talk."** This is one of the most critical success factors in aligning your team and your clients to your vision together with a consistency of approach. You must act and behave fully in accordance with your vision. Any indication that there is a 'disconnect' between your public face and internal behaviours means you will lose face and confidence internally. This factor comes up time and time again as being the key thing that will destroy your credibility and affect the team's effectiveness or performance. When your team sees that you take running and leading your business this seriously then you can easily encourage 'forward thinking' and creativity in your team, where you have one. **Liz** and **Gary** are examples here.

How do you take responsibility and acknowledge your own mistakes? Martin and **Richard** to name two mentioned that they take ownership of theirs. Is this something you do easily or do you need to work on it? Blame costs you your credibility. Your peers, team and clients will notice, although whether they say anything is another matter. It keeps your team members on the defensive and ultimately sabotages real growth. Don't try to be 'superman' or 'superwoman'. Lead also on being human. This makes it ok for you and your team to use 'failure' as a learning experience. Most extraordinary leaders and teams have used this as a stepping-stone to greatness.

A lament I continually receive from managing partners and business owners is lack of time. Everyone, including Lord Alan Sugar and Sir Richard Branson, to name two, has 168 hours in the week. **Schedule thinking time** in your diary and protect this space, as you would time with a client. The length of the time depends on the leadership activities you are doing or wanting to do. As a business owner you are leading your own business as well as a team (if you have one). If you are in the middle of changing your business operations or trying to grow your business in any significant way, then have a daily slot. This can be a short strategic review of 15 minutes to ensure you are on track. (And yes time spent on this in the shower can count!) John Adair who has written excellent books on leadership has found that this 'thinking' time is the one activity that is not done enough. If you are the sole business owner then part of this thinking time should be spent assessing your ability to influence the actions, beliefs, and feelings of external suppliers to support any development projects you have initiated or require for your business. A vital skill here is delegation. How are your delegation skills?

Taking care of yourself and your team. Nearly all of our Stars said that they had an approachable and supportive manner in respect of their team leadership. If you want a healthy team then you have to demonstrate this in your own approach to work. Eating healthily, exercising and not overworking on a daily basis has to be modelled as well as encouraged. A balanced team mentally and physically is less likely to make mistakes and is the blueprint for success. **Jodie's** approach to staff care is part of her 'Thriving' brand.

Only **Kirstie** mentioned regular team meetings and **Gary** said he walked the floor and sat at reception. Where you work in open plan offices like **Jade** and **Noreen** (to name two) then you can spot issues relatively quickly and take appropriate action.

How to lead change for your business

> 'THERE IS NOTHING MORE DIFFICULT TO PLAN,
> MORE DOUBTFUL OF SUCCESS
> NOR MORE DANGEROUS TO MANAGE
> THAN THE CREATION OF A NEW SYSTEM'
> **NICCOLO MACHIAVELLI**

I have listed nine steps below to provide you with a tried and tested process to developing your new vision for your business or your part of your business. This may be a new LegalTech product or website or indeed any other new venture.

1 **Preparation.** Before developing your new vision or key objective(s), time should be taken to assess the climate and need for change. Document the business analysis tools (such as the PESTLE/SWOT see **Section 5 Chapter 5.2**). **These can then be used to document your 'journey' for future reference when you write your book!**

2 **Sharing.** Seeing the above data will help you think through and anticipate key elements of change to ensure that the potential solutions can be included in your plan. This is a very productive use of your time. Where you can involve everyone in the 'change' because being part of the process gives everyone a sense of ownership and belonging. For those who are sole practitioners, this could include family members. At this stage you need to describe the change required as completely as you can so that there is as much clarity here for both you and your team/family. Another question that is important is assessing what is the appetite for change? For example, a discussion of expanding the business may include more time away from the family and you can then assess the impact. They may want to support you in the short term but something may have to change if this is going to be for the next five years. Or if that is the case then you may need to review what you and family need – a cleaner – outsourced ironing – help from the grandparents. Then allow time for you and the team/ family to reflect some more on the new vision/strategy.

3 **Planning.** Once you have a vision/strategy and have thought through the key elements, then bring your team together for the next step – to start the planning process for the change. **Listen!** Listen and acknowledge that you have heard them. Respond to what you are going to do with their input. This is where you want to involve

your 'dissenters' and flush out their concerns as to what will work and what won't. Establish celebratory events for achieving significant milestones. Best practice is that planning should at least take 20% of the time spent on any change management arrangements.

4 **Agree realistic time-scales for the change you want or need to introduce.** I, and my clients, found this was very common around website changes and design. It is easy to underestimate the preparation and the external delivery time for this. Whatever the change you want to introduce prepare and plan for time slippage as this can prolong uncertainty and may give 'resistant' team members a reason for noncompliance. Further if this involves staff with fee earning work, then there may have to be discussions (and some form of remuneration/recognition for the short-term extra hours required to implement the change). This is especially true where your fee earner may be moving into a management role due to maternity leave, illness or as career development to take them to the next level.

5 **Review your resources.** Bring in outside help for the whole or part of the process but retain responsibility. When **Noreen** introduced a new client relationship management system and an accounts package, she arranged training for the whole team including her accountant and me. This gave the team the ability to ask questions from the expert trainer as how best to use this on a strategic and operational level.

6 **Consider contingency plans** at this stage for anticipating and coping with the unforeseen and any setbacks. Think about the skills required for the transition and the new ways of working – what training/coaching is required.

7 **Communicating.** Decide how you are going to communicate progress – by email to the team – face2face in the team meetings via presentations? Your communication plan should cover the beginning of your change project, during and after the project you are initiating. **The cost of gossip is high; forestall it through clear accurate communication.**

8 **Implementation.** Start your new change 'project' when you say you will and deliver the new methods/processes or products to your agreed timetable. Do allow time for the unexpected as it is normally impossible to plan for everything. Initiating a training programme that will give people the skills and opportunity for more team building around your new technology product or service. Allow time to help people to let go of the 'old' and acclimatise to the 'new' and they may need coaching to

embed the change. Think about incentives to encourage the adaptation you require, and encourage your team to look for opportunities where they can contribute to or be involved positively in the change 'project'. The people in your team who make this work should be 'formally' recognised and rewarded as well as praised.

9 **Tracking.** It is important to track the impact of the changes you have introduced. If you encourage your people to find out what is working and what is not this will prove invaluable. The de-brief stage is vital and often forgotten.

If you are not in charge how do you lead?

For those that are contemplating leading their team or own business then you need to start your leadership development as soon as possible.

A question I am often asked is how can you do this when you are not in charge? There is a myth that you cannot lead unless you are the business owner or in 'charge'; and that is simply not true.

There are three key areas in which you can lead.

1 **Values and qualities.** The first starts with you; your values and the qualities you bring to your work. So do you know what your values are; and are you leading with these? If you are struggling to identify these then, list what is important to you in your working life. Review your knowledge of your reputational capital within your team and clients, as this is a good place to start.

For example are you known to be:

- Client focused?
- Approachable – friendly?
- Trustworthy – a safe pair of hands?
- Authentic – real and genuine?
- Enthusiastic – positive attitude?
- Confident and humble?

If you are, you will be 'role modelling' these values and qualities. Or are you known to be the opposite of these?

As you can see these values and qualities have nothing to do with being in charge. It is said that you become like the five people you most spend time with

2 **Knowledge and expertise.** You can lead with your knowledge and expertise. Whether you are the 'go-to' person in your office or not you will invariably lead your clients in the legal landscape in which they are seeking your advice and guidance.

3 **Knowledge of and understanding people – internal and external.** The third area is about people – if you don't like people it is going to be very difficult to lead them!

So how well do you know your colleagues or clients? How good a listener are you? Do you talk over colleagues and clients or wait impatiently for your turn? Sometimes they just want to be listened to.

If you think you are a good listener (and most lawyers tell me they are) – try an experiment. Next time you are listening, give the person your full-undivided attention and be in 'receive mode'. **Do not construct your answer or search for information to share as you listen.** Then when they have told you the whole story – repeat back to them what you have heard. This ensures that you have an opportunity did understand and avoid any misunderstandings. It tells your speaker that you listened to them. It is curious that lawyers think that they are showing listening skills when taking notes, and the client feels like they are just speaking to the top of the lawyer's head! Not a great way to build rapport.

If you are looking to expand your leadership skills and are not given an opportunity within the current organisation in which you work then look for possibilities outside.

John Adair *'In fact there is **quite a lot** an individual can do outside his/her organisation – **in spite of it** – to grow as a leader: for example **community experience, reading & thinking** on the subject and **observing** the good and not so good leaders.'* Your local Law Society and the Junior Law Division are always looking for committee members or charities in your area may be looking for a trustee.

YOUR TURN

Personal leadership plan(s)

Set out below is some mini-plans for you to start your own leadership journey, if your current organisation does not have a leadership programme for you to join.

1. Personal leadership development goals

Identify which competency or skill from the earlier exercises and information in this chapter that you want to develop, and how you will do this and by when. I recommend that you choose no more than three at a time.

	Competency/skill	What will I do to achieve it?	By when?
1			
2			
3			

2. Personal leadership action or project plan

This is for you to record any leadership activities you want to practice or where you are involved in a project or major transaction where you are given more responsibility to grow. There is also a column for you to record what you have learnt.

	Activities to practice	What project/ transaction?	What did I learn?
1			
2			
3			

3. The percentage of time I will spend over the next 6/12 months on 'leadership' activities is when I am in charge is?

4. The percentage of time I will spend over the next 6/12 months on 'leadership' activities is when I am not in charge to prepare myself is?

CHAPTER 5.4
GOOD PEOPLE EQUALS A GOOD TEAM - *NOT NECESSARILY*

When to expand - how our Stars chose

Nearly all of our Stars who have started out on their own have expanded, some in their first year whether planned or not. Only **Andrea, Ann, Geoff, Jane** have no intention of recruiting any staff whatsoever.

Of those Stars who have recruited staff, they generally have a mix of solicitors (employed or consultants) and legal executives/paralegals/ admin staff.

Andrew, **Bill**, **Gary**, **Ian & Matt**, and **Rachel** have all taken on trainees. **John**, **Ian** & **Matt** and **Kirstie's** model is based primarily on consultant solicitors.

Andrew, Gary and **Liz** have expanded the ownership of their organisation at the time of publishing.

Bill, Ian & Matt, James, Jade, Laura, Richard, Simon and **Thomas** set up in partnership from the start with someone they knew – three of these are in partnership with their wives.

The important question is what suits you and your type of business and the strategy you have for your growth? It should be noted that just because you want to expand, recruiting the 'good' people is exceedingly challenging. This is so whether you are recruiting consultants, solicitors (newly qualified all the way up to partner level) paralegals or from other disciplines such as marketing.

Therefore the remainder of this chapter focuses on the Stars that have staff.

The team challenges identified by our Stars

These are the challenges identified by our Stars when in their interviews:

Managing workload within the team:

- **Andrew** *'run up to a big trial and everyone will stop what they are doing and help.'*
- **Liz** *'the biggest challenge is coping with the workload. Sometimes we have*

to turn things around with very tight deadlines for very demanding clients.'

- **Cathy**, **Noreen**, and **Jade** developing their staff's technical skills in busy environments.

Finding the right people:

This is a common theme for those who have teams and those who are looking to expand. This can be a real issue if you are niche. **Bill** *'I have been looking for another construction partner/director – even used a headhunter. You realise you are looking for someone like yourself. Problem is finding someone with ambition and ability to build rapport with clients.'*

Another example is if your business model is different. **John** *'biggest challenge is getting the right candidates who want to join and are not worried by the consultancy model.'* **Kirstie** *'Convincing some great in house lawyers we meet to make the leap and join us is our greatest challenge given that lawyers are typically a risk adverse group.'*

Creating a team and a common approach

- **Gary** *'Business won't work until we all are cooperating like wheels on a car'*

- **Ian** & **Matt** *'the biggest challenge is cohesion. The other challenge with any fundamentally consultant-led practice is not letting something to develop or when they do getting a hammer and smashing the side out of it but you cannot force people to do it – have to persuade people to open the doors'*

- **Jade** *'I would say having come from different backgrounds, is making sure we're all working in a way, which is efficient for everybody. So for example my business partner Rodney is 73 and is used to having a secretary that he types for. Whereas I come from a firm where we don't have secretaries we have assistants who had their own role, it's just bringing us all together so that we're all working in a way, which is roughly the same and not confusing for the support staff. So yeah bringing it all together as a team so we're all working in the same way with the same competencies and standards.*

- **Laura** *'I would say that the biggest challenge to a small business is when you do have members of staff leave for whatever reason that might be. Because I think that it leaves people feeling unsettled and uncertain about what's to come. We have learned that's communication again is key so that they know they have nothing to fear. They know what the* *players and you involve them in that plan. And so we've been very keen to do that. So we've had when we have had people leave we have been be able to say right well you know this this is what's going to change I'm not going to change. This is what we're looking to do.'*

- **Noreen** *'making sure that everybody gets on and works together to achieve the best possible outcome.'* **Rachel** *'everyone has different skillset and qualities – making sure work gets allocated correctly to play on those strengths. Working collaboratively.'* **Thomas** *'Challenges = staff management, making sure everyone gets on with everyone, ensuring no friction and that it is a nice place to work.'*

Other challenges identified

- **Peter** *'so our biggest challenge is geography. It's a huge problem. A huge nightmare problem and we are constantly working on it. The logistics of multi-site offices offering all of the services that we do. We have 11 offices. We haven't got 11 employment lawyers, we haven't got 11 commercial lawyers, we haven't got 11 conveyancers, we haven't got 11 wills and probates solicitors. And unfortunately 'Joe Blogs' when he walks through the door, he's responding to our marketing. He's walked through our little door in Guisborough or Beverley or wherever and he expects to be able to have an appointment face to face that day with any of those disciplines.'*

What training, if any, did our Stars have to prepare for leading and managing teams?

Of the fourteen Stars who have teams, only Gary attended a 'formal' training programme – Harvard and Elite Programmes. Ten have had training and/or coaching with me at different times during their journeys on a range of business, leadership and management topics. These included Management Stage 1 & 2, as well as customised coaching or training programmes. Quite a lot of our Stars have used coaches and mentors whom they have mentioned in their interviews.

Some Stars use books/podcasts and support groups to supplement their ad hoc training **Andrew**, **John** and **Peter**. **Laura** states she is *'self-taught with books and Law Society small firm events.'* **Martin** and **Richard** have had vast business and management experience at 'partner' level during their careers but the actual formal training was ad hoc during this time.

It takes time and effort to build really effective collaborative teams and I would recommend that you take some training and/or coaching especially if this does not come naturally. Knowledge of how to build and manage including communication and delegation skills will save you time and energy.

Dos and don'ts of leading and managing your team

Clearly whole books have been written on this topic so I have confined myself, given the spacing constraints, to list of do's and don'ts as a prompt for you to see if you need to make any changes to your activities here.

Dos

- Be visible.
- Give lots of sincere praise.
- Be polite.
- Take an interest in them/genuinely care about them.
- Trust them.
- Inspire them.
- Motivate them.
- Grow/develop them by providing some structure to the process and a clear end goal of the development.
- Keep your promises to staff.
- Celebrate success.
- Apologise when you make a mistake.
- Be honest and respectful straight talking.
- Make the challenging decisions fair and transparent.
- Communicate your vision for the future to provide direction for your team.
- Enthuse about your work, team goals and the organisation's values and goals.
- Role model the behaviours you want and expect to see in your team.
- Not let your personal life affect your work or leadership on a day-to-day basis.
- Be consistent and predictable.

Don'ts

- Bad mouth your partners, directors, or your team members.
- Make promises you can't keep.
- Take the credit but do take the blame.
- Assume an open door is enough expecting your team to tell you when they are unhappy or have a grievance.
- Try to be liked all the time.
- Only trust the people who always say yes or agree with you.
- Give your staff unpleasant surprises.
- Feel you have to justify your actions.
- Be afraid to roll up your sleeves and help.
- Think you are too important to do menial jobs.
- Be a bully.
- Be one of the gang or treat your team as you would a friend.
- Delegate all the unpleasant activities or imply a job you can't or don't do is easy.
- Make the easy compromise.
- Leave things till the last minute either in respect of your own work or work you are delegating.
- Disregard work/life balance or any signs of stress within your team.

Developing your team

Once you have set up your team, the next step is to develop them and nearly all our Stars stated this was their intention as they were keen for their people to be developed. What this that looked liked in practice was not necessarily easy to understand from the interviews. Therefore here are some suggestions for you to review as to whether they would suit you and your team.

To psychometric test your team or not?

I know that most lawyers are unfamiliar with these and no Star mentioned them in the interviews. Large corporate organisations have used psychometric testing for decades; *'indeed I have an extremely large file containing all the ones I have done over the years'* **Ann**. Each organisation has their own favourite. Myers Briggs and subsequent variations such as, Insight and Disc use four basic coloured categories. A great favourite with teams is Belbin. (In fact this was one of the most popular exercises in the Management Stage 1 & 2 that I taught for the major training providers.)

Psychometric testing is popular in industry because it is a relatively quick and easy process to unlock a wealth of information about your personal and leadership styles as well as team cohesion. The idea of preferences is the basis of any psychometric testing so it is not about finding out if you have the imposter syndrome or lots of weaknesses! Armed with the information on behavioural preferences, quickly leads us to excel at our strengths.

In my experience, assessing teams using this tool enables leaders and managers to lead and manage their teams more effectively as they can see in a colourful team map, how strong the team is in one category. It also provides information to assist smooth communication, to and within the team, which then enables the team to solve problems faster and make better decisions going forward.

Are competency frameworks useful?

Who uses these? **Ann** *'I experienced a whole range of legal and non-legal competency frameworks when I was leading my in-house legal department. I became involved, as a Senior Manager, in the revision of the then current one in 2000, and loved every minute of it.'*

Whilst most of those with staff say that they care about staff development very few had specific development plans for their people. From the interviews, as the SRA recently found in their survey, nearly all Sole Practitioners and small firms do not use the SRA Competency Framework for developing their Solicitors. Only **Noreen** stated she used this system for her own development as she employs paralegals. Others such as **Samira** and **Gary** have adapted the SRA system to their needs.

For those Stars who operate law firms, this was their view:

- **Bill** *'It is very difficult to use rigid frameworks. We are a niche practice – building up competences is subject to the work we do.'*

- **John** *'I wish they hadn't have changed it. It adds another level of assessing what you do and don't know. Everyone is aware of it; I ask everyone to maintain his or her own training records. We use a lot of videos. Different for everyone in relation to experience and area of law you are working on it. I do staff alignment to see what their goals are.*

Rather than what's fit for me because if you grow as a business I want them to be happy rather grown apart and never knowing. So that could be financially time the family holidays it can be so much as sport is for use within the office and ask for that in pop'

- **Liz** *'I don't use that competency framework but I do encourage soft skills training and development. Maybe I should look more closely at that.'*

- **Peter** *'we do. I think it's still very much early stages. In our strategy away day with senior management we talked about SRA Competencies. The SRA competency framework has only been in place for two years now and I think there's been a learning exercise on everybody's part. I think what we are seeing and we're going to develop this further in our appraisal process, is to bring that competency framework alongside our standard appraisal process so that not only are we looking at our appraisal paperwork but we're also looking at the competency framework.'*

- **Richard** *'no we have external compliance people who are very aware of that and I would like to think we are always on the right track.'*

- **Thomas** *'we don't use the competency framework. We have an appraisal system, which is good. Why wouldn't we support people's development?'*

Those Stars that have non-solicitor staff use the following methods:

- **Jade** *'three month appraisals and every file is signed off'*

- **Miguel** *'It's not formal, but I'd encourage everyone to continually be looking for ways to improve themselves. It's always been something I've taken personal responsibility for – even when employed. I can probably summarise it as "defy the odds" and "step up" and do something every day that scares you.'* **Ann**, **Andrea** and **Kate** also take personal responsibility for their continued education on a yearly basis.

- **Noreen**: *'sitting in the same office allows me to work out their strengths and weaknesses, and as they are new and still learning, we then agree the next steps on their learning journey.'*

- **Rachel:** *'making sure they get enough technical training. Networking events that may have a training element e.g. speaker. Plenty of webinars. Cost expert to make sure we were doing our costing right which also gave us reassurance.'*

Team successes our Stars have so far experienced

Our Stars that said* awards were the biggest success included **Jade**, **John**, **Laura** and **Rachel**. The Stars who recognised their team's working together to achieve litigation wins or completions were **Andrew**, **Liz**, **Noreen**, and **Richard**. **Samira** and **Thomas** stated it was the team that they had built.

Others included:

- **Jodie** *'being recognised as punching above our weight. I mean I often speak to my team about this as well as we are a small firm. I think we do have a perception from a lot people that we're bigger than we are. I was speaking at the Mindful Employer Conference last year and the delegates thought I was representing a large corporate firm, at the time I only had one employee!'*

- **Kirstie** *'our greatest success is in the number of successful women we have in our team. Women make up 50% of our team but of our top ten billers last year eight of them were female.'*

- **Martin** *'biggest success has undoubtedly been the paperless/familyflex operation. It is too early to say about the LegalTtech products being developed.'*

***Most of our Stars have either been shortlisted for and/or have won various awards, which can be found listed on their websites.**

CHAPTER 5.5
GAZING INTO THE CRYSTAL BALL - WHAT DO THE STARS SEE FOR THEIR BUSINESS IN THE NEXT THREE YEARS?

This is the question I put to our Stars, as there are many different perspective on where business and legal services are headed. In reviewing their answers I have divided these into the following sections:

Continuing to practise law in a traditional way

General Expansion plans: Bill wants to expand internationally; **Jane** wants to expand her client base; **Jade** wants to move into commercial property; **Richard** wants to become more recognised in his chosen topic; **Geoff's** focus is *'how can I best serve the interests of my clients'*.

Specifically looking to expand team wise: Bill and **Claire** want a slightly larger team of specialists; **Jade** wants to expand to include lawyers with commercial property expertise; **Jill** and **John** are expanding using consultants; **John. Liz** and **Noreen** want to expand their teams and offices; **Peter** wants a number of things such as consolidation; and growth of lawyers, volume of work, turnover and profit in our geographical areas. **Thomas** is aiming to diversify into other areas for his dental sector such as wills/probate and therefore seeking team members with this expertise.

How our Stars are using technology and/or social media to develop their business

This is what our Stars were planning at the time of the interview:

Technology to support delivery of legal services

- **Andrew** loves the mechanics of social media and website tracking to inform business decisions on the practice of law and looking to diversify the legal practice and increase cash flow.
- **Gary** is looking at new products to continue to change the face of law and perception of lawyers.
- **Jodie** is investigating technological products to sit alongside employment law service and mental health campaigns.
- **Martin** is perusing a reduction in fee earning hours using new LegalTech products for his clients.

- **Rachel** is continuing to expand her online offerings in her business.
- **Noreen** is researching the marketplace for AI systems that are applicable to her legal services.
- Whilst **Simon** is LinkedIn savvy he is considering going online but in the short term is looking to expand his specialist team, so again watch this space.

Technology to change working practices

- **Jodie** and **James** are using technology systems for remote working and reduce working hours.
- **Ian & Matt** want more sophisticated systems to enable them to compete.

Social media

- **James** is going to continue to use twitter and his fixed fee model to stay ahead of his competition.
- **Laura** is staying niche but aiming to become more tech savvy
- **Samira** is getting to grips with marketing especially social media, so watch this space.

Practising law plus other things

By this I mean expanding into other areas outside the core. **Andrew** had just launched the 'The Rich Lawyer Magazine' and Truth Recruitment at the time of interview. **Gary** is fanatical about his educational hub and the risk solution part of his business, which continues to expand.

Moving out of law

Those of us, who are in the training and coaching field, see our personal and business development as a must and will continue to explore this going forward. It has the added benefit of developing our clients too as we take what we have learnt in these fields to them. (**Andrea**, **Ann** and **Kate**).

- New training and coaching products delivered online. **Andrea**.
- Reviewing the possibility of virtual reality training products for lawyers. **Ann**.
- To continue to develop her electrical business and build up a property portfolio. **Cathy**.
- To build a Safeguarding academy. **Kate**.
- Building and expanding a recruitment business. **Miguel**.

CHAPTER 5.6
IS RUNNING A LEGAL BUSINESS FOR YOU?

Advice from all of our Stars in their own words to those wanting to set up their own business

Ann *'find your passion, as it may be that your business lies outside your legal training. Take business skills as seriously as you would the law, whether you decide to branch out to forge your own path or remain within your current organisation.'*

Andrea *'just do it. I think I faffed around for too long, not doing it and doing other things, pretending I didn't want to do it. So just do it and work on yourself. When we go into this or into any business we spend so much time on questions like – have I got the right website? The right leaflets? The right business cards? Actually what really, really matters is doing the work and doing really good work. You can have a successful business even if you don't have this or any of the things we think we need. Get rid of the beliefs you don't need or these will stop you. The more you work on this the more you can see through that.'*

Andrew *'I don't think running a business or being an entrepreneur or a law entrepreneur is for everybody. I speak to lots of lawyers who may want to work here on a self-employed basis and for some of them it really is the wrong choice. So when some people have worked here on a self-employed basis, they quickly find out if it's for them. You have got to be really self-motivated to do this. You have got to be happy with things being not perfect if you are a perfectionist I am not sure it is the right route. I also think it takes so much energy out of you, and I hadn't factored in that. So I was lucky to have started when I was four years PQE because I had some more energy. I could work until four in the morning then I can't work past 7.00 pm now.'*

Bill *'do it earlier. We set up 11 years ago and I should have done it four or five years before then. I think that the 'forties' is a good time. Some people set up earlier and that can depend on what they want to do. For me, my clients need that depth of expertise and longevity in my field. Don't set up on just your own, although I know that there is a load of sole practitioners. Trish and I work very well together. If you set up with two or three other people then if nothing else, you are sharing the cost of your business. So every time you employ someone, you are sharing the cost. And that also gives you checks and balances because you're different. You will be working with different speed – have a different background. Once you have a common denominator because you have set up together, will mean that there will be lots of different things spinning in people's heads. If you do that with a good group with you may have arguments.*

I would say that arguments are not necessarily a bad thing. Be really brutally honest and open with people, that's the only way.'

Cathy *'if anyone else can do it then you can do it! I sometimes get worried or nervous about new things but the thing that helps my confidence most is just thinking about all the other guys who have managed, if they can do it I can do it!'*

Claire *'there is no earthly point in setting up your own business if you're unable to have conversations about fees, chase up fees, manage cash flow and be quite hard. During my first year of business I had a few bad experiences with some bad debt and in hindsight I had gut feelings about the clients involved, it didn't feel right. But I was still in that bigger firm Mind-set, where you take any work that comes your way, as there is generally pressure from others in the organisation for you to do that. Big lesson learnt for me was that if I don't want to do it I don't have to do it and I don't have to justify myself to anyone. It is a really good shift. If it does not feel right, I don't say no generally, I just don't follow up. Gut feel is usually based on something tangible.'*

Garry *"what I find is that Star Wars movies and that Tolkien books planted the seeds in me about going to the stars and doing things differently. I wanted to do that. When is the best time to start up a business – it's never the best time. The best time is now when you make the decision"*

Geoff *'everybody should work for themselves! Different models suit different people. There is a natural perception, probably, that when you are thinking about starting out as a sole practitioner, whether it is feasible in this day and age. These thoughts arise, I think, because of the traditional business model. So if you work for a large commercial firm, the margins, the overheads, negative thoughts, cash flow, employees – getting cash or work in, the working capital requirement. All of those things are quite challenging to get right. And two of the four firms I worked for as an employee before I set up on my own went bust. The reality is, that starting out on your own is administratively straightforward but there is quite a bit to it. If you can get through law school and get a degree you can set up on your own. In particular, there is a perception in large commercial firms, that there is not a lot of work around; and there is a lot of discussion about the fierce competition. The reality as an SP is once you have your toes in the water; there is a lot of work out there. You may need some lateral thinking or changing your hourly rate for your target audience. The amount of work for lawyers to do is colossal, as far as I am concerned. That is a major concern when you are starting up on your own. You know, is anyone going to use me for my services. The reality is that there is a huge amount out there, access to justice in my line of business, court work, and people using the court service, those kinds of things.'*

Matt *'funnily enough I was just speaking to someone I know last night. It was someone I worked with, and he brought his wife with him. She was a junior lawyer. So what I was telling her was to stick it out a bit longer if you are getting decent enough experience. Just keep your head down. My view is that with the benefit of hindsight, I could have done this and gained fantastic experience. For me at the time I didn't have enough resilience and family life to keep me going through running a business. So if you can get through the early years, that's where you get a good grounding and good experience; and hopefully get a bit of a following because you 'get' your type of clients. That's where you develop your skills as a lawyer.*

Ian sees this as two questions – *'what would my advice be to someone wanting to start their own practice and what would I say to someone who is perhaps more junior – why am I doing this? From my own experience in a London city firm I thought that things weren't particularly brilliant whilst I was there. Actually, when I left I realised they were flipping fantastic really and the way it was geared up, the culture and the support structures. The reality is that you can only make a judgement about your experiences in your 'rear view' mirror. You can only connect it all up backwards. You are going to make some decisions and you are going to make some 'mistakes'. You are going to make some because you are only going to be able to assess the situation as you live it and that is quite hard – that is okay. You will learn an awful lot.*

If you think this is not working for some reason – try something different– try a different practice area – there is no disadvantage to doing this. It's cheesy but true. The 'why' is important? Why do you want to do it? Freedom, flexibility and money, then I am not sure that your own practice, necessarily delivers that. It certainly doesn't offer this straight off the bat. There needs to be something else that is driving you. You need to understand what that is, before you step off, because if you can't answer that question, if you don't have a compelling answer to that question – then there are other options out there that may be better suited for you. Maybe quit law – world doesn't end if you decide to not practise law anymore. Get the answer to that why.

Jade *'write a business plan and do it properly and take your time. It really helped me when I first met Rodney. It was a bit of a leap of faith so useful then just spending that time. So I think it was about a year's worth of planning whilst I was still in employment. Just taking the time to get everything down on paper filling in the blanks so we would know the certain areas we struggled with and when we needed the accountants help do the forecasts. Use I.T. professionals and get it all on paper. Do your research and then when you see it in black and white. This provides predictions and the worst-case scenario; and you realise that it is achievable and that gives you the confidence to go for it.'*

James *'well firstly something that you think can be unique for your market. Find your USP and do a lot of research. Spend a lot of time working out what your competition is – who's out there. If anyone is doing it – are they doing it in a particular way, whether you can do it better? Go all in – be the first one – just don't go at it half-hearted. When we set this business up there were restrictions on how we got going but once we finally cut the cord it was all we did. We did spend months just focusing on getting this place up and running so that when we got our licence we could really hit the ground running; but that was just the frustration of setting up the business because the SRA started to take up to six months processing first applications for a license. Very few employers would be accommodating and paying you a salary whilst you doing that – setting up a competitive competitor practice. So we knew that we were going to literally six months out. And it is a case of what do you do whilst your living that six months? Do you do nothing? So that is where the whole social media thing came in because we were maxing out on that. LinkedIn was a big part of that. Whilst we couldn't set up a Twitter account for our new firm that nobody knew about the question was how could we still bang on about what we were doing and where we were on LinkedIn. So keep a presence. I think things like that has been a real boon for what we were doing.'*

Jane *'have systems in place. Be very systematic when you are setting up, e.g. letter templates. I have a bank of templates I use. Beware of risks. As I have said I am risk-averse. I do things to suit my temperament rather than down another route, which would not suit my temperament. To also have fun! You have to take the leap of faith. Think outside the box. I had someone say to me I can re-qualify and me thinking why not?'*

Jill *'be kind to yourself, you can only try your best. Try to enjoy and appreciate the benefits of running your own firm.'*

Jodie *'I would just say 'just do it' because I think what can often happen is that you can procrastinate and you always put stuff off. I had to do it because of the situation I was in. But I think I probably should have just set up as a firm from the beginning and not been a consultant first in hindsight. It helps you to test the waters to see if this is something for you. For me it was a much more confidence thing for me. So I think if you are thinking of doing it make sure you have the right team around you to do that.'*

John *'I think it came at the right time in my life on the basis that I was very happy at Blacks. Whilst I did think of partnership there, this has worked out much better – there's a lot of freedom working for yourself. I would say develop a network as early as you can, because as you grow in experience in the level of cases that you deal with, they will grow with you in those organisations. If you are looking after their best interests then it is a good basis to build* *relationships that last. I don't work with anyone I don't like; I am not very good at hiding my emotions. I don't have to and I have that luxury. Doing it earlier – probably not for me, particularly as I had a very young baby at the time. My wife was working. So I think if you ever were planning to do this, I would start networking as soon as possible. And have a plan of action to do that. You have the time to do it. When you have small children you have less time to do that.'*

Kate *'Keep going – I think you have to accept every part of the journey, whether you enjoy it or not. Honestly there is quite a lot of what we do that we don't enjoy, but keep in mind why you are doing it. What is it that you want to achieve, what it is you want to accomplish and why you want to achieve it? If that 'Why?' is strong enough it will keep you going. A very good friend of mine who is one of my ambassador friends, he and I were having a conversation a few weeks ago. I was in a bit of a dilemma about certain things. He said there are two types of work – there's the bills work and the thrills work. Your bill's work pays for your thrill's work. So sometimes you just have to suck it up and get on with it.'*

Kirstie *'You need to work out what your appetite for risk is and don't do it if your partner is not 100% on board with your decision.'*

Laura *'If this is their dream, and as long as they're prepared for a lot of hard work and they don't expect an instant reward either, then they should go for it. It's a long process and there are going to be plenty of challenges along the way and you will have that moment where you say is it worth it? It would so easy to give up but actually if you just stick with it I promise you won't regret it.'*

Liz *'I started out with a proper business plan and I would say that anybody who didn't start a business without a proper business plan is looking to fail. I started with a business plan and I do think that's really ultra important. An accountant friend with one of the big four accountancy firms said to me when I started, always have a benchmark in key performance indicators in your business and that fact it took me about five or six years before I really got my head around that and implemented it. And I didn't do that and that was a big mistake. I do wish that I'd implemented it at the beginning because I think I would have held myself more accountable for things that I did early on and things that other people did for me. So I think that's useful. That's what I'd tell my younger self if I were to start it again.'*

Martin *'I think if you ask anybody what they're going to say to their younger self I think most people come up with the same answer, which is I'd let myself know that actually it's going to be fine. You're going to be ok. And I think I would say that anyway. Whatever course you take you is going to be ok. Different things* *happen. I've never yet had a door close where another one hasn't opened. And sometimes those doors closing felt awful. I felt like they were the worst things in the world to have happened, and yet looking back I can honestly say that it just sent me down a different route. And I've sort of bounced back and moved on. Classic example actually is the exit from my old firm, which sadly tends to be the same thing each and every time when lawyers leave lawyers – they don't seem to be able to let go nicely. And despite my best attempts to do that, that again was the case and in the end I literally handed my entire shares back to them for nothing. And I took the view that actually I don't want this fight and it's too much of a distraction so you can have it all back for nothing. Because I've got – again – the vision and belief that I don't need it.*

I think from a commercial point of view you clearly have got to have a product and service that people want. And I think that's key that you pick the subject matter you love and is commercial and the rest is just about application. So I think for me, going back, I'd say don't worry about – there's a huge amount of things you don't need to worry about and there's things you do need to focus on to make sure you've got a business that actually people want and people need. And focus on what you know and what you love – you can develop anything else.

There's a quote I saw on LinkedIn the other day is: 'if you're the most entrepreneurial person in the room you're in the wrong room'. I think I may have changed it but the point remains the same. I think it is absolutely right, if you're not stretching yourself or surrounding yourself with people who are not of the same enthusiasm, drive, passion and then expertise. So what I don't do now, is that I won't deal with people or work with people who don't have the same values I'm talking about in business. You need all those pieces to sit and think I'd really like to work with you and I am no longer going to try and fit 'square pegs in round holes' to carry people along. Life's too short. Let's go speak to people who can make things happen and keep things moving. That's another thing I would probably go back and say, bring humour and be yourself.'

Miguel *'you could listen to Everybody's Free to Wear Sunscreen by Baz Luhrman. Great advice!*

1. *Read several good books – the first one is Start with Why by Simon Sinek. And focus on why you are doing this – it has to go beyond making money. Secondly, The E-Myth Revisited by Michael E Gerber, which is great and will really make you think about how you turn your skill or talent into a business you can scale. What you do as a business owner in the very beginning will change as you grow your business.*
2. *Have a personal vision as well as a company one. Look at it every day. If you don't you'll get so busy that you will forget it.*

3. *Develop and articulate some core values and make sure they are shared with and by anyone you work with. It sounds cheesy but you all need to be on the same page. If you define what you are and a 'way' of working, then when you're not around to dispense advice, as business owner, the chances are that people who work for you will get it right if they stick to the values.*

4. *Make a commitment to read one book a week if you can or listen to Audio books on journeys. It's a massive time saver.*

5. *Get a coach. Running a business can be lonely and you need people to learn from and hold you to account.*

6. *Join a group of like-minded business owners. If you're having difficulties, some of the people you network with will have had exactly the same ones and learning from them helps you not to have to reinvent the wheel and get it wrong.*

7. *Accept you are always learning and you don't have all the answers. It's okay to be wrong. One of my mentor's encourages his people to "fail quickly", change what's not working and keep reiterating. That's part of the fun although it may not always seem like that at the time.*

8. *Delegate and coach people. Get comfortable with it. Being coached helps you coach others. Aim to get out of your own way as much as you can. You have to accept that there are things you shouldn't be doing and you need a "Don't Do" list, just as much as you need your "TO DO" list. Accept that your role will change as a business owner. You move from being operational to being strategic and focusing on keeping the business on track. It sounds really obvious but is often not that easy to pull off. If you have been operational all your life then running a business is going to feel VERY different.'*

9. *Master marketing – it's continually changing and will drive you crazy. Following on from that, even though you believe in what you do and are good at it, just accept that every once in a while you are going to piss someone off, since everyone is different and they might be having a bad day.*

10. *Embrace technology. It's simultaneously one of my biggest bugbears, when it goes wrong, and a massive help when it goes right. Don't be afraid to try new tools.*

11. *Be comfortable with risk. The greatest risk is to take none. Remember that fear stops you living, not dying. Maybe it will work out, maybe it won't but the journey will be the best thing you ever did.'*

Noreen *'if you want to do it – you should do it. I think a lot people will try and talk you out of it. I think that you need to have the confidence to believe in yourself and you can do it. I started with nothing in the sense that I was* *working in the public sector before I set up so I didn't really have a client base as such. And as I've progressed I got myself premises – legal work and clients, and then I realised whom I needed to work with and build strategic alliances with certain companies, which would help my business grow. That's what I've done. So it's just a journey that I've done with very little from the beginning.'*

Peter *'Well, don't be afraid. I think there are two types of people out there. There are lawyers who love the law, who are passionate about getting their nose stuck into a book, dealing with a problem, fixing it, advising on options, etc. There are other lawyers who love relationships with clients and the two don't necessarily meet all the time. I am very privileged to be able to do a job running a firm where we have huge sways of clients across the most beautiful county in the country. I didn't think I could do it. I was a bit scared – ok I was a lot scared. I was very naïve. I've made some humungous mistakes. But I've had some great successes. I've had an amazing journey so far. Would I do it again? In a heartbeat! Would I do it differently? I would change hundreds of things along the way. So if there's a single message – do your research, get a business plan, get the finance in place and go for it. And every time you get knocked back, pull yourself up, dust yourself down and get on it and do it again because business is a journey and you're not travelling to a destination. You've got to enjoy it and if you're not enjoying it then change to something you do.'*

Rachel *'just keep going. Often feel like it is like being in a really dense forest and having a knife to hack away and get though it.'*

Richard *'started off in 2002 and I was naïve. In a way it is good to have that. I would say if you do it, make it your life and soul – live and breathe it – you have to show absolute dedication. If work-life balance is important to you then I am not sure that running your own legal practice is something for you. I feel like my mortgages drive me and I owe a duty to my staff to lead by example.'*

Samira *'my advice would be to just do it, don't look back; there will be many, many lows. But one of the biggest things is to build the right team – it has taken me seven years to get there. Each time when something was not working out was a low I guess. Just have to keep going. Don't worry about business plans. Sometimes I say to my staff, lets just do it, once you begin things start falling into place.'*

Simon *'have a belief in yourself that you can do it rather than listen to the negative voices and surround yourself with people who are positive not naysayers.*

Speak to people who are already doing it and see who helped them. So I got Steven Marge's name from Jez and Gareth Milner, well everyone seems to know him. Got recommended to you from Jodie. You will get people you trust recommending people they trust.

Have an office as it does make you more focused. You get so much more done. Anyone that is thinking of doing it – do it. '

Thomas *'you speak to a lot of lawyers and a lot of my friends are unhappy with their careers. I know some people at bigger firms who are on a treadmill and can't see where the next stage is in their career. Wage slaves and all this sort of thing. They are just a number and I know that not everybody gets an opportunity to do what we did. Even if there is a sniff of an opportunity, grab it, just do it.'*

Your Turn

Professional, personal and management assessment for setting up your own business

This is a simple personal assessment for you to identify your technical, business and soft skills. You may want to collect feedback from designated peer group, team member and your boss depending on the system used by your organisation.

	Strengths	Areas for Improvement to set up my business	Business/ Personal Plan
Technical Competency			
Business Skills			
Leadership			
Management			
Relationship management			
Interpersonal skills			

Your Turn

Your business story starts here ...

SECTION 6

THE YORKSHIRE LEGAL STARS WHO HAVE FORGED THEIR OWN PATH

THE PURPOSE OF THIS SECTION

Where possible I have included as much of their original 'story' as recorded in the interviews or provided in writing, specifically excluding the answers in **Section 5. Chapter 5.6.**

N.B. All of those Stars interviewed have significantly developed their business, their services and products, and websites between the time of their interviews and the publication of this book as not one of them has stood still

Overview of the segmentation of the interviews

The interviews are in alphabetical order in four segments as follows:

1. Fourteen legal business owners with a team at the time of interview

1. Andrew Gray
2. Bill Barton
3. Gary Gallen
4. Jade Campbell
5. Jodie Hill
6. Laura Clapton
7. Liz Ward
8. Martin Holdsworth
9. Noreen Khan
10. Peter Gibson
11. Rachel Roche
12. Richard Cramer
13. Samira Cakali
14. Thomas Coates

2. Four legal business owners with consultants delivering legal services

1. Ian McCann & Matt Dowell
2. John Bailes
3. Kirstie Penk

3. Six legal business owners with no team at the time of the interview

1. Claire Murphy
2. Geoff Peter
3. James Thornton
4. Jane Winteringham
5. Jill Rucklidge
6. Simon Robinson

4. Five business owners who have moved out of law to run a non-legal business

1. Andrea Morrison
2. Ann Page
3. Cathy Cockin
4. Kate Young
5. Miguel Florit

FOURTEEN LEGAL BUSINESS OWNERS WITH A TEAM AT THE TIME OF INTERVIEW

1. ANDREW GRAY

Solicitor and owner of Truth Legal (personal injury, medical negligence and employment law) www.truthlegal.co.uk

Why practise your legal expertise as a business owner?

Multiple reasons. The main one being frustration with the large law firm I was working at prior to setting up.

Without a shadow of a doubt, six years on I was still angry about how I was treated. I was worried about my son being born – my second child – and the arrival was in early December.

They had two weeks paid paternity. I was phenomenally busy at the time with Christmas being so close. This would have meant a month off.

So what I proposed was I'll take the first week off, and then take the remainder of my paternity leave later. I thought well that makes sense from the work point of view and from my point of view. My wife's point of view too. My wife's mother was going to be with us for the first week with my first child.

My immediate manager thought it was a good idea too. It just was stopped by the powers that be. And it came back with no. I had to take them together otherwise I would lose it.

I'm furious because of the way I was treated and it also then brought a few things into sharp focus, which was the amount of work I was expected to do, which I thought was unreasonable. Also the cost targets were bonkers. I was getting paid one sixth of all my cost targets. I thought that was just ridiculous. I was travelling two hours a day, which could be put to family time.

My parents run businesses and still do. They're in their mid 70s and are still in businesses so it's kind of got me thinking that maybe I ought to give it a go.

I was four years qualified with potentially a high legal salary and my wife on maternity leave. We had almost no money coming in at all. There wasn't that much to lose in some ways, which at that time which made it easier to do, as I was more junior. I was probably a bit more cocky about it overall but I was also lucky because, generally I was in a niche area of personal injury work called assaults at work. I was passionate about helping those who were assaulted at work. For example nurses being assaulted by patients or children who assault their teachers.

I researched this type of work by checking out Google for assaults at work. The only firm that was listed and ranked was the one I was working for. So I thought I can help people more effectively and cheaper and be ranked too. And that's what happened.

What is your best and worst business habit?

I'm sure I must have multiple bad habits; you would have to ask other people really.

I come up with too many ideas and so I throw a lot of darts and some of them land and some don't. I think I am a bit unusual in that my head will not stop producing ideas – that's all it does – in fact all it's ever done since I was a kid. As a result, I am sometimes at odds with other people I work with and they kinder have to get used to it. I have had another idea.... I have had another idea....I have had another idea.... After a while they understand that I am generally talking about all these ideas as I operate at this level as I don't want to stand still. It does get them ready for change, and they adopt change a bit faster because they are going to have too. So it's a good thing and a bad habit.

That is why I want to recruit more people.

Is it a bad habit to not be able to switch off from work? Don't know – hard to say.

How do you manage the 'highs' and the 'lows' of being a business owner? (Stress management) and/or what are you doing to build resilience?

So my degree is predominantly in philosophy. Well that's where I got to try to think like a Stoic. And so for example only on Tuesday we had to discontinue a trial two days into the three allotted, when the circumstances changed. It was a difficult case from the get go and we thought it is likely that we would lose. Well when we don't have after the event insurance and we have something like £50,000 pounds on the clock with £12,000 in disbursements. So we lose £50,000 pounds. Right. But that's just where it goes. But also we got hit with a £12,000 pound bill and I'm kind of unfazed by it because you know that's litigation.

We're in litigation and we'll have the highs and lows of a roller coaster. So losing a trial is always a great thing. I just had to praise my colleagues because of their hard work even though we did not get the result we wanted especially on a no win-no fee case. It's easy enough to take your client to trial when they are paying you to do so, but a different matter when it's your money.

So when it is more than 50/50 then we win half and lose half, which is kind of our coverage here in these types of cases. So when you lose like that and it is outside our control we still do a post-mortem to see if we would do the same thing again. But financially it was horrible. It is balanced when we have successes as you get lucky breaks too. Don't get too excited by your successes and conversely don't get too worried about anything. If your colleagues see you not be so emotional when you win or you lose this creates a better atmosphere.

Who do you turn to for support inspiration and why? Who would you like to thank for their support and why?

I use a lot of podcasts and books predominantly. An example would be this guy called Seth Godin who's a marketing general philosopher I suppose. What he thinks about the school of life, which is something I really like. I like authors Tim Ferriss and Alain du Botton (another philosopher).

Definitely thank my parents who loaned me £30,000 pounds. I have paid back £15,000 over the last six years and that was really helpful because a person doing business.

We made a loss the first two years even though we billed a lot simply because we were setting up. The loan made it possible because dealing with banks was horrific.

Definitely my wife as well because she just ran the house. It seems unfair, even antiquated our division of labour. But that's how it has been. She has had a steady income and managed the house. She's supporting the kids so we have a platform that works.

And Georgina – she has been pretty solid through out. There have been hundreds – you, Ann, having been on your one-day management course.

Did or do you have a personal or business vision?

My vision has remained pretty steady. As business is an extension of my values, I'm really glad people were comfortable with that. I believe you should shout your values from rooftops so everybody knows. It was important because you're entering a personal injury world. We only represent those that are genuine. And also my colleagues apply these values as well and so buy into the concept that we are not representing all and sundry. We didn't want to do that. And we are at one with our ethics

My vision is that I'd like to build things. I wanted to keep growing, growing, growing. I think we help a lot of people. We gave away about a quarter of a million pounds worth of free advice last year, which is an incredible amount and I am more proud of this more than anything else. Therefore the more profitable we are, and the more staff we have, the more people we can help. So growth not for the vanity purposes, not really for financial reasons, its so we can help more people.

Did you have a business plan when you first started? If so what worked what didn't?

I did. In fact I had to have one because I needed to show one to the SRA and I think I got it down to one side of A4, for me. I've got it somewhere just for comedy reasons because I don't think your business plan really ever survives its first interaction with the customer. I had to I had to put some rough numbers on there and those numbers might have been a little optimistic but my best educated guesses at the time.

What are you doing differently from the organisation you have left behind and/or the competition?

First we offer the similar kind of employee benefits based on flexibility and what is in the bank account.

We tried to be so flexible as to when people were needed in the office – we try not to be clock-watchers – trying to make it more of a hot desk environment – working from home environment so that it cuts down commuting for them. People are most productive and do record their most hours at home. Working from home and being flexible makes a 'people happier' environment.

Another difference to my previous organisation is cost targets. We wanted to make sure that these were reasonable and manageable. So we agreed for those that are employed it is a third of their salary. We do pay bonuses so that we can reward those that work really, really hard. For example, if they billed £12,000 over their target they would get a £4,000 bonus – so people can earn well here.

Because it is personal injury work it is important that everyone collaborates and holidays are covered, court dates and so on. I think it is the tradition in other PI law firms that whichever fee earner has the file at the settlement claims all the costs for their target; which means that no-one really collaborates because if you help someone with that file you don't get paid for that time. Here we make sure everyone is paid for the work that they do. So it makes sense to work on other cases as well as your own.

We ensure that everyone is up to speed on all our matters so that they can even recognise them by the tone of the voice on the telephone. We don't want it to be that the client is not recognised and one of many that is being processed by many different people. I think we have achieved that.

Difference between competitors

Huge difference. So we have always specialized in what we call switch solicitor cases or change solicitor cases and personal injury matters from those clients who are really miffed with the level of service they were often getting from unqualified paralegals who have got 550 cases. This is the most I have heard of and we don't have 550 for the seven of us here.

When it gets more complicated, those un-qualified people with too much work have an impossible job handling that kind of work. So we've always specialized taking those files off the firms who do this. So we've actually seen what claim firms do which is unusual because claimant lawyers don't know what the other claimant lawyers are doing. Why would they? So we have seen some good practices out there and some dreadful ones.

So I think firms like ours that are specialist, we have smaller volumes of cases for qualified people (solicitors) and good people, which is why the service level is different and why the reviews are different.

(N.B. Certainly one of the stories I will mention here is when I came to your five-year anniversary party I met one of your clients who practically worshiped the ground you stood on. This was because you were helping them to get justice and support for their child and their previous lawyers had not served them well. They were also over the moon at being invited to your celebratory party.)

See also answer to the business plan question.

What has been your greatest success to date?

I have spent a lot of time with the family. So that is huge. Less commuting and if there's any issues with the children to the point that they need to be collected from school I can because I don't have a boss. So the kids are seeing a lot more of me than they would be if I were still in the city commuting and doing longer hours.

I was around but still doing emails on my phone so present in the room but not with them. That has changed. I have managed to take the kids to school three or four days a week for the last six years, which certainly I could not have done before.

I think business-wise – well the reviews we and I have got are amazing. We've got 35 '5' star reviews since I started recording them recently. That's amazing and becomes marketing itself. And I think the longevity of people I've worked here as well which is nice, as it becomes more of a family atmosphere. Georgina and I have worked 5 ½ years together – actually I have lost count. Most people stay.

Where do you see threats to your legal business?

Without doubt this government I can't stand this government. Where do I start? We don't do legal aid work. Due to the decimation of Legal Aid work we have to offer so-called free work. Free legal advice to make up for Legal Aid being canned. In addition the budgets for Citizens Advice Bureau have been decimated as well.

There have been changes the Jackson reforms came in 2013 trying to get ahead of those. I think the government is in the pocket of the insurers and every time they have a sneeze the government says 'bless you'. We are forever terrified of what this government is going to do.

Another of the big changes they're going to do is to change small claims limit of £1,000 to £5,000 for road traffic accidents. This means that of the circa 70,0000 road traffic accident claims, I reckon 65,0000 of them will not have someone involved on their behalf and are up against insurers and their lawyers. The biggest type of con over justice I have ever come across. It is disgraceful behaviour.

They have also illegally, definitely illegally introduced employment tribunal fees at a very high level. So previously there were no tribunal fees payable in an employment claim and politically I think that was wrong anyway. I think there should have been a small charge. In fact the government made the charge £1,200. So when you've lost your job because you're gay, black, Christian or Muslim or whatever it may be as to why you have lost your job and you have to pay £1,200 to bring your case against a well-funded opponent who may not even pay you even if you win. It's dealing with all of that at a time of vulnerability. The Court kicked that one out thankfully so it's a ' topsy-turvy' world.

So trying to diversify into different areas and also praying for change in government. So there's that. So I think that the government is the biggest threat.

What is your personal brand? Name your top three qualities, which enable you to run a unique legal practice.

1. Transparency with colleagues – they know how we are doing.
2. Knowing my strengths and my many weaknesses
3. Delegation – apparently many business leaders find this hard, but this has been easy for me, probably because my colleagues are better at the tasks than I am.

Why your firm's name?

Its genesis is that I am a Quaker. Quakers have five testimonies – five things that they broadly believe in. I don't believe in all of them. One of them is equality. Every one is equal, live more simple lives (not flashy – never bought a Ferrari or anything like that). They tend to believe in pacifism, although I am not a pacifist entirely. They also believe in sustainability for the environment and look after it as much as possible. But also truth, as Quakers are renowned for being truthful. They never swore oaths, as their word is their bond.

So I try to mimic what Roundtree and Cadbury have done for their business in that they looked after their staff; and their staff looked after their customers. They were all transparent about their business. The Quakers also were called, at one point, friends of truth. So when I was in the business planning stage, I was reading a book about Quakers and came across gospel truth. Whilst it was quite a boring book, I genuinely woke up in the middle of the night at 3.00am in the morning and decided to call the firm Truth Legal. It has resonated with us really well from the 'get-go'.

Read a book from a marketer Seth Godwin called 'Purple Cow' and he said – there was so much noise online you need to cut through. My name is Andrew Gray so couldn't be more of an obvious name.

It is so taken and so Google unfriendly. Also how do you spell Gray – is it with an 'a' or with an 'e'? And then what do you do when you bring someone else in? Does it become Andrew Gray and Partners and to promote non-solicitors and we would have to be an ABS? Thus a change of brand and name and it seem bonkers to do all those things.

I did not want to use the word solicitors as at the beginning there was only me and that would imply there was more and be untruthful.

Truth Legal ticked the Purple Cow box because 'WOW it's a Purple Cow'. It had an ethical bent to it and it worked in the personal injury world. On Google there was nothing with Truth Legal combined. The last thing is that I liked the five letters and the five letters together and it seems to put them on top of each other – they work.

How do I feel about it now – is that it should have the word solicitors in it so that if you were Googling solicitors and it says Truth Legal – are they solicitors? So do we go Truth Solicitors Legal or Truth Legal Solicitors? But can't change it now.

Is there anything specific you do to manage the quality of service?

So that's a great question.

So I do file reviews and the bigger you get the more difficult it is to manage quality. It's so important to hire the right people and make sure they are trained and that the training they attend isn't about getting the 16 hours CPD as it was in the past. But the training has to be continuous.

For example I'll get a list of blogs in the morning from Lexology and I will ask all the lawyers to sign up to Lexology to check their area of law. I recognise that they can be so busy they can't find them. So today's a case in point. There was a news blog about contributory negligence in cycling and I circulated that around my colleagues to get them thinking about relevant case law.

Every day, it's thinking, well we're in a place where we care about continuously learning; and I encourage the lawyers to look stuff up. This is another way we are different from the big firms, as we want enquiring minds.

We have currently been trialling an office manager to help us set up relevant processes to be more efficient.

What interpersonal skills are important to be successful with your type of clients?

So I used the robot test. I tried this out with Georgina who's the second member of staff I took on. She applied to be a trainee solicitor and was working at a big insurance law firm. She was acting for insurance companies where they might get into their head all claimants are like scumbags. It's a lot more complicated than that. When Georgina first came for an interview with me, we did a 14-hour job interview. Part of it was to see how Georgina interacted with the claimant. So I had a client of mine explain what I was doing following Georgina signing a non-disclosure agreement.

Gave her the file to take away the existing witness statement, which the client was comfortable with as I told him I had someone who was very capable. Just to see if she could empathise because that was the key thing for all of us. Do you care about the your clients? Do you advise and empathise. I don't want to them be anaesthetised just to finish the case.

I want them to say – I'll admit it – 'that was disgusting. Have you seen what happened in that case?' I want them to be moved by what they hear and if they are not moved don't work here.

Marketing online (websites, Twitter, Facebook, Instagram, LinkedIn, YouTube or other)?

All of them but by far the most useful is the websites. Again gave away great free content online. Be honest/transparent and have some personality – write or be helpful.

Google likes FAQ because clients like it and Google does because it gives enquirers online the right answer.

I have a digital strategy. You know we spend a lot on this. My job really, is well, to look after the lawyers. A lot of the clients are active and we need to drive the market. I listen to multiple marketing podcast and read articles on a daily basis

How do you help people – by posting the best content? So I run the strategy. So when I think of articles to write I look at what enquiries are coming in. If we can't help people because they don't know where to begin, then we may be able to if we write the article and the answers. Then they might call us first as we have shown that we know their pain or problem.

We've got three websites anyway and one of this is a Polish version. Our lawyer just translated different articles with a different vibe to it to cater for different cultural questions we get from social media. It's just more difficult to manage this part because I don't know what words mean.

Digital strategy – we will spend around £1,500 per month either on other blog writers – 'S' marketers and web designers. Then there's also my time so it is a big part of our strategy really.

This hopefully will mean that we should be more immune to any shocks. So we don't have any Insurer who sends us our work – we do have one claims management company. Work comes from lots of different places so we are a bit more protected and can plan it a bit more. I've worked in places where there has been one big union client or one big insurance client and can pull the plug on that firm. We don't have that vulnerability.

Offline marketing:

I was introduced to BNI by another lawyer. When I went along, there was one of the most mind-blowing or most useful experiences since setting up. I realised the true meaning of commercial and business perspectives. It was so perfect.

It was like being in a Force nine hurricane where 30 odd people come to pitch or talk to people. You see people who are not professional give great pitches but the professionals give it the worst.
So I found BNI not great for generating leads for PI and employment law but I went for the business acumen that you gain from talking to others. This wasn't my first reason for going. But that was the reason to stay. Friendships with other business owners who may not be in your field was another reason because when you are a business owner, it is good to have like-minded people to talk to. Many business owners seek help from their peers and can know what's going on in the world or you meet some more interesting people. Highly recommend this even though I have now quit as I have been ill recently.

How do you lead and manage your team. Have you had any training about leadership and management? What would you say is your best/ worst quality?

First of all from you, Ann. I attended your Management Stage 2 (which was compulsory six years ago) and I found your coaching useful at that time too to keep me on track.

Now it tends to be blog posts from Linked-in, commenting podcasts, that kind of stuff on a regular basis. But some of it needs to be trial and error anyway.

My job really is to up-skill people who work with me. So making other people directors, putting someone in charge of the HR – in charge of billing so I am doing less and less. I'm trying to in a sense to write myself out of the business because that would then be a real business. You know you've got business when you don't have to be there and it still ticks over. This happened and when I was poorly in March (2018) with five weeks off work and every thing worked. I am so proud of my team.

Worst qualities – I have so many weaknesses it is hard to pick one. Best – optimism, particularly in humanity.

How do you develop your team? Do you use the SRA competency framework for example?

No don't do it. I like the idea behind it. I thought it was always simply bonkers to stick to 16 hours training and do wills to make up the points when you didn't do wills. Wrong. Wrong to do all the training at the last minute under the old system I think it has to be continuous.

I also like the fact that the new system includes the fact that you read stuff, you write stuff as part of your training. It should be continuous and it needs to be built in and be integral to the organisation. Learning all the time is imperative.
I am concerned that some of our lawyers don't fully get it.

What are the biggest team challenges and successes?

Team challenges are generally around running up to trial, for us to be fully ready go to trial. Things don't often go to trial they just settle or discontinue beforehand. Things happen such as Royal Mail delivering late and someone driving to court with the right document. That's a challenge because you can't predict litigation as a force of business. Everyone has to stop what he or she is doing and work on one matter. And it is delicious to watch everyone do it. So it is also a team success to see everyone working together.

Where do you see your legal practice going in the next three years?

Where will the firm be? Yeah, well what we're finding is that our brand was a bit ahead of its time but it seems to have found its time.

So our web visitors on own Truth Legal site could well be over 500 per day with bounce rate of under one per cent which means that 495 people out of 500 were meant to be on the site and were on it for a couple of minutes.

So we want to diversify for cash flow reasons but also to offer our way of doing things in other areas of law. We think that people want so much more from their lawyers and companies these days. Examples of Ben and Jerry's or Innocent Drinks, which gives 5% of their profits away.

The world is changing a lot. People want to use more authentic and more transparent products and services. So I'm hoping that one day that the lawyers will allow me to put all their salaries on the website. They're not with me on that one yet. But I am happy to put mine on there.

2. BILL BARTON

Solicitor and joint owner with Trish Barton (Solicitor) of Barton Legal (Property – construction and commercial) www.bartonlegal.com

Why practise your legal expertise as a business owner?

Simple answer is control. The legal profession is a contradiction in that it relies on groupings of talented individuals in partnerships or Limited Liability Partnerships and the rest. This then creates a lack of individuality and so having your own business allows you to make decisions more quickly and not worry about the politics.

Another reason why we set up is that I felt I did not feel as though my clients were given enough love or TLC I have also said to my clients that this is my mobile number. I expect you to use it if there is a problem. Call me at a weekend. If you call me with a problem at the weekend, I might tell you that it is not a problem – you enjoy your weekend. If it is a problem I have taken it off you and you can enjoy your weekend.

What is your best and worst business habit?

Too long hours and not leaving work behind. Availability is a double-edged sword – *see above*. It is the selling point to clients but no real holiday for me.

How do you manage the 'highs' and the 'lows' of being a business owner? (Stress management) and/or what are you doing to build resilience?

Attitude – I happen to love the work I do. Can't expect to love everyday. But I love my clients even the most challenging ones. My wife is the co-director. Children are a big release. My children bring me back down to earth – do not give a 'monkeys' about how big of a deal I have done.

We try and celebrate success and failure. We try and celebrate a good month and equally if you have a failure. Actually whilst I did say celebrate you have to look at it. Ok that's happened and how am I going to learn from it and not repeat it? So what can you do? Well you know what – it is a lesson. You are constantly learning. You take something from that so it won't happen again. Turn negative into a positive.

Who do you turn to for support and inspiration? Who would you like to thank for their support and why?

Family and long term friends. Firstly it's my wife and my children on advice on doing things.

Then long-term friends who are within the profession and connected generally. They're the people who have an understanding of what you do and what you are going through. Sometimes they can help you through as they have been through that. I think it's how open you want to be. Sometimes one of the biggest problems with support is how open you are going to be. Are you actually going to tell people that you are having a hard time? If, as lots of businesses do, they just tell you that they are always fantastic that is disingenuous.

The first proper boss I had was Frances Kirkam. She was great and I am full of admiration because she is incredibly well respected for the lawyer and judge she was. I think having respect from peers is phenomenally important especially from another lawyer – that makes a big difference.

Did or do you have a personal or business vision?

Wrote on a whiteboard when we first set up – only business plan we have had – get clients, do work, get paid, retire. That is the full extent of the business plan we have had – encapsulated everything. How you do that is micromanaging your commercial goals on a year-by-year basis.

Did you have a business plan when you first started – if so what worked and what didn't?

See above answer.

What are you doing differently from the organisation you have left and/or the competition?

This comes into a variety of things you have raised. We have a large volume of repeat work, longevity of clients. I have got clients from when I moved up to Leeds 20 years ago. I worked in Birmingham originally. So some of my clients I have acted for, for 20 years. Then its, what I talked about before, you have to make your clients genuinely believe that you are there for them. There's too much networking syndrome. People go in and pass out business cards and think they have got business. It is not how it works. For example, Italian clients (I have a number of these) expect you to go to dinner, have a bottle of wine, discuss things to get know you to see if they like you. You might have two or three of those meetings. Because if I like you and could spend a couple of hours with you, I am more likely to give you work. That's the approach rather than coming in and saying, right I will do this work for 50% less than somebody else. There is always someone cheaper. We are not interested in undercutting. We aim to provide the same quality of service as people had when I was at DLA or any top firm but we add to that a more personal and proactive approach. The clients know you can phone any time and we will help them.

Where we don't do that work, I won't say I am sorry but we don't do that. I will go and find the person in one of the firms we know that can deal with it. Make sure that they can handle it and I will put them together. Because it doesn't matter if I am not doing that client's work but I don't believe that when you pass the client on to another firm, you lose the client. I think you can enhance the relationship, your client knows that you trust them. It is a two-way thing. That builds it and I am lucky that I have kept the same mobile number for 20+ years. I put in people's names, the details about them and the name comes up on your phone and you have their info at your fingertips. Clients really appreciate picking up conversations where they left off. Clients hate having to tell each solicitor – this is my background and this is what I want to do and these are the important things.

Q. Do you have fixed fees? Yes we do a huge amount of fixed fees. Most commercial property work is fixed fee. We are very unusual in that we have in the last four or five years done a lot of construction work and we act for about seven/eight law firms. They have a schedule and that describes the work. So contract drafting/ review/ appointments/ warranties. If you had five appointments there is a fixed fee for the first one, which reduces. Anything you can do like that is all on a fixed fee.

I also do cap fees. So on large energy projects, I'll say to a client right I will charge you this much provided it completes by this date. So you do cap and collar. Again clients want certainty. If a client can define their work precisely – I'll define my fees.

You normally can't define your work in litigation so that is on an hourly rate. Over the last 18 months we have worked really hard to do fixed fees for different stages so that you can say pre-action protocol is £X, for CMC is £Y. For example we have agreed there is going to be four witness statements. The other side say there is going to be three. Right, we'll agree we will do this many and that none of them are going to be more than 20 pages. So you agree with your client and if you have to change that then you go back to the client; but at least the client has got an idea that in the next four months, some of this work is fixed and some is on a purely hourly rate. Most people are reporting to someone else.

What has been your greatest success to date?

It goes back to what I said before. Long-term repeat work and referrals from clients, which is one of the loveliest things, even if it's not a big job. Currently we are doing a big piece of work in relation to HS2 £150 million pound worth of work and it is a big job. They were referred by a client who I have not done anything for about five years. Haven't spoken to them in that time just sent out newsletters. That is fantastic.

We have entered awards – not sure if these are important. Our ranking in Legal 500 and Chambers is important. It shows, again, industry acceptance. I know because I have been in their position and have been phoned up about others. So I know the people do phone up and check. Our clients tell us they have had a phone call, and that again is really important to us

Where do you see the threats for your legal business?

Brexit – because a lot of our work has been international – German and Italian. German client left due to uncertainty. London is an international centre for legal clients. The uncertainty – companies do not know what is going on. Businesses like to know what is going on. Even if a yes is given then that project might take two years before solicitors are instructed. I see that as still being uncertainty. What is going to come out is our biggest threat, the rest we can manage.

What is your personal brand? Name your top three qualities, which enable you to run a unique legal practice.

We provide a really personal service, and we project manage. It is an all-embracing service. Where a client wants a service that we do not do, we work with a lot of other firms. We will say to a client: here is a choice of other law firms who do that work by asking the following questions. Do you want location? Do you want expensive (some do)? Do you want another niche firm? You decide this choice. We can instruct and they can deal with you direct or we can manage that process for you. So that you deal with us and we'll cope with all these other bits which are quite common in energy projects. So you get this all-embracing service so that we can stand out more. Knowing our clients.

Our corporate colour is purple. Which is a quality colour we choose 11 years ago. It is becoming more common now.

Honestly I don't know which three words best fit me. You as a business owner are different from what a client sees. So as a business owner – resilience, proactive, passionate (we love what we do). From a client's perspective they would see resilience differently. They might say something like steady.

Why your firm's name?

We landed on this name really quickly and I know that people agonise over a name. Barton Legal is like Ronseal – does what it says on the tin. We are Barton Legal a specialist legal service company.

Is there anything specific you do to manage the quality of service?

We have intermittently sent questionnaires to clients. Generally it's from speaking to clients and asking if everything was ok. I learnt a lesson from consultants' years ago. When you have a lot of things on – call all your clients on Friday afternoon, just to check with them. If they've got a massive problem, this allows them to get their problems off their chest. They don't then spend the weekend on it and you are on it.

The best way is having regular contact over the phone with clients, avoid emailing too often. You can hear the client's tone of voice and understand their perspective. I also ask other people. If we have a client who is seeing a consultant on a piece of litigation then I will check with the consultant to see how they are. Any gripes or groans about us. If so you don't confront the client but you resolve it. You might say sorry if you think it is appropriate. It is dealing with things in a proactive personal manner.

What interpersonal skills are important to be successful with your type of clients?

Being able to be sociable, interpersonal skills are key. Being able to listen and understand or recognising when they are bored, worried or frightened. It is knowing how to never make anyone feel uncomfortable. As far as you possibly can making people feel comfortable. Finding people's names out before a meeting. It's a tiny thing that does not take a great deal of effort. Lots of partners told me this trick, it is not new. If you deal with people as though they are a commodity, they will treat you the same way. If you treat people generally how you want to be treated, then that is a much better approach.

Don't do things that your mother/grandmother would be embarrassed about. All of those things are important although we all fall down from time to time, I am far from perfect. You support and encourage others whether it's your team, your staff or other solicitors. Nothing to stop you if you are a really 'big enough' solicitor to help and protect someone from another firm. It's a whole range of things. These are not peculiar to the legal profession – just life skills.

It used to be that you sat in a room with your principal and learnt these. It is now old fashioned and we have moved away from this. I think that there is a huge number of solicitors who are over-promoted. I think that there are a lot of people who are partners who shouldn't be partners because they are not rounded. They have been promoted for other reasons. And the legal profession is a bizarre one where just because you have been there for 15 years, you are a partner, and someone says you can now run a business. So when did you do your HR training/employment law or your tax or your corporate? So you are now running a business shouting and screaming at people. It doesn't work. The person who changes the ink in a machine is as important in a company as the top most partner, because if you don't have that person, I am willing to bet that senior partner or director will have no idea how to change the ink or to reconnect the computer. You need all of those things.

Marketing online (websites, Twitter, Facebook, Instagram, LinkedIn, YouTube or other)?

We use our website. We normally publish a newsletter every quarter which links back to our website. Other people's websites or others writing articles which link back to our website.

I should use LinkedIn more, two members of staff look after Twitter to post things. No Facebook or Instagram.

For YouTube – submitted videos for Yorkshire Legal Awards – they didn't get anywhere. We asked our clients to film their own videos just on their IPhones– some said it was excruciating. There should be a link from these to our website.

Offline Marketing

Increasing international clients by attending conferences abroad.

A lot of networking – part of various networking groups – BNI. Nature of work, property and construction, people expect knowledge of local businesses including trades e.g. plumber/builder. We only focus on commercial property here and I think it is really useful to be part of a local community.

I am a member of lots of institutes such as the Chartered Institute of Arbitrators, TEXA. Industry ones such as the Law Society. Networking to me is about building long term relationships, I am not generally very good at going into something once a month which you don't make work.

IBA is something I have been working on for last two/three years for international work. So I am now on the International Construction Project Committee. I spoke at last year in Sydney, this year I will be speaking in Rome (2018). That is something that has led to CLINT – Construction Law International. I will do book reviews and articles. That gives you credibility in your industry and gives you connections. You exchange emails sharing views e.g. from Peru/America. That's brilliant – gets your mind fizzing.

How do you lead and manage them? Have you had any training about leadership and management? What would they say is your best/worst quality?

I probably swear far too much. I try and balance it between being very, very honest with people about their performance. I don't think it helps to say you have done a brilliant job if it is not. Actually praising staff is no different from praising children. There are times when children and staff are incredibly frustrating. You know something is broken and it wasn't done by anyone. You might lose your temper but other times you love them to bits.

Yes it's like children, you have to be there, trying to inspire, balancing it with discipline and TLC. Not letting any of us get too inflated with our own importance. Trying to remind them of a lot of the core things we have talked about. Make your client feel special. I am always trying to say don't just think about the piece of paper you reviewed. What else is there – think about other proactive issues you could be working on.

Again, as with children you don't give them the answer. You are giving them the hints and they come up with the answers, themselves. That works, and sometimes people get things wrong, and you have to decide – is some of that my fault? Is there any benefit in shouting or is it worth saying – do you know what – what are we going to learn from this mistake? We are not going to make that one again are we? Then again, it is not hiding it. Humour sometimes helps and you want them to get over it and not feel too embarrassed about it. Get it out in the open.

We have a lot of office socials – there is a great café round the corner. I take people for lunch on a regular basis, drinks after work. Families are a difficult comparison but it is similar to that.

Have you had any business or management training?

No. I have not had any leadership or management training except a long time ago Management Stage 1 – maybe Stage 2. If you are a solicitor over a certain age it's likely you've picked it up. If you have made a reasonable stab at it, you've progressed. And if you didn't make a reasonable stab at it, then you probably didn't progress.

How do you develop your team? Do you use the SRA Competency Framework?

No I don't. I think it is very difficult to use rigid frameworks. We are a niche practice and I only do construction and engineering. Trish only does commercial property, our staff will do a mixture of the two. So building up competences is subject to the work we do. We try and give people far more ownership and involvement at a much, much earlier date. That's based upon Trish and I thinking is that person incompetent to do that? And if the answer is yes – go on.

We normally have a team meeting weekly, although frequently it does not happen. We will sit down in the construction side, pretty much every morning and discuss what's going on. Trish does the same. We try and map out what is coming up for the week. This helps us apportion work between the lawyers. I like most construction lawyers do contentions and non-contentious work. You learn from each. Lottie is our paralegal and I took her to a meeting yesterday. This is the first meeting she has been to. She was doing the notes and therefore understands how a meeting runs. The politics and the 'chit-chat'. That helps her and then informs her in thinking about other meetings. We try and ask – did you get that? I constantly ask, as we are very, very open.

What are your biggest team challenges and successes?

Growth. I've been looking for another construction partner/director – used a headhunter. You realise you are looking for someone like yourself. I have a 'pond' of clients and I am looking for someone who is like-minded with a slightly different 'pond'. Finding people who have that desire, I have interviewed a few lawyers who have said I have it cushy where I am. They seem to have less ambition than I do. That's sad.

So growing the business and finding people whom you can graft on to your firm and who get on with people. That is the highest competency in a small firm – getting on and fitting in and be part of the team and having ability to build rapport with someone.

A success would be my current assistant Tom. He did a different degree and he 'paralegaled' with us for six months. Went away did his law conversion course. We kept him on throughout his studies and his law finals. He has done his training and is qualified and I would say he is way ahead of the curve in terms of what he can do because he knows the clients. He has hands on experience and last year he ran a three-day trial. Counsel was happy with him. This is not the experience he would get in a large firm. We are cost-effective.

Children and flowers – you have to do so many things to nurture them, and to persuade them to blossom and grow. If you do that really well, you bask in their glory in a different way, rather than living their lives for them. I love coming across my trainees who are now partners in law firms. That's rewarding.

Where do you see your legal practice going in the next three years?

In anything, if you let the negatives and doomsayers get you down, you are finished. We are a niche practice. More firms are realising they need to not dabble – for those wanting a quality service, here we are. We have links across the world with firms, and with Brexit now is the time to go directly to Europe. Building more links with international law firms will benefit and show them the benefits of English Law and our expertise. Most English law firms are way, way ahead of any firms in any other state. We are building genuine relationships.

I have to be optimistic. I hope to grow with three or four more solicitors. Our work will have larger percentage of international work. Like to see the junior lawyers coming through and doing that themselves and blossoming. Being in a position of getting a great piece of work.

If solicitors don't forget where they come from and they remember that the client is paramount then the legal profession has still got a great future.

Anything else you would like to add?

Communication: I worked very hard to drive Leeds Market itself as the Legal excellence centre outside London. It's contentious but you have to start somewhere. I love Leeds city, having worked in Manchester and Sheffield; and I am a 'brummie'. I really want to see Leeds flourish. The more I can do to make Leeds the centre of excellence the better. I'd like to see more solicitors being really been proud of what they do and be confident to stand out. Same as your children. You want them to go out and be proud of your family name.

(In our discussion Bill's unusual heritage and time as Leeds Law Society President came up and I have asked permission to included this here.)

My great, great grandfather, Sir Edmund Barton, was the first Prime Minister of Australia from 1901 to 1903. He was one of the primary movers in the years beforehand, of the debates across what were previously entirely autonomous states, in a time when pony and trap and the occasional train were the only modes of transport – unless you walked. He covered thousands of miles encouraging and persuading the people and governments of each state to support Federation.

This may not seem important to people outside Australia, but he remains famous to this day with many public buildings, streets and open spaces named after him. A recent campaign to encourage schoolchildren to learn about Australian history was centred on Sir Edmund.

As a result when I was in Australia in 2017, I was interviewed on TV and radio and invited to a private meeting with the leader of their parliament. Huge honours.

It was perhaps the stories told to me by my grandmother of Sir Edmund that inspired me to become a solicitor. Whilst I am nowhere near his level of intellect or importance, I am proud of the contributions I have made as a solicitor, of my own law firm and in representing Leeds as a director and President of Leeds Law Society.

As Leeds Law Society President, speaking to a lot of managing partners I explained to them that we should use the term solicitor more than the term lawyer. We have a protected name and we need to be proud to use it.

We are a quality service. Law firms and solicitors need to collaborate and communicate on a very open and honest basis. So that law firms can share experiences good and bad so we all benefit from those, instead of squabbling with the SRA and other authorities. Let's do this.

3. GARY GALLEN

Solicitor, CEO, and owner of Rradar Limited (a specialist Litigation and commercial legal practice using digital tools and an educational led strategy for business risk and services) www.Rradar.com

Why practise your legal expertise as a business owner?

I believe I have always felt I have been a business owner, no matter what I have done in any event. I have never tried to abdicate that responsibility. What frustrated me the most was that I had a responsibility to help people and I dealt with people in crisis, in difficulty and at the problem stage involving the criminal code and criminal law.

I can honestly say that I have never in 30 years of working in the criminal justice system actually come across genuinely bad people that deliberately set about doing genuinely bad things, accepting the risks of being caught and when they got caught, then trying to find the cleverest person they could to try and avoid the penalties. I am happy to say that most of the people I dealt with, actually when you unpacked what they'd done, who they were, what their pressures were, and why they had done what they had done – they were not bad people. Most people – they don't know what they don't know. An incredible amount of people would bumble and stumble and get stuck in things. Even when I did the 'high street' criminal work, you would find people who were addicted to drugs, alcohol or other things. I can't help myself I like people. I like stories. I would prefer to help rather than cast off and consign to the scrapheap. I want to help. It is just in my DNA

What Rradar has enabled me to do is to remove some of the frustrations working as a partner in a major firm i.e., as an owner of the business with many hats. I wanted to feel that I was more in control in making those decisions to achieve those values and that vision more effectively, because there was frustrations and difficulty as I was pushing for change. The legal profession needed to modernise and that was one of the frustrations. I found out that I was trying to lead – be responsible, own what I was doing and deliver something but I felt I was being constantly held back in the organisations I worked for.

So I felt it was an obstacle, so I tried to change it all to achieve the success of doing it without those frictions. This meant I had to step out of the legal profession to build the educational technology business then re-enter the legal profession at an upstream point with a different mindset, a different set of beliefs and value set about giving information, about sharing knowledge. I think going back to why lawyers are there in the first place – they were teachers, educators, the law is not meant to stop – it's meant to allow people to know how to do the right thing in the right way at the right place and not getting into difficulties.

Lawyers seem to have lost some of that navigational and educational skill and it became more about the lawyer, the knowledge and the income.

As time has gone by, it focuses the mind on the fact that I am not going to be around forever. I would like to think that I could leave my mark and leave it somehow improved and better. And let people know what they can achieve, what they can do rather than they always be thinking they can't – but they can. It is a big perception issue I am battling against, law is only there to stop the bad behaviour. So if you are a good person who wants to do good things, what we should do is showing people how to stop people being hurt – for example that guy's hand on a machine, which has no cover. That's the health and safety rule. So what we're doing is giving an understanding of the impacts of behaviour because people want to go on in a good way. So let's try and take them in that good way but we should be more like universities – more like educational establishments and share knowledge – does that make sense?

What is your best and worst business habit?

My best business habit is, well you can take this one of two ways, a long time ago someone I respect very much admired my stubbornness. And I suppose it's that resilience – you don't give up. I have learnt from different methodologies in leadership books well from the military. And sometimes what they look for is not what you expect that they look for. They are looking for the person who won't quit, who will help others, the person who brings the team on. It is not necessarily the person – the one guy who runs and gets there the fastest – before anyone else, who doesn't look after anyone else or bring the team along etc. So stubbornness to make sure you don't quit and you see things through. Its really an important part of the character and I think the clients that I have always worked with – the recurring comments that I am proud of – we know what we are going to get working with you. For example, you don't quit and what ever can be achieved – you're gonna find a way. Because you are determined, you don't give up, you don't let it go. A dog with a bone and that's what I think you have to be.

Bad things are going to happen, no matter how smart you are there are obstacles and you have to recognise that you don't know everything. You've got to flex your style, you've got to learn new stuff, you've got to coach, help educate and communicate. You find yourself repeating yourself over and over again but that is your job as a CEO. You have got to try and help people get on your wavelength and understand what you are trying to achieve. Why you are trying to achieve it. Embed that in them. Understand with their different character and behaviour why it is important to do it. And what key role you need them to carry out because you can't do it on your own. So you have got to bring good people with you. That stubbornness in all things – that need to educate and move forward and what you must always do is to move forward. Its not getting knocked down as Mohammed Ali said. A hero of mine says – 'getting knocked down isn't the problem – staying down is the problem – get yourself back up'. Always move forward and learn from everything that you do.

There is a phrase that gets bandied about in a lot of books – fail fast and I hate it. And I think it's so wrong and it should be learn fast. Yeah – it's just a different Mindset

Even though I embrace technology I always write down key learning's – so it's one of my habits and I recently wrote about this on LinkedIn. I keep a journal. It is about semantic learning however you do it.

You can be the greatest lawyer in the world but if people can't understand what you are talking about then you are going to lose every case – you are not going to be great with your clients. Courtrooms are about simple communication. You have to leave the law to one side unless it is a specific legal technical point that you are explaining to the judge. Otherwise you are trying to bring people along with you. I dealt with a very difficult murder case very early in my career and the prosecuting counsel was a QC – a fantastic gentleman. And we had an extremely capable QC– now a High Court Judge – working for us with an amazing intellect. But he was a little bit cold. He was a little bit about himself and too much on the technical side.

This was at Lincoln Crown court so it is the old style court – very intimidating. At a crucial point when our client was giving his evidence I looked at the jury box. And when the defendant was giving evidence I again looked at the jury. You'll know that jury members are given a pad and pencil to make notes and key documents in a folder. I noticed that one of the younger members of the jury had his eyes closed and was looking at the ceiling, and he was trying to hold the pencil between his top lip and his nose. Everyone else had his or hers open. I had watched the jury everyday during that trial looking for body language, looking for indicators and for what was resonating. And when their QC got up to speak, he never looked at the judge he never looked at anyone else – he was not interested in the advocates etc. He looked everyone of the jury in the eyes – he changed his tone, he had a laugh – he was a great orator and a very good actor. He was very polished and our barrister was very, very cold and most of the time he spent looking at the judge and he lost our jury. What I learnt from that experience is that if you can't communicate, if you don't understand who your audience are – if you don't understand that there are lots of behaviour and character types then you are always going to be struggling; and then you are going to always have conflict in your own personal and working life and business as well. That skill of awareness and this business is trying to communicate with people and law needs to be communicated.

So we are trying to build a completely new education methodology. That's why we have teachers, why we have audio specialists – video specialists – photographers – technologists. All sorts to help take that technical content of the lawyers and help move it so that it becomes owned, understood, practised, embraced and people are confident going about the work they want to do. We exist to serve. Business is not there to serve – it is the other way around.

How do you manage the 'highs' and the 'lows' of being a business owner? (Stress management) and/or what are you doing to build resilience?

Interesting.

I enjoy the time with the children – that is incredibly important to me. And trying not to be anyway dictatorial and I think I have done that because with my kids I know exactly where I stand in the pecking order. If we had a fish and a cat I would be below them as well.

It's to get them to embrace learning – different and to try to have an entrepreneurial spirit because I think that is pushed out in schools and education and business and the workplace. We read books, you and I, and people ask us what is our USP. What a ridiculous phrase. And they say to embrace difference etc.

And there is a big push on social media to campaign and divide a city and we see what is happening in American politics – Trump. You see the fears of change everywhere.

What can we do to try and build some balance to that? And it has to be the next generation coming through. We have got to be the best advocates – it is the legacy – what empowerment? What understanding? What possibilities? What opportunities are we leaving to those that follow?

And we have had some brilliant lawyers who have changed the world – look at Nelson Mandela. He was legally trained. In the Houses of Parliament the single most dominant profession is law. So we can be great orators and I think there is a great responsibility on us. So with my children – how can I take what I have learnt and the mistakes that I have made, and somehow pass it on to them so that they don't get frustrated with learning or with the education system and recognise that that is the key to unlocking their lives?

Who do you turn to for support and inspiration? Who would you like to thank for their support and why?

I meet people who give me moments of inspiration – lots of those if you bother to look for them. I had mentioned Professor Steve Peters and I love being in Steve's company and talking to him about issues. It might not be one individual that inspires you and that you constantly look up to.

I have not been a CEO starting up a company before so I need a chief marketing officer, a chief technologists a chief legal officer, a chief financial officer etc. You are managing and you are building.

My two daughters teach me a huge amount and separately my son. My son is profound in terms of disability specialism with an exception type of Down's syndrome including autism. His ability to smile and learn new things is tremendous. And what I have learnt – it is not about how much time you spend with them but the quality of the time definitely. What do you do with that time?

I don't care too much about the trappings. I want to be out in the real world in other people's lives and see what you can learn and adapt to do things. They like to live their lives out in the world as well. The challenging questions that they come up with are tremendous. Olivia and Grace embrace technology; friendships – understanding micro influencing – instagram – the positivity. They also teach me some of the negatives such as the 'body shaming' before it was in the news. I have heard this for six-seven years out of them. So we have great relationships – great conversations very much inspirational to me. I pity the boy that is ever going to befriended by those two girls because they are both very, very self-willed and know what they want out of life. And I hope that that very much continues.

There are some of the people in Leeds ask me why the quotes on the building – that you will see around you and also in Hull. Just look around as to what inspires my character as I have tried to incorporate these into my building. Nelson Mandela – Plato – Gandhi – Leonardo Da Vinci. These are people who were definitely unusual and saw different ways and were not frightened to stand up and speak out. Prepared to take the consequences for standing for something different.

A current one – the Nike ad just been released with Mr Kaepernick has not been able to get a quarterback role since he declined his renewed contract last year. That is a very brave stance.

I don't like just following blindly. For example I didn't vote for them because my dad, my granddad etc voted for them without applying any intellect, any understanding to what you are doing – following orders without any thought isn't good enough for me.

But there is one moment I suppose and I am talking a lot. I queued up to watch Star Wars. (Ann: I was in Leicester Square to watch that when it came out.) I am still trying to build the first hologram lawyer. I suppose we are like the Jedi trying to bring balance to the universe and it blew me away. And in the same year I discovered Tolkien and the Hobbit. So I read Tolkien every year and I watch the Star Wars every year. If you look what Tolkien wrote about the story of overcoming, such a tremendously rich and layered book. Actually I can still discover odd things now from continuing to read it. It is relevant still year on year. And Star Wars – look at that franchise and how it moves forward.

It's the two things that have affected me deeply in my life about being courageous, about thinking and looking different. Its about finding your own feet in this world and don't be limited by your own imagination. The author Tolkien and a visionary filmmaker Mr Lucas. I think they are two of the best business books AND stories you could ever come across regardless of all the ones following on afterwards.

Did or do you have a personal or business vision?

I suppose I did yes. And I had procrastinated which is something that I hate but I had recognised it. But my son Daniel had been in and out of hospital – we almost lost him on a number of occasions but we had fantastic support and care to revive him. Great Ormond Street were brilliant. I couldn't blame Daniel – when is the best time to have kids. But what I realised is that I had wanted to build and create something since I was a child. Found out my dad was dying of cancer whilst I was young and still a student so I was travelling to look after him whilst studying for my degree. He actually lived through that year despite the two strokes – that stubbornness. That period of time made me reconfigure and change where I was going in the timelines because I was looking my dad, and helping mum. I still went on to do the degree.

Met my wife and had three children but the second child Daniel was the one with the special needs. That was like a small nuclear bomb going off in your life – totally alters your perspective on life. So I made the decision – this is not working – I'm frustrated. Clients love what I do but I can't do it where I am in the structure I am in and too many other people saying you can't do it – It will never work because they didn't believe it. They could stop you doing what you wanted. But my clients kept asking – can you please do more and more of this? So the decision was made and I moved out.

So I've always wanted to do – the seed was always in there. Getting past looking after father, then I needed a job to keep my mother in her house so she would not be kicked out of the house when her husband died, then Daniel came along and I just had to get to the far side that he was big enough and robust enough.

I got lots of offers from lots of law firms and I went to a couple because they made promises. In fact they couldn't help and its not because they were in any way bad people or anything. They actually couldn't help themselves and they couldn't do the kind of step dynamic change I want to do. And the vision was purely I could see how we could make it better.

I think that two decades or more inside law I knew how to break it and reconstruct it. Technology and the Legal Services Act came together. Technology gave me the means to scale it into an educational model. Empowering a complete new platform for the business and the Legal Services Act allowed the de-regulation so I could embrace a completely new model. I am not playing at this and I am going to do it 110% and invest my whole being in it.

Did you have a business plan when you first started – if so what worked and what didn't?

So resigning – working through the gardening leave developing my plan. Investing all your own money in it – re-mortgaging the house, maxing the credit cards – phone cut off and this that and the other. All you have to do to go through. It was just a brilliant journey because it was such a release – it was what I wanted to do; both my heart and intellect were completely and utterly aligned.

We are moving to that digital transformation journey, moving large groups of corporates across on that journey where they trust our technology, trust our virtual assistants, trust our platform and our templates and our communication because they know there are humans in the loop.

They know that if it goes wrong there's not a robot that comes to sort it out and that the technology is not an open bit of social media. For example, Googling it in the hopes of getting the right advice.

One of the challenges is building an end-to-end solution and trusting people to embrace the digital platform and the education, communication and the delivery through that because they know at the back of it there's real proper people that know what they are talking about. Not taking lawyers out of the loop, keeping lawyers very much in the loop but raising the standard of the conversation. Creating better communication and discussion about what they can do and where they can go rather than all about the crisis and what has gone terribly wrong.

What are you doing differently from the organisation you have left behind and/or the competition?

See answers to the two questions above.

What has been your greatest success to date?

Two things, which are intrinsically linked:

1. We are reaching more and more people – feedback is coming in that we are making a difference.
2. Quotes – People often talk about how great it is to find a business that actually delivers what it promises. That was also emphasised when the team did a charity walk for a Down's syndrome. A lady tweeted what a lovely group of people to meet on a charity walk. Brilliant to be doing what you are doing for charity and how fantastic that you are doing this for your employer and the business that you work for –the two are so aligned. If the people believe in it and the clients believe in it then that is what has to align because clients can tell when you genuinely care or not – maybe get away with it for a certain time. Little things like unsolicited evidence show me its working.

Where do you see the threats for your legal business?

There could be many – as the CEO, I can't be complacent. Must be constantly moving forward and constantly be innovative. Won multiple awards. We are 5% of a business plan, 5% of an opportunity – so the biggest threat for me would be sitting still and not realising full potential. So we have got to keep on pushing and moving forwards. There is so much change in the world, so much opportunity, it is learning, that adaptability. We're a blend business, by that I mean we take education and psychology with law, risk management and insurance world; and then were putting it through a new educational technology with a human in the loop – so it's still human.

We are split into three industry sectors, which are quite traditional, and then we are bringing a new vehicle, which is our solution into it, which people find quite difficult. People find this difficult to understand so I am constantly questioning myself on whether I am using the right language etc.

What is your personal brand? (Name your top three qualities, which enable you to run a unique legal practice.)

Stubbornness – some would consider this a negative but I think this is a positive.

Persistence – I don't give up. The learning attitude = this skill of reading, thinking, sitting having debates and conversation.

Problem solving – need the stubbornness and learning to be able to do this.

Started off in my career with linear learning – have to learn everything from A – Z. What I have learnt in my career and from dealing with humans in cases and pressures of work is that adaptive thinking is what you need. You need to be able to take conflicting thoughts and ideas, hold them in your head, find out ways of making them work and deconstructing them and taking them to pieces which goes to what I try to teach people. What is the outcome we are aiming for? And then try to work backwards. So do you know how to think forwards and backwards? Its like chess in many ways I suppose. I find that so many people can only think one way or at most two. What I am trying to teach is that you need to be able to hold more ideas and thoughts in your head especially if you want to be a business leader.

Why your name?

I did not want anything that was like a normal law firm name. I wanted to build something about – a regulation radar – a responsibility radar – a risk and reward radar – it was about navigation and radar. Earlier I also used to do CPD teaching and things like that and lectures to the profession about criminal law to build my brand and network and opportunity for business. I used to talk about RRA and the double R advantage – rules and regulations and how you cannot avoid them – if you don't want to get caught offside in football, then learn the damn rule, then you can play the way you want to play. The laws are there as we as humans cannot be trusted to do the right thing all the time – so we keep on having to manage behaviour.

This is where it's great, some people in the firm would be shocked and say you can't do that with a brand name but that's where you need a sense of humour in life.

Is there anything specific you do to manage the quality of service?

I always make myself available to the people in the business and to the customers – clients, brokers and partners.

I think at the moment it is something that I am assessing as we have gone from being in my conservatory, to one employee, to a group of ten employees to then having the second floor in a building, 50 staff then a 100 staff – I want to keep close to it. When I'm in because I am constantly pulled in different directions for the business to be with partners, business, opportunity etc as we are scaling and growing the business out, I recognise that I have not got as much time around the people in the business.

I'll sometimes go on reception in the morning I'll put the music on and have croissants and welcome them into the business; and walk around the business. We had a live gig at the business – first practising law firm to have a live gig. That brings you close to your staff and close to your people. When I mean I don't like to sit in my office, I like to be where the action is happening. I also do spend a lot of time with the clients about what we do and how we could do it better. This is through meetings and presentations. I have not just got one view of the business. They will email and telephone me at night. I like to have a 360-degree view of what is going on.

We do not get many complaints but when we do I go and speak to them so they know they have my attention. That may get more and more difficult to do as I build the business in more locations and potential countries. This provides us with much learning and much resilience in insuring it never happens again. We the have all the component parts and data that has come out that is then shared with the broker, with their accountant, stakeholders and investors and we started from that and that was what was the core from day one. From day one it was about taking all that learning from every single case, every single telephone conversation, live chat, communication download and turning it into educational learning and training development programmes. Less people were ringing us after they had a problem be cause they then embraced the learning and they saw the complete other way to work with us rather than ring us when they were in trouble.

What interpersonal skills are important to be successful with your type of clients?

We have fantastic communication; understanding and awareness skills combined with regulatory navigation skills.

People recognise the learning and development paths with us; and so clients are purely coming for the learning and development with us and not just because they are in trouble.

Marketing online (websites, Twitter, Facebook, Instagram, LinkedIn, YouTube or other)?

Do we embrace it? Yes we do. Is it a good means of communication? In many respects, yes. Do we have to be able to communicate with the entrepreneurs of tomorrow? Absolutely

We try and put our personal signature on those platforms wherever possible. We have professional rules and conduct standards – cannot share data, appropriate protection and security. You will find Rradar pushing in more and more directions and embracing those platforms. Me personally? LinkedIn and Microsoft as I have worked with them. Twitter is what I favour – not right for every type of message.

Personally I have serious issues with Facebook so I will never be on that, I have issues with my children as they have been forced to go onto it because there are certain groups, sporting associations and clubs – I have raised this with their school and said to them you are making my young children, young teenagers, before they have left school, go on a platform. Not the only parent that is upset about this. Why should they as a school demand that they move onto such a platform? That was dictated due to ill-informed decision.

Offline Marketing

None.

How do you lead and manage your team? Have you had any training? What would they say is your best/worst quality?

Different associations and courses I have been at. I read a lot, everyday. Many books throughout the year. One of my disappointments about these new books that come out is that there is next to nothing new in any one that you read. I have been to Harvard. There is a programme I have embraced whole-heartedly which I am trying to bring to my clients and other businesses. This opens up all sorts of programmes such as the elite programme from the London Stock Exchange Group – heard of it by fluke through clients – first practising law firm that is allowed on the elite programme. This is an 18-month programme of in depth training.

Ability to cross think – holding those different things and finding a way to make them work, which I have mentioned before.

I have had to learn more patience in this business than I have ever had to before. I want to do things quickly and make decisions, I have learnt that skill over the years, in court rooms and police stations you deal with there and then on the spot, there is no place to hide.

I have never been frightened of the responsibility or the decision-making but what I have to learn is what you just mentioned – I see things differently to others and having that awareness allows me to see outside the box or just ignore the box altogether.

How do you develop your team? Do you use the SRA Competency Framework?

Yes we do – not the only thing we use. I say to my people you will be judged by the rules stated by the SRA so there is no harm in trying to understand it and adapting it to hit all those targets. 99.9% of the time these things have got purpose so do not ignore them.

What are your biggest team challenges and successes?

Because we have recruited 90 people in just under a year and continuing to recruit, this alone provides us with challenges. We now have our first HR manager Andrea Willoughby and who with Heather Brown knows what this area is all about including the different team assessment models.

Just reassessing everything. Revisiting all again and figuring out what is the right thing for us as a body. Business won't work until we all are cooperating like wheels on a car. All of those are under review at the moment – have different consultants working with us.

Where do you see your legal practice going in the next three years?

Set out to leave a legacy and change behaviours in the world, certainly the perception of lawyers and law.

4. JADE CAMPBELL

Solicitor and co-owner of Lester Campbell (Residential conveyancing)
www.lestercampbell.co.uk

Why practise your legal expertise as a business owner?

Well the obvious answer is to give you control of your own destiny. So obviously working for other firms and working hard for other people it's nice to put your own ideas into motion. Have that freedom and basically control your own destiny – that's it.

What is your best and worst business habit?

I think I'm good at mentoring other people in leadership and training. And worst is probably that I get sucked into the fee earning and find it hard sometimes to find time to take a step back and look at things almost like an outside person. And it's finding that balance between running the business and getting swept away with the fee earning. Definitely.

How do you manage the 'highs' and the 'lows' of being a business owner? (Stress management) and/or what are you doing to build resilience?

I go on lots of holidays and really try to go to the gym just to distress. Make sure you find time for that and catch yourself. Work hard – play hard.

For resilience I just keep fit because for about three years I really got out of the habit of going to the gym and I just found that I was really stressed all the time. Just literally going to the gym three or five times a week, it just takes your heart rate right down. So I find that's what works for me. And then also as I say the holidays I have to have something to look forward. On holiday I don't deal with work unless it's something really urgent.

Who do you turn to for support and inspiration? Who would you'd like to thank for their support and why?

Business partner and other professionals are like-minded people to me, bosses, colleagues, friends, family, anyone.

I would like to thank my business partner Rodney Lester, as he's made all this possible. He put the initial investment in cash. I wouldn't have been able to do it without him and also his guidance from having run a firm for many years prior to this. Also he gave the confidence that you know that you can do this, having not run a business previously myself. So definitely Rodney and my partner for supporting me because we didn't know how it would be if I wasn't earning money. So obviously he was very supportive as well and told me to go for it.

Did or do you have a personal or business vision?

See answer below.

Did you have a business plan when you first started – if so what worked and what didn't?

Well, because I've managed conveyancing departments before, not only for my last employer but also the job before when I applied for the management role, I had to do a business plan for the department. So I had to do a forecast about how I saw the department going and look at different business models – what their strengths and weaknesses were. So obviously I had a little bit of practice doing that sort of planning.

Then also having managed a team for quite a number of years I've seen how it works in practice.

What this enabled me to do was see what works and what didn't from my perspective, as my previous two employers were very different firms; and I felt that both had different strengths and weaknesses. I've tried to combine the best from both and also tried to give a bit of a fresh look in terms of what never sat right with me as an employee. The sort of things like fixed pricing and publishing the price on the web which is a big thing at the moment with a lot of sites but it's something that I also felt passionate about for a long time so that was in the business plan from day one. And it's nice to put those ideas in motion as well.

What are you doing differently from the organisation you have left behind and/or the competition?

We are a small niche practice competing primarily with volume conveyancing factories and established high-street firms. Our overheads are higher and we have less capacity for volume and so the plan was always to focus on a quality personal service and target customers directly, building on existing contacts initially. The vast majority of our clients are existing clients or recommendations from existing clients. We do also work with a few select and mostly local introducers.

The idea was always that we build the business one client at a time rather than source high-volume bought-in work so that we can maintain quality but also keep it at a price, which is transparent, as we are not paying steep referral fees or being dictated to on price by volume introducers.

What has been your greatest success to date?

Hitting the ground running. When we opened our doors as a conveyancing firm the one big concern was whether we'd be able to get on the lender panels and we actually achieved that fairly easily. Some of them were challenging but fairly quickly we were able to get on all the lender panels, which was a big help in just maintaining relationships with clients and agents and building that reputation. Massive relief.

Where do you see the threats to your legal business?

I think we are in an industry where the profit margins and rates are very tight. It's difficult to get the balance. The biggest challenge is maintaining that level of service while still being competitive and not out-pricing yourself in the market definitely.

What would you say is your personal brand? Name your top three qualities, which enable you to run a unique practice?

I think it's our personalities – we are very direct, face-to-face. Very hard to put it into three words. Trying to think what I put in my business plan – efficient, personable and approachable.

Why your firm's name?

We wanted the name to reflect that we were solicitors and not just conveyancers as we felt this gave us more credibility and also the flexibility to branch out into other areas in the future should we decide to do so. Had we chosen a name that reflected that we primarily offer conveyancing services it would have restrictive and perhaps given the impression we were licensed conveyancers and not solicitors with wider expertise and deeper understanding of the law. We chose our surnames, as this is a traditional format and quite frankly couldn't think of anything else we both liked better!

Is there anything specific you do to manage the quality of service?

Our conveyancers have been trained in house and all files are checked at partner level until the partners are confident that they can work independently. Thereafter, monthly file reviews are conducted and all files have various checklists to be completed at various stages, including a pre-exchange checklist, which is signed by a partner, all files receive a second pair of eyes before contracts are exchanged.

We try and accommodate clients' preferences in terms of how they like to be contacted so email/phone whatever they prefer or if they want to come to the office. However our offices are not very disabled-friendly as we are upstairs. It's not my responsibility at the moment but it's difficult for disabled people to go so we still do home visits for the disabled or elderly. And if a client wants to pop in on the way home we are quite accommodating.

We try to keep them updated throughout the transaction, explain the process and will do a final report. That sums up everything in one document and just keep in touch with them throughout.

We do send our client feedback questionnaires on all transactions and we also enter awards that we ask people to vote for us. So we are getting feedback all the time and we just kind of learn from that feedback really. And there are probably things we could do better to get people to return the feedback files more. We have also participated in mystery shopping activities and regularly enter awards based on client feedback and judging a panel, which provides invaluable feedback from outside sources.

What interpersonal skills are important to be successful with your type of clients?

I think we have to be very approachable and down to earth where we're dealing with everyday people that are buying houses. Also builders and developers don't want to deal with stuffy lawyers

We have to be available whether it is on the phone, by email or in person. We also have to communicate with all parties connected with the transaction such as the estate agents, mortgage advisors and other solicitors so that the process is transparent and understood.

Marketing online (websites, Twitter, Facebook, Instagram, LinkedIn, YouTube or other)?

We have set up a Facebook page, Instagram, LinkedIn and Twitter. Despite having quite a young team we're not that social media savvy; and we've been lucky enough that all our clients come to us anyway. So it's probably going to be next year that we'll look at getting some sort of marketing budget together and possibly get some sort of a grant to help fund a marketing campaign because ideally want to go to clients directly rather than via introducers. And I think social media is the way to do it and that's a project, which will probably come into play next year.

Awards and we when we get shortlisted we do put them on social media. We try and promote the social media pages. There's ways we can do that better.

We had a promotion one year. A Christmas promotion just to get some instructions through the January sale if you like. So we used Facebook for that but because most of our clients are recommendations anyway. We've not needed it. Although as we grow up it will obviously come in handy. So I've been quite lucky in that respect.

Offline marketing

We do have a PR strategy – I can't remember. (Laughter) We always said that in the early years we wanted to lay the foundation. It was never about growth. In the early years it was more about getting the model right. Getting the profit margins and the work levels right and the systems right.

Thereafter we'd start to put more focus on marketing and growing the team. We felt strongly that we did not want to rely on volume conveyancing to make a profit. We have therefore done very little marketing to date and have instead focused on existing clients, repeat business and recommendations with a view to growing the business organically

How do you lead and manage your team? So have you had any business training or leadership and management training?

Whilst I am very hands-on I try to lead by example. So just give them opportunities to have a go at doing something for example a title check. We'll do this together initially and keep checking it until they get it right.

The reason I am hands-on is that without any specific training manuals in place yet we check everything so we're happy that they've got it and I'm happy for them to go independent.

No I have not had any training except what I've covered in the manager's roles in the past so obviously I've seen management training but they're not business running training.

What would they say is your best and worst quality as a leader or manager?

Rodney would say I am good at mentoring and training the team and being supportive.

I think one of my worst traits is that I'm generally very calm but occasionally I can blow a little bit about if I'm getting stressed because I got so much work to do. And it's finding that balance again. In an ideal world when we are little bit bigger then I can take on more of the business side; then I think I'll be a better manager and leader because I have more time to do that.

How do you develop your team? Do you use the SRA Competency framework?

No they're not solicitors so no one knows what's in it.

We do regular appraisals. We have three monthly appraisals and at the moment every single file is signed off. So there's complete control done that way. We're very lucky in that the two junior conveyances we have both the LPC. They are both bright and they are not daft. They'll ask questions and they're very switched on. So yeah, very proud of our junior conveyancers!

What are the biggest team challenges and successes?

I would say having come from different backgrounds is making sure we're all working in a way, which is efficient for everybody. So for example my business partner Rodney is 73 and is used to having a secretary that he types for. Whereas I come from a firm where we don't have secretaries who have assistants and everybody has their own role and it's just bringing us all together that we're all working in a way which is roughly the same and not confusing for the subpart staff really. So yeah bringing it all together as a team so we're all working in the same way with the same competencies and standards.

Our biggest team success is that we've won a few awards. So we've entered Richard for 'Rising Stars' twice and he's come runner-up twice. We entered Sidhra for Conveyancer of the Year and she was shortlisted for that. In 2017, we won two awards: the Silver Award for Yorkshire Region Conveyancing Firm and The People Award to Jade Campbell; and in 2018 we won the *Bronze Award for Yorkshire and The Humber Region Conveyancing Firm.

I think it's just a nice atmosphere in the office they all get on we work hard. It's very open and we just crack on and everybody does their bit so everyone's got a good attitude to work and I think everybody enjoys work as well at the moment. So that helps.

Well I think if you enjoy going to work then when you have to put in that extra mile to do well, you want to be there don't you. So it has a knock on effect. So we're a small team but we all feel bonded and go on with it. So yeah the great team we have.

Where do you see your legal practice going in the next three years?

In the next three years. I'm due to write the next three years' business plan so I'm probably not as switched on with this, as I should be.

Certainly I think the conveyancing team, I imagine that would probably double over the next three years. One at a time.

The commercial property department really is just sort of ticking along in the background so I'd like to put my focus on how to help Rodney to get that going really.

And one of our employees got 100 per cent in his wills and probate exam on his LPC. So he will be leading our wills and probate team supported by Rodney and his wife Eileen who is also a wills-trained lawyer.

5. JODIE HILL

Solicitor/Barrister, founder and owner of Thrive Law (Employment, Mental Health (Thriving Minds), HR and Thrive Women)
www.thrivelaw.co.uk

Why practise your legal expertise as a business owner.

Because I wanted to break away from just being a lawyer in a traditional firm.

So what I wanted to do was create an atmosphere that I felt that I could grow in and also create an environment that was flexible; and was a good for women and for people with mental health problems as well as create a law firm with a good quality reputation.

What would you say is your best and worst business habit?

So I think my best business habit would probably be that I will give anything a try. So I'm willing to adapt to change, which a lot of lawyers aren't.

However I'd say probably my worst one is that I'm probably all over the place at times in terms of spreading myself too thinly sometimes, because when you do start up you have the initial pull of so many things to do and what do want to I spend most of my time on?

How do you manage the 'highs' and the 'lows' of being a business owner? (Stress management) and/or what are you doing to build resilience?

I probably manage the lows. I just ride the highs. Also give yourself credit when you do something good. Because being a business owner you kind of get half the opportunity for somebody to appraise you and tell you that you've done really well. So you have to do that for yourself.

So what I do is I actually reflect on a regular basis where I look at what I've done. What are my takeaways that week? What were my challenges? What were my wins? And I have all of these different categories in a book that I write down. So those are really, really helpful. More so because if you're not in a corporate environment where you've got this structure where you are told what you've done is really good. It can be a bit demoralising because you feel like you're constantly grafting with no feedback. And so that's really helped me to create self-awareness about what's working and what's not.

And then it also helps with the lows because when you look at these you can then say well actually I/we did all these other amazing things this week too. So it puts it into perspective rather than just dwelling on one issue. The other thing I do with the lows is bounce off certain people to get different perspectives. I'm always trying to not just react to a situation and to try to remove any emotion from it so I can provide a measured response. So if I feel as though there is a particular low point or a particular challenge then I try to deal with it by balance and for the people to check that I'm dealing with it in the right way – in a measured way.

How do you build resilience?

I listened to quite a lot of professional self-help book books all on the audible apps. So some of them you gave me e.g. Tony Robbins. I've gone back to some of them and actually started listening to those again. And I find that that just kind of refocuses your mind a little bit and takes off just thinking about the business, and it helps you to refocus on self-care. The other thing I do, is do a lot of exercise which I find gives my brain a little break from all the business world and the law. And also obviously makes you feel better so that helps me to build my resilience.

Who do you turn to for support and inspiration? Who would you like to thank for their support and why?

You as you know. Ceri Widett (Barrister at Exchange Chambers) who is also a huge inspiration to me. She's been a mentor really early on because she was Barrister. I used to work with her so she's kind of been there from day one for my journey for more of the legal side whereas I feel like you've been there more from the business side and from a

coaching aspect. It's really great to have the two different perspectives and I would suggest I would suggest to anyone setting up to surround themselves with people who offer value and support.
For my financial education and needs I would like to thank Julie Bickerdyke who is guiding me through with ease, as this is not my forte. Abby Coleman's been really supportive as well. So when I was just setting out she gave me a platform for my blogs and access to her readers. That was good.

My friends and family (thanks Mum!!). Massive shout out though to Gemma Gray, she's my best friend and we have known each other since school, she's so fiery and so amazingly supportive with every aspect of my life. My go-to-person. Everyone needs a Gemma in his or her life! I would like to thank my fiancée for being supportive when I left my old firm and I was really unwell through to becoming a consultant then setting up a business.

Did or do you have a personal or business vision?

Yes to a degree because I did sit down and write a business plan for where I wanted to be in the next three or four years. But it was more about creating the right environment for me to work in and then attract like-minded people to share those values. So the key thing for me is to create a brand that reflected me and I think I've done that now which is really good but then also transitioning that and attracting the right people that's a massive challenge in itself. So the vision is more about creating a workplace of those types of people who share my values and I have a truly diverse firm with a workforce to be reckoned with.

Then we've got an event that we're planning for October on Mental Health via the Thriving Minds part of my vision. Off the back of that event, what we're looking to do is to create an online community where people can basically share what has and hasn't worked in business. This is focused on mental health and well being purely because there isn't a network out there at the moment. There are a lot of business networks but there isn't something where business owners engage just about mental health – about what works and doesn't work.

And then we want to follow that journey on with further workshops and sharing of resources. And also if they've trialled anything that they would discuss at our events about how what they did actually worked and how did they tweak to get it to work if at all? So it's really just about helping people grow old along the journey so there's quite a lot of free stuff that we do on off the back of events.

The idea for me is then to grow the business to a point where it is says is obviously sustainable but also can run without me or with very minimal input from me so that I can then develop other areas of the business whether that's to do with training or well-being or everyday behaviour. But also I'd like to go off and have a baby at some point in the future so my legal business needs to accommodate my personal vision too.

Did you have a business plan when you started – if so what worked and what didn't?

It is too early to say what has worked and what didn't with the business plan that I have written.

What are you doing differently from the organisation you have left behind and/or the competition?

We have a very strong presence in the mental health sector. We are not afraid to give an opinion on what we believe is the right way to do things and to put our own stamp on things.

Whereas, I think, a lot of traditional firms because they do lots of different areas it's very difficult for them to do that as in such a targeted way. We are a niche employment firm with focus on mental health and women. We also offer flexible working which links in with those working mums as well. So it's opening up the roles that we have to a much wider workforce within the legal sector, which is probably more women as well, which is nice.

In terms of our clients, we offer fixed fees and retainers so people pay by direct debit. We are accessible and easy to contact which I know is often the opposite to other firms where clients struggle to get hold of their legal team.

We've set up different tiered packages for the HR so you've got different levels of support available to businesses; and we also help employees on a fixed-fee basis. I think we've offered those bespoke solutions based on the challenges and pains of our clients. And I think one of the things I've certainly talked about in business, these days, is the client's journey. I have actually started this as part of our marketing strategy. We have a nurture sequence in which we have a database whereby when people become a client or a contact they go into the sequence and they have a series of – they start a journey basically. So that journey starts as a welcome this is what we do and then it sends them details about the campaign that we're doing – about the mental health first aid training.

We've just done two documents that can be downloaded from my website. One is about how to manage stress in the workplace. And the other relates to mental health and we've got another document coming out so there is a journey there.

Everything that we do is mainly cloud-based. So we're developing an app at the moment whereby we're hoping to deliver legal services through the app. Actually I am spending some time developing that and I am going on an app development course in September with a friend of mine. She is a coder but she's learning at the moment so she's getting me onto this course just so I can understand the back end. And that's totally different to what most other lawyers do they just outsource it and just get somebody to do it. I'm really interested in learning how that works so that I can really understand how to make the most of it and then see how that can help my business in terms of automating some of the procedures. That's how we do things differently.

What has been your greatest success to date?

I think there are two things. The first thing for me was getting the brand right and that being received really well – not just among the public but amongst the lawyers. We have had so much feedback saying 'we actually love your brand' but that's a huge thing as lawyers are so sceptical at times.

And the other thing was to take on my first paralegal employee, so now I have three employees.

Where do you see the threats to your legal business?

The threats will definitely come in from other HR consultants and other firms that are trying to go down into mental health right now. So I think we were one of the first firms that ever really specialised in this type of work. I'm seeing, now, a lot more firms trying to do training around it and trying to push into the sector because it is topical. But for us it's more about being authentic and just making sure that we stick to our values and we continue to push that message forward. I think as long as we do that, we're not going to be damaged by any potential competition because we're probably not targeting the same people.

What would you say your personal brand is? Name your top three qualities, which enable you to run a unique legal practice?

One of the key things that we wanted to make as part of our branding was transparency. So transparency in terms of advice and costs around time comes in with the fixed fees and online non-legal jargon.

Thrive Law is obviously a law firm not a wellness company. We collaborate with a lot of different organisations. We have a huge referral partnership with loads of different organisations who are really good on that so we can add value to what our clients need in this area.

We are authentic and relatable – I think me sharing my own story breaks down some barriers and builds trust for clients to approach us.

Why your firm's name?

Yes I think the name reflects my brand as was trying to say what we want is for people to thrive in the workplace and that that applies to both employers and employees. So the employees are thriving because they have a well-structured workplace that deal with things properly and know the correct training but the employer can then have a thriving workforce because the employees are happier. I want everyone in the workplace to Thrive. Thrive Law was the most apt name as this is my 'why?'

Is there anything specific you do to manage the quality of service?

I outsource my compliance so I'm very keen on making sure everything is completely SRA compliant and to the best of our ability. And so everything is audited on a regular basis. I've got someone on retainer to do that but also I'd review the files and keep an eye on everything.

We also work very collaboratively as a team so even though Imogen is a self-employed associate and I have a paralegal. We will all discuss and share knowledge on best practice law and service, to make sure we're all singing from the same hymn sheet. One of my sayings is that 'that there's no stupid question and always ask the question because actually it could make your advice so much better and it could avoid any potential problems.'

And then there are the awards and being shortlisted in my first year.

What interpersonal skills are important to be successful with your type of clients?

Friendly and empathic. I've experienced some of the issues that maybe I'm dealing with for my clients so I can have that perspective from both sides. What it's like to be an employer and go through that but also what it's like as an employee and maybe why people react in certain ways to situations. So I think that helps to have that empathy in the perspective.

Availability. And so for example I allow people to text me or call outside hours, being flexible is important.

Marketing online (websites, Twitter, Facebook, Instagram, LinkedIn, YouTube or other)?

I use social media a lot.

My website is currently being built. I don't get any walk-ins because we don't have a sign outside our office, as this is not how I want to attract clients.

I actually have had a client off Instagram and Facebook and Twitter this week. Then last week I had one or two from LinkedIn. So I am beginning to see clients starting to use these channels to reach out. It is also great for online networking and then some of that does convert to sales. And I think you need to be consistent with it. So if you just post random stuff or share stuff but don't have an opinion then it doesn't always convert to sales. Where you become more than powerful is being a leader in that area. So it's about doing it in the right way and in a more strategic approach as opposed to just having these platforms. This is especially true for the law firms that have Twitter or Instagram and don't use them

I've just set up a YouTube channel. I'm going to start blogging my journey, which I just thought would be quite helpful for people but also just doing tips and things. So at the moment I don't know how well that's going to be received but with the rest of the social media. I have found that everyone's really receptive to that. So it's great for promoting us, our values and what we do. So we have e only had it for three weeks and we've got 250 followers already. We're hoping for more engagement as we progress. We've had an enquiry through there already. So yeah it's really good for us. We're really enjoying it and we're starting to build our own media hash tags as well.

We do have a social media planning meeting every month whereby we discuss and agree what we're going to post. This will include posts of specific events or it's a specific day of the year that's relevant to my clients. At the moment we are trialling a 'Wednesday Appreciation' of inspiring woman. We basically link up to that woman and we say – wow we should appreciate them. Just promoting a bit of diversity as well. So we agree a month in advance and then we do reactive stuff as when required.

Offline Marketing

I've been really looking over this during the last two weeks because I've had an intern from my old school so she's done PR and she's doing PR marketing. She's helping us with social media and just basically doing more reactive stuff which has been really, really helpful. This is just short term and here after that point they will have to pick it back. But we do have a strategy in that.

So, at the moment, the marketing strategy we've placed it on hold. We're partway through it only because of the event that we're doing. This event takes precedence and a lot of our strategy will come from that event. This is because it will depend on the engagement that we'll get from that. So what we've decided to do is focus on this critical event because we were now well on with our social media strategy and we know what who are our target audience. Once the event is done, will then pick up the overall strategy and review how we can continue the relationship with our attendees; and convert some of those into clients.

The TV and radio stuff is kind of ad-hoc but is getting comments. Obviously going on the Sky News was really helpful to raise my profile. I still have people saying 'oh my God – that interview', in a good way. You know it's all a bit of a whirlwind when you go and do it all live as you don't get to know the questions in advance or anything. Nevertheless it does give you such an amazing reach that you just don't expect it to have. And then I was on Look North on the issue of discrimination and appear online too a lot in the press. So yes those things really help to raise your profile although I wouldn't say they necessarily get clients per se.

Public speaking on these matters and probably the Sky News has produced a few clients. In fact I had a tribunal case referred to me and they have had a solicitor because they wanted me to do it instead. This was due to the fact that the solicitor they had didn't understand mental health and they hadn't pleaded it in the right way. But it was great that they picked me because of my understanding so that that was nice. That's obviously getting the right message out there. This is really good because I speak at events such as the Mindful Employer Conference; did a couple for two of insurers one in the North East and one in Leeds at their inclusion and diversity events.

So holding workshops about the importance of mental health first aid is basically just explaining how to speak to people with these issues. As I said earlier we want to build a support network and these events plug that gap. I've just opened a whole new audience to thinking in a different way- so it's touching different people in different ways. It doesn't necessarily mean that they'll become a client but then they might know someone who becomes a client. So that's kind of how I'm doing at the moment – just splitting my time quite evenly between this and doing the legal work and running the firm.

How do you lead and manage your team. Have you had any training? What would you say is your best/worst quality?

I asked them about how they would like to be managed. They are candid which I respect and want. They said that my best quality was my approachability and management style and what they meant by that was I gave daily 1-2-1. Part of this is that not only will I'll summarise what I want them to do but also give them practical guidance on how to do things, without actually telling them how to do it. Yeah so that still gives them the opportunity to learn. If they get things wrong they feel I give constructive feedback. I think there is a preconception in the law that the boss just shouts at you. I said at the beginning 'there's no question that's a stupid question' I would rather you ask all the questions you have. When I give constructive feedback they feel that they can then ask me more questions
They also said that the fact that I make them go home; and I wouldn't let them come to work early as a matter of course. I have a really firm belief that if you can't do your job in the hours then we must have a chat about workloads. Obviously there's an element of flexibility and on a Friday we might go home at four and then if we've got an event everyone stays to cover the event.

The worst trait, well, it is sometimes my lack of instant availability. I am so busy all the time as this is a start up and they feel that my time is very precious. Sometimes it is hard to regroup and discuss where I'm at and that makes sense. But when we did it's worth it and we do make progress. So I think because I'm not in the office all the time, it can be challenging for them from time to time, when they can't immediately bounce things off me. This is why I have the initial conversations to ensure that they know what and the how of the next steps.

I am going to sort out an office manual to cover the basics, especially as I am expanding the team quite rapidly.

Do you use the SRA Competency Framework? How do you develop your team?

There is a loose training plan depending on where they are. Again I am going to undertake appraisals shortly so that will give them an opportunity to discuss what is working and what is not. With your help Ann, I then want to set out that these in writing and when the team is expanded we can have a team-working workshop, as a collegiate environment is very important to me.

Thank you for bringing me up to speed on the SRA competency which is not needed for my firm at the moment but when I expand it will be.

What are your biggest team challenges and successes?

I mean I often speak to my team about this as well as we are a small firm. I think we do have a perception from a lot people that we're bigger than we are. . I was speaking at the Mindful Employer Conference last year and the delegates thought I was representing a large corporate firm, at the time I only had one employee!

When I explained that we were a small firm, they said "we didn't realise; your brand and your image it just gives off that you are a really, really big corporate firm". I think that's a huge success in terms of how we are perceived by others despite having a really small and relaxed atmosphere in the office we are giving a real corporate message still.

Also a lot people want me to do things for them personally because I am the face of the company so I think that's a big challenge when your clients are expecting you and you know that somebody else might respond. So it's just about managing expectations of people even though they've been referred to me. I might not be the one that deals with their matter personally.

Where do you see your legal practice going in the next three years?

Online I think AI is going to play a massive part in the legal sector. We're really slow in the legal sector look at the FinTech, and the way that's gone, look Sage and Xero and all the other accounting apps that we've got. We haven't got anything in the legal sector that dominates legal services delivery.

Although I don't think lawyers are going to be replaced by an AI. I think some lawyers will become back-office lawyers. Maybe less face-to-face contact with the interface to clients being more around computers. This is true for the team as well because people can access work and services wherever they want, rather than having to come into an office. I think it will complement and automate what a lot of lawyers do. So I think the type of legal practice that we are we would like to lead the way.

6. LAURA CLAPTON

Solicitor and co-owner of Consilia Legal (Family and Employment law) www.consilialegal.co.uk

Why practise your legal expertise as a business?

I think throughout my early career as a lawyer I didn't quite feel like I was being fulfilled in my role purely as a lawyer working for somebody else, as I was keen to be involved in the growth of the department. But I was frustrated by the difficulties in implementing change. I had a lot of ideas and some of those ideas I was able to implement in another firm. This had a successful outcome for the department and for the firm and helped with growth.

And I think ultimately, whilst I felt pride in what I had achieved, as I was working for somebody else's business, I wasn't necessarily benefiting from that change. And because my role is still seen as being limited to the legal one and I'm not the business owner of that firm – and therefore not the one that's going to and really benefit from the changes that I implemented.

So I think I just wanted to be more at the forefront of a change. And then as I said to actually benefit from those changes. That will be made that is unusual but you want to benefit from change.

Is it possible for you to just expand a little bit on the change that you initiated?

Yes. I mean I am a big advocate for alternative dispute resolution. So I trained at quite an early age is to become a mediator. Historically mediators generally were family lawyers who then became mediators later on in their careers. But I was very keen to do that early on, so from qualification.

So whilst working in a firm I was instrumental really in actually creating a mediation service offering within that firm that didn't do that previously, including the branding, and the marketing literature, the website and making new contacts. Trying to ascertain who were going to be our key referrers and trying to build relationships with those individuals and other organisations and really a part of every single aspect of making up that brand and creating that department. And I did feel a sense of achievement, don't get me wrong, I did feel that.

But I just felt that I wanted more of them and I wanted to be able to continue to do so to continue to implement change. Particularly in how these ideas have been put into practice rather than just be one isolated opportunity. And so I think that, that really is what triggered the thing that I wanted to move on to be a business owner myself.

What is your best and worst business habit?

I think my best habits, both business and personal, is that I'm not scared of change. Changes are for me a positive thing. I'm always looking for that next challenge. I think not being afraid of change helps me to take on challenges and progress to the next big thing, not just in business but in my personal life as well.

And so I think it is a strength of mine is that, as a business owner is that I'm never complacent just to stay in and concentrate on the present. I'm always looking as to how do we need to keep moving to make sure that we don't fall behind, and just be conscious about the complexities that may come into the market that we need to just make sure we're ahead of the game. This is also important for staff that as business owners our 'forward-thinking' be strategic and not just settling for how things are even if things can be very good. That would be what I would consider is my strength

A negative and I think a lot businesses owners would probably share these things is not relinquishing control. So taking too much on myself, even though there are perfectly good people around me that are more than capable. I think it's difficult especially at the early stages when you've built something for nothing to allow somebody else to take control of an element of what you view as your baby in a new business.

How do you manage the 'highs' and the 'lows' of being a business owner? (Stress management) and/or what are you doing to build resilience?

I'm very grateful and lucky to have very strong family and friend support network and I do call upon them as a sounding board. They are people who will listen to me. And they're very good at putting things in perspective for me. It reminds me about what is going on and that is really important and also in reminding you what you have achieved and focusing on the positives.

And I think I do that in many cases where there is a negative situation, I very much like to tackle it head on – deal with it and then just move on. Not letting that linger and letting that negativity stay with me. So I do try to box it. Often you know there are challenges and things don't go the way that you hope. So its just dealing with it and then just drawing a line and moving on from it and trying to turn any negatives into positives. First it's about my own approach but as I said the people around me make sure that I don't get too wrapped up in my own self-importance. You know that actually they help me to put them into perspective. You know actually we are really lucky to be in the position that we're in.

Who do you turn to for support and inspiration? Who would you like to thank for their support?

My husband he's really laid-back. He listens to me talk about the business on a daily basis and he does so in a very supportive way and he never moans when I'm working unsociable hours or long hours. He's the person who reminds me when I am feeling down or have low moments or the challenging moments that he's the one to lift me back up by saying 'look what you've achieved and that you are capable of achieving great things'. I take a lot from that.

I take a lot of inspiration from my father because he's a business owner. He still runs a small business and so from a very young age I was involved in that. So whilst I was training to be a lawyer, I was also working on his business. I started working for him when I needed to fund training as a lawyer. But also it really helped me to understand the workings of a business regarding a completely different industry. I learnt about the accounts, the marketing and sales. So that was a really good experience for me.

I have also to thank my business partner Marie. I've got to thank her because she's been as fully as committed as I am in making this business a successful one. And I go back to her and I think we really pick each other up. And we each have different challenges both business and personal so we try and support each other.

Did or do you have a personal or business vision?

I think the business vision changes over time. I think initially it was just to be able to offer an alternative dispute resolution, as I am a big advocate of that. It was to have a practice that, that was our strength, that's what we were known for. That was our reputation that we offered high-quality mediation services and then we would go to mediators in the Yorkshire region. And that was really the offering that I wanted to be able to put out to the legal market.

And I also, initially thought that the vision was that we would always stay niche and specialist in the areas that we delivered but that we would look to grow maybe geographically and look at having an offering in many different regions within Yorkshire but to always stay true to what we are. I think that is the way things are going and I have seen that since we set up business four years ago. All of the specialised departments in these firms coming onto the market and it does seem like that is the way that things are going.

And so that was I suppose my actual business vision in terms of personal vision and again I think that has changed over time. I think initially it was all about the business and the work making us successful. As time goes on it is about striking a balance. So to have a good work-life balance and to have a business that has a talented team within it.

Can you create something that actually you could step away from and it still works perfectly, still runs perfectly naturally and allow you to then have a good work life balance and spend time with the people that are important to you, do the things that that you see in your dreams and desires like travelling? Certainly I'd say in the first two years I had very few holidays. We will actually work in the business every day of the year. In fact it wasn't until we employed a team that we trusted that would look after the business that enabled us to actually take a break. A break that really helps you come back and feel refreshed and raring to go. And that's how I feel like, in some respects, I've achieved up to some degree and this last year actually has been a big turning point.

Did you have a business plan and if so what worked and what didn't?

We needed to have a business plan as part of our SRA application process and the business plan was great in terms of getting our ideas and our views down that we had for the business. A reference point if you like and a year down the line you look back at the business side and think: 'well yes we did implement some of the things that we said we wanted to d'o but actually what we found is the growth, we experienced was a lot sooner than we expected.

So that brought other challenges from that quick growth. We hadn't expected to take on another employee so that hadn't been factored into the plan, such as HR and other aspects that go along with that.

So actually, in a positive way we outgrew the business plan quite quickly. What that has meant is that we have actually had to review the plan. We do that at least on an annual basis to make sure a new business plan is still fit for purpose.

What are you doing that's different to the organisation you've left or from your competitors?

And in terms of our unique offerings, I think that we do a lot of marketing that is possibly unusual or not conventional when it comes to law firms. So it is the same as I said before I'd like to think that we are quite forward-thinking. We very much acknowledge and try to nurture our online presence and that is really important to what we do. We are very big on our soft digital marketing and our social media platforms, our website.

And just having a bit more of a human touch to what we do and the things that we post. Yes we've got informative legal pieces but also just a bit more about us. I think what we try to do is to have a bit more personality behind who we are what we do.

We do fixed fee work. So we try and get away from the hourly rates that historically law firms have always gauged profitability by or how they've built client bases.

Also just in terms of how we work as a team and how we gauge performance. So again I think we take a much more holistic approach in terms of how we gauge our team's performance – it's not just about billable hours/chargeable hours.

What has been your greatest success to date?

I think in terms of how we gauge our success is that we actually employ talented lawyers that work with us and stay with us. The fact that they wanted to come and work for us and I think for us that was a real sense of pride that actually we were seen as a reputable law firm amongst much bigger much more well-established firms. So, for us, I think first that was one element of it.

Other elements of it were being able to have a good quality way of life and actually to develop our existing junior members of staff (including offering them training contracts). When as I say I want a work-life balance, it is also something we also want for our team as well. So I think that people that have been within the firm have been our success. In total there are eight of us; and we are growing.

Where do you see the threats for your legal business?

We do need to be mindful of technology and how that is going to have any impact upon what people expect from legal services. So I think that it is important to ensure that we keep changing the way that we practise to ensure that we don't fall behind.

So for example in family cases now, the government has launched an online divorce system. And again there is going to be more in the future. We need to remain attractive for our future clients so that they come and deal with us in a different way; and it's not just this tradition of coming to a solicitor's office and sitting down in person.

So we try to say it is more of a practice that works with technology around rather than against it. We've got very good case management systems that we use. We're constantly making changes and improving our website. And we need to consider all sorts of online offerings we should have in the future but still be able to have the High Court legal services and the personal approach. It is getting that balance just right. But yes we aim to be moving with the changes in the legal market definitely. Could be a threat if you don't or if you're trying to ignore it.

What is your personal brand? Name your top three qualities, which enable you to run a unique legal practice.

In terms of my personal brand, I would say approachable, which I think that's a good thing in terms of my professional connections, that feel quite happy to pick up the phone and ask me a question about client or ask if they can pick my brain. They know that they can do that. The team know that they can approach me about any questions that they have and I have an open door policy. And just in terms of my clients, that they are comfortable ringing me and knowing that I'm going to be at the other end for them to listen and they're not scared of asking questions.

And I think my legal expertise. I am a specialist in family law and I don't try and dabble in any other area. I very much focused on what I know I'm good at.

The third one I'll say is that I'm pragmatic because I am big advocate of alternative solutions. I'm always thinking about how to adopt a solution for a client that's going to avoid litigation and going to reduce costs and it's going to reduce hostility. The legal market and the clients know that, that's the approach that I take. Therefore they know it will be a non-confrontational approach to the work that I do and that their clients will feel at ease with me.

Why your firm's name?

This is the reason we chose the name 'Consilia' which means 'working together' in Latin. We believe Consilia represents who we are and our relationship with our clients.

At Consilia Legal our team share a mission – to work with our clients to best achieve their goals. We do this by providing pragmatic, creative and commercially sound advice to suit each individual client's budget

Are you doing anything specific to manage quality of service?

We assess our quality of service through client feedback and feedback from our referrers. We undertake annual client surveys and request feedback at the end of each matter. I'm pleased to say that we are rated 5* on Google by our clients. The feedback we receive from referrers is also invaluable and the fact that they continue to refer clients to us is a great marker that they are satisfied with the service we are providing to clients.

We also do regular file reviews internally to assess both quality and risk.

What interpersonal skills are important to be successful in your type of legal service?

Approachability has already been mentioned. Being mindful of the best route that will reduce costs and have the least impact on the mental health of the client.

Communication is key. It's really important that you communicate well and you communicate often. There's nothing worse than clients feeling left in the dark and they don't know what's going on in their own life. Divorce could be one of the most difficult experiences that they go through and just be mindful that you might know what's going on but that doesn't mean that the client does.

Marketing online (websites, Twitter, Facebook, Instagram, LinkedIn, YouTube or other)?

We do use all the different types of social media platforms. I'd say we have two main purposes in terms of what we do. One is to inform and therefore we do a lot of articles and blogs on the website and through social media.

And the second one is, as I said before, about getting our personality across. If we go on team events, if we host training events or social events, a charity or what would inspire our team – you know

congratulating our team members when they achieve something. So it's very informative but also getting our brand across in a in a personable way. So that's how we generally use social media.
We are regularly updating the website. We know the importance of that. We measure rates based on rankings. On mediation we have appeared not yet appeared on top of Google but we're definitely on first page; and that was a great achievement when that happened. With the other areas again we're just monitoring our rankings and again the aim is to get onto the first page of Google. We do use Google Analytics so we can analyse who's coming on our website and if they are coming on the website – are they staying? So we can see if the website is meeting the users needs and everything else. That is something that we are conscious of and we monitor it on a regular basis.

Offline marketing

In terms of general marketing, I mean we tend to steer away from paid advertising or radio and all that kind of thing. We've, sort of, explored that in the past and for whatever reason we've decided that it wasn't right. It is all about the people and our brand.

So it's about getting out there and showing our team and who we are. So a lot of the marketing that we do is about hosting and running seminars and training events. So for example I run a lot of mediation workshops for lawyers to come and find out about mediation so that they can advise their clients as to what it would involve – what the benefits are.

We as a team are involved in a lot of marketing through training and we have our own networking events for niche law firms. So we meet on a regular basis with these other firms. We invited the ones that also specialise in one or two areas to dinner. We share ideas. We discuss challenges but in a very informal setting and we give each of them the opportunity to be able to refer clients to areas of practice that that firm doesn't specialise in. And so we're a strong network of other professionals that are going to refer work to us, and that for us is a great tool to showcase what we do.

How do you lead and manage a team? Have you had any training? What would you say is your best/worst quality?

As a manager I would say that the way that I manage is through support and encouragement. I'd like to say that I don't micromanage and I hope my team agrees!

In terms of control, it's not necessarily about being in control of everything but taking on the burden 'the whole monkey on the back kind of thing'. People pass it back to me, and they think I'll sort it out. And I think sometimes I have to just give it back and say 'Right, see whether you can find the solution first.'

I think that they would definitely say I'm supportive and encouraging but that could also be a negative trait as well because I think sometimes I could challenge them a bit more and mother them less.

As I said before I operate very much an open door policy. I'd like to think that if ever any of the team made a mistake or we had an issue that they would feel that they could come to me and it wouldn't be about blame. It would be about finding solutions together and transport them through that difficult experience but also giving them the freedom and the autonomy to run on with their own ideas, even if sometimes I'm not sure they are going to work. I think it's still good to let them experience that and then they can have feedback and reflect on actually why didn't that work – how might do things differently? And so even if I may have a slightly different angle or different idea and stuff because it's good to let them run with their own and get that experience.

So have you had any leadership or management training?

Initially no. And it was literally the blind leading the blind when we first set up. Well you are moving at a million miles an hour and actually nobody has ever done it before. And we just wanted to get on with it, you know, and really just make it up and let's see what happens. We'll just let fate take its course.

And then things start to settle down and then you start to actually think strategically and that's when we decided that we needed to educate ourselves. So reading books for business owners and attending Law Society events and training that is specifically for all small law firms who are also practitioners. The annual small firms conference. And obviously doing things such as making sure from a compliance point of view.

We recently had some training that was not just about team culture but about leadership culture for myself and Marie and looked at how the team views our leadership as well. We're very keen to continue to learn and develop our leadership skills. And then we do view it as being a fundamental for us at this size. It really important and there is a lot more to learn.

So best quality is the fact that I am supportive as discussed earlier. Again I think I am not challenging people enough. Not to throw people in the deep end necessarily because I've had that experience. I think it is maybe you have to actually give the team a bit more responsibility to allow them to develop to themselves.

How do you develop your team? Do you actually use the SRA competency framework?

We internally have our own career progression for our team. And so we define success. That is really important so that the team knows where they are going in and they have their own goals and ambitions which hopefully are within this practice rather than elsewhere. So we very much used other frameworks in which to be able to devise something to show them how their career could progress. What they would look to be achieving and demonstrate at that point their 'step-ups'. The team are very aware of that. We are very encouraging of them going and developing externally.

Obviously the mandatory requirements that they do on family law competency or on the trainees for the professional skills courses are fully supported. So even though there is no CPD we still have our training records which are used and which we look at to develop them. Why they do what they do and what the benefits they are getting from that if they get involved in things like BNI, Chamber of Commerce and everything to help them develop as individuals and develop their own brand. So we encourage them to do that.

What would you say is your biggest team challenge and success.

And our biggest team success, and I think you have to say that we were all very proud this year, is when we were nominated for three awards. And particularly when you are up against much larger well-established law firms. So I think we all felt a real sense of achievement.

And I was actually on holiday at the time when the team messaged me to say we shortlisted for these three awards and everybody felt said a sense of achievement, as we were all involved in the process.

And it was reflective of where we've come. So we were nominated for an award last year. The whole team went to the event and it was a really good way of thanking everybody for their support and for wanting to support us through this journey. So we'll be going again this year.

Whether we win or not, just the fact that we've been basically acknowledged that what we're doing is good work is a great sense of achievement.

I would say that the biggest challenge to a small business is when you have members of staff leave for whatever reason that might be. Because I think that it leaves people feeling unsettled and uncertain about what's to come. We have learned that communication again is key so that they know they have nothing to fear and you involve them in that plan. And we've been very keen to do that. So when we have had people leave we have been be able to say 'right well you know this is what's going to change'. This is what we're looking to do.

We're very open about when we are recruiting. You know the last thing we want to do is recruit somebody and then, you know, the team don't find out until they are sitting down at their the desks on Monday morning. It is about involving them in that planning process as well. Then they feel more settled, comfortable and valued because you actually want them to be involved in that process.

Where do you see your legal practice going in the next three years?

I think it's going to be niche specialist firms, particularly for the type of areas that we do – private client services and employment, HR as well.

The next thing that will happen over the next three years is that competitors will come into the market offering similar services as small-specialised niche practices. That is one way and I think the other way is that firms will become more savvy in terms of how to effectively work with technology including their digital marketing strategies and everything else. So we have to fully prepare for that in order for us to be still considered a leader in our work in our particular field.

7. LIZ WARD

Solicitor and founding Director of Virtuoso Legal (Intellectual Property, Commercial and IT/Technology) www.virtuosolegal.com

Why practise your legal expertise as a business owner?

Well that's an interesting question because legal expertise and business owner in my view aren't two talents that sit very comfortably together. There are lots of people who are very good legal people and a lot of people who are good business people. And I don't think, unless you really try and merge the two, that the two skill sets naturally sit together and I'll tell you why. I think a lot of lawyers are trained to be risk-averse.

They're trained to think in very sort of linear ways and they're taught to be ultra-cautious in lots of business decisions whereas entrepreneurs and business owners naturally tend to have a different skill set. They tend to be much 'bigger picture' people and not so into the detail, which is a skill set, you learn as a lawyer. And of course the one thing you can't be as a business owner is risk averse because business is inherently risky. So I think when you are a lawyer and you go into business that you have to kind of discipline yourself on both fronts. You have to discipline yourself against being too entrepreneurial and out there otherwise you can catch a cold. I think it's difficult to be a good business owner. I recognise that these are big generalisations.

What is your best and worst business habit?

I think my best business habit is to keep a very close eye on the figures.

It's also my worst business habit because it means sometimes I'm impatient with things. It means that I'm always looking for the financial return and sometimes that's a long time coming. I hope, I'd like to think, I get the balance right but I'm not sure that I do. But a lot of lawyers are very poor with finances. They don't think things through at all. They don't look at what the real issues are in business that drives the business forward. They don't look at innovation in the enterprise in the same way. But innovation and enterprise come with a cost attached to them and it's sometimes easy to think you're going to get a return on investment but it may take quite a long time. So those are my best and worst.

How do you manage the 'highs' and the 'lows' of being a business owner? (Stress management) and/or what are you doing to build resilience?

I think that comes with experience on a personal level. I've ridden my way back from a number of disasters or near-disasters. I've had my back against the wall on a number of occasions and every time you do that you almost go through a kind of a 'sea change' in your experience and what you take from something. I'm a firm believer that there are no mistakes in life but there are lots of learning opportunities and it's about turning those around and managing your nerves whilst you turn them around. You can't always do it. Sometimes everybody has sleepless nights. I've had lots of sleepless nights about you know paying the Inland Revenue paying my staff making sure that everybody is happy at work.

The lows really for me is all to do with finances because you know the old adage that cash is king. That's so true in a business and unless you're really, really good at the old BS. If you know that the figures are right and you've not got the income coming in, I think it's very difficult to maintain any kind of mentally stability while that's going on. I mean, and I know you will appreciate, that is a common theme in every business owner that I talk to.

I did a short presentation last year when it was my ten year anniversary and I made one or two jokes about the time that the Inland Revenue man was sat in the basement of the offices which he wasn't but I joked with another friend who runs a law firm who was having similar issues paying the Inland Revenue. Everybody came to me afterwards and said that so resonated with me. It doesn't matter what business you're in, the finance is the one thing you can't afford to get wrong. It is the one thing that you constantly monitor. You have to constantly monitor your overheads – constantly monitor your margins – constantly monitor bills, monitor outgoings – what you're charging people and what's profitable for you – what's not profitable for you and making those decisions all the time in lots of ways. Many of the other things that you do in business are much more straightforward, but the financial issues are always the most challenging.

So how do I manage the stress? That's a good one. Sometimes I resort to a bottle of gin. Though I'm past all that. I realise that actually having a few drinks doesn't make anything any better. The way that I manage stress is to get out in the outdoors – get out into the big wide-open spaces.

I also like to have a plan. I always work to a plan and I think if you've got a plan at least you've got some kind of direction. Having a goal and if you can see the end of the tunnel or if you have a vision as to what the end of the tunnel actually looks like, you can get there a lot faster. At least you can travel there in your mind and that gives you a certain peace of peace of mind as well.

Who do you turn to for support and inspiration? Who would you like to thank for their support?

In business, I have a number of people who inspire me. Tony Robbins is the obvious one. Tony Robbins is a big inspiration for lots of people. There are others and I am in a WhatsApp group for another.

I also have a business coach who puts another dimension on things and somebody like yourself too Ann. Because again you're a great touchtone – you're great at bringing a certain level of rationality or reasoning or insight and experience to a situation. So I've got a number of people really that I can touch base with one way or another.

Did or do you have a personal or business vision?

This has been refined over time, although it has always been based on being the 'best' at what we do.

We are currently pursing relentless customer service, and identifying value at every opportunity as our vision is that Virtuoso Legal intends to become the number one intellectual property law firm in the UK over the next five years. This is going to form the bedrock of our vision going forward.

Did you have a business plan when you first started – if so what worked and what didn't?

As I have said, I think it's really important to have a business plan.

There were lots of things I got right from the very start. I set up sat with Sage as my bookkeeping system. Also I set up with a very good cloud based case management system and time-recording system. This is 11 years ago now. So there were lots of things even in the early days I thought through and I think it is worth thinking about all these kinds of things. If you're going to go into business thinking about what do you actually need from day one?

I got professional IT support because again I realised that if I didn't have professional IT support and I lost documents or my PC or my laptop malfunctioned in some way that I was really snookered. So I got that right.

I think another thing to bear in mind is that your outsourcers at the beginning are not necessarily going to be with you when you expand. For example the professional I.T. support that I started with was a very, very small outfit that really couldn't service my longer term needs; and that's what happens in business you grow. Your needs change and you occasionally have to move away from suppliers which is quite difficult because sometimes you've developed a personal relationship with them. But it's not only about the relationship you have with them it's about what they can deliver to you and you have to be able to differentiate between the two. So I've moved to quite a long way away from where I started.

What are you doing differently from the organisation you have left behind and/or the competition?

What we do here is radically different from what other law firms do. When I went into the law 20 years ago I'd already been in industry.

I looked around at the legal profession and I thought: 'how on earth does any of this operate?' because it seemed to me that it didn't operate with its clients best interests at heart.

And it also seemed to me to be a hierarchy that wasn't necessarily built on merit; it was a hierarchy that was built on people who'd just been there for years. I know it's changed now. Also they didn't have proper financial information, which I had always been used to in industry. I remember going in to my principal's office and asking who are your best customers? What are your margins? What are you doing here for marketing? And they look rather blankly at me. You know he wasn't a man who even took anybody out for lunch. I think once a year he went to the cricket with somebody. That was the 'be all and end all' of his marketing efforts. And I just thought I'm not sure how any of this functions. It doesn't seem to me to be a normal business where you know everybody has to work out getting new instructions.

We start trainees here from day one with an expectation that they're going to at least network with other people even if it's for their own benefit. So that's one major difference between myself and a lot of big law firms.

Also from day one we skilled people up in all sorts of skills, as you know I'm very, very keen on soft skills and I'm very keen that people are able to talk to people in a way that is relatable and understandable and not use lots of legal jargon.

We operate here on what we call the Kaizen philosophy. Now the Kaizen philosophy is the same thing that was pioneered after Japan in the Second World War and rebuilt a lot of Japanese businesses. In fact the principles are still used by the Nissan plant. The idea is that everybody gets an opportunity to feedback and improve everything that's done everyday. So it's a philosophy of continual change. It's a philosophy of continual improvement. It is a philosophy of continually scrutinising what we do on a daily basis and saying can we do this better. So we look at everything on a regular basis. I get fee earners within my team to champion elements of what they do to teach the people and to skill them up in what they do. And that again is all part of Kaizen philosophy and just building on that.

I'm implementing some changes here where we will do a profit share for everybody. Everybody will be a stakeholder to a certain extent in the business. There are ways of structuring this so that it works for everybody and it certainly builds a team.

One of the big problems and one of my big bugbears in a lot of legal practices, actually in all professional practices, you see people who are leading lights. There are some people who will bill two to three times the amount that other people do and that's great; but what it means is they're not sharing. What it often means is that they're not delegating and they're not working as a team. So they can be the star performer and be the goal-scorer and they can be the one that leads from the centre forward but actually if you really want to get ahead you have to build a team. It's about having the defenders as well as the attackers. It's about having a goalkeeper as well as the goal scorer and I don't think a lot of law firms operate on those principles and I think that's a big mistake. I think it's a very old fashioned way of dealing with things to have those kinds of meritocracies and that silo type attitude to work. I totally understand why professional firms do that and they will say oh look at so-and-so billing twice as much as everybody else. But the fact of the matter is we've built a team. If somebody is billing twice the amount of a similar kind of work then you have to ask you ask yourself the question 'why are they doing that when you're a team? Why are they not delegating tasks downwards? Why are they not sharing their expertise with other people and that's the thing from my point of view that I think a lot of law firms get completely wrong.

The other thing too that we are completely different from every other law firm is the structure of us. To my mind a partnership a traditional law firm partnership where people put money in and share the profits is completely outmoded. I am a big believer in sharing the profit. I am a big believer in sharing some of the burdens. I am a big believer in lots of people working together in a collaborative way. But the traditional model just does not work. You know I think it's totally wrong in private practice for younger fee earners to re-mortgage their house to inject a quarter of a million pounds loan into the firm to allow somebody more senior to exit. I'm sorry. I call it a Ponzi scheme because you're not building value in the firm, which is very different to here. My strategic objective is to build value within Virtuoso Legal by building a good base in terms of people, the reputation that we've got, the digital marketing that we've got. We are not just getting clients and referrals in on one basis its right across the board to make Virtuoso Legal a much 'greater sum than its individual parts' and so few law firms understand that.

What has been your greatest success to date?

My greatest success to date – I think building the team that I've got. I've got a really excellent team now and I have some very, very good junior people who've come through who see the vision in the same way that I do and that I think is great. I've obviously inspired people enough to stay after qualifying which is always a good thing; and I've given them a way of viewing things that I think is a way forward that I think is very kind of 2018. I think very few law firms are very 2018.

Where do you see as threats to your legal business?

I think things like artificial intelligence. I wouldn't call them a threat I'd call them something that I've got my eye on in the corner of my eye. I'm aware of the fact that artificial intelligence is going to take some of the tasks away from lawyers or even make it easier for us. There are all sorts of opportunities out there.

Other threats are the global financial situation. This is something we can never get away from – if our clients are prospering then we're prospering and that's simply economics.

For IP, it is Brexit. This is definitely going to have an impact. Yes for sure it's going to have a negative impact in lots of ways; with intellectual property there are lots of harmonised legislation. So for years we've been able to file one trademark application and get trademark cover in 28 countries using an E.U., trademark. That protocol is up in the air. How that's going to land? Again it's the same with patents. I mean there is a European Patent Protocol and at the moment a Patent Court has been built in London. Will this court give decisions that will cover the whole of Europe? Now that sits outside the EU legislation interestingly enough, so hopefully will still go ahead. But at the moment that's all slightly up in the air. So yes Brexit is going to pose some interesting conundrums/threats/opportunities. I think it is the question of how you view it. I know you agree.

What is your personal brand? (Name your top three qualities, which enable you to run a unique legal practice.)

Tenacity. I think staying power if you haven't got staying power then you'll crumble. There are a lot of challenges in running a legal firm, which may be over financing – over overstaffing – over systems – over regulation – new offices.

You've really got to have tenacity and I'm a bit stubborn. I think that helps me.

Number two is actually being imaginative. And I think if you really want to be a good businessperson you have to have that imagination. You have to be able to think differently from the way that other people think. And if you don't think differently then you might as well just be employed.

The third quality is I think I'd like to say I'm a good lawyer. I've had great training and experience. I've met some fantastic clients. I've worked with some fantastic people and that's all rubbed off on me. So I've been cultivated in the right sort of biomass to bring a certain skill set here and that's really useful. I think it helps to be a good lawyer because you set the standard for the people that you work with – you set a standard in terms of training – in terms of expectations – in terms of attention to detail that other people want and can see to emulate. And at the end of the day clients expect you to have that level of knowledge and detail particularly in a boutique practice like ours.

Why your firm's name?

Virtuoso Legal – I wanted a brand name that wasn't just me! I thought Elizabeth Ward and Co or whatever just wouldn't cut it in this day and age. Virtuoso indicated a brilliant skill level – which we have, and it also wasn't just about me. If you want to build a brand and a team then in my view you need a word that evokes your service and not one person.

Is there anything specific you do to manage the quality of service?

We have collaborative working and we have a buddying system. There are automatic checks and balances and in part one of the things that we're really working on at the moment is task management. So we work on task management again collaboratively so that notifications go into our case management system and several people are notified. This is so that we are all standardised in the way that we use our systems for task management and that kind of thing. So that's what we do for quality assurance.

We do have an operations manual but we're looking at bringing it up to date with all those things in it. And so again people who come to work for Virtuoso Legal there is a Virtuoso Legal way of opening up a new file, cataloguing things on that file, dealing with deadlines, dealing with final dates, dealing with money, going into the account and accounts being paid. We're only a small firm and it's a work in progress.

The great thing about being a relatively small firm with such a 10/12 fee earners as we are at the moment is that we can continually work on improving that process. I think one of the big problems identified by quite a lot of candidates I've interviewed recently is that in larger firms you get some lawyers adopting technology but not all. You get some people who really embrace new ideas and new technology and then you get the other end of the spectrum where people are a bit more senior and they don't change their ways very quickly.

Which particular interpersonal skills are important to be successful with your type of clients?

Having a real insight and knowledge into innovation and brands is really useful to them because they can talk to the clients in their language. Because I've got a background as a biologist in the pharmaceutical industry, clients love it that I understand the technology behind that particular industry and I can use the same language as them. So that's a really useful skill set to have.

Having empathy, I think this is the number one for any lawyer.

Understanding what the clients want. So many lawyers are just responsive. They don't really reflect on what they're doing they're just responding to a need. And I think sometimes the understanding of the importance of that can be underestimated.

Marketing online (websites, Twitter, Facebook, Instagram, LinkedIn, YouTube or other)?

I think if you have a marketing strategy it's got to it's got to be multifaceted. And a lot of it's under the radar. People see things like for example; they will see what we do in terms of social media because we're very active on LinkedIn. We do a lot of blogs on Lexology now so that's all very visible to people. We do a little bit on Facebook and Twitter. Not a huge amount. We could do more.

If you want to contact journalists for example you can't beat Twitter.

As I mentioned, a lot of it is invisible like search engine optimization for keywords, pay-per-click campaigns, and also things like Google reviews. Just constantly keeping on top of our website and its visibility profile with so many people looking via the Internet these days. Some people will seek out a referral for a lawyer and that's fine. We've got to tap into those and some younger people will just go online. Who comes to the top of Google? And rightly or wrongly people who really didn't know what they were doing were claiming that space in the past. On our digital offering we believe that a Virtuoso Legal were light years ahead of what anybody else is doing

Offline marketing

Yeah. We rely on traditional marketing techniques meeting the lawyers or the lawyers are actually our best source of referrals.

So it's important for us to be joining the right networks and the right groups whether it is the trademark attorneys group or going to international trademark conferences.

I have written a book called 'If you're so clever why aren't you rich? We hold seminars and have set up an IP knowledge base on the web. My firm regularly contributes articles and lectures on the commercialisation and defence of intellectual property.

We do podcasts, as you know Ann, because you were interviewed for one of them.

How do you lead and manage a team? Have you had any training? What would you say is your best/worst quality?

Best quality – I am quite innovative and inspirational. I'd like to think so.

Also its very much part of my DNA that we work collaboratively and have that collaborative feedback. I mean not that it matters to me I'm a 100% shareholder in this business but my two directors are involved to a fairly detailed level even though they don't necessarily have the financial responsibility of making this firm perform to its optimum. But they know it's in their benefit and I want them to know that it's in their benefit not just my two directors but also the whole team.

One of the things that I really encourage staff to do is to give 360-degree feedback that's occasionally uncomfortable. Because you know sometimes people say things and you get 'that's not me I haven't done it'. But actually if people are doing it for the right reasons, they're doing it because they want to be honest with you. They want you to know something and then you need to take it in the spirit in which it's intended and not be thin-skinned about it. You know go away and cry in a corner because someone just criticised you. I try to encourage constructive criticism all the time I'm always saying to staff –' okay well that's the problem. What do you suggest we do about it?'

My worst quality is sometimes I can be a bit dismissive of people. I think I perhaps I take a really umbrella view and don't realise that some feedback is profoundly personal and they can be affected by something I said which wouldn't affect me. Sometimes I don't necessarily get where they're coming from. I'm not that callous but I'm a bit kind of like not understanding my impact.

Have you had any training in terms of leadership or management?

Only what I've done myself. I mean I think I'm all about growth mind-set and about improving myself every day. It is all about growing yourself and being comfortable in that growth mind-set making those changes. Doing those things that you need to do and moving on.

How do you develop your team? Do you use the SRA Competency Framework?

I don't use that competency framework but I do encourage soft skills training and development. Maybe I should look more closely at that.

What I would say is that you don't work in this firm unless you embrace technology and you embrace change. And it's that growth mind-set that's really important to me. If I was to summarise actually how were different from other law firms. We all have a growth mind-set. That's what we are all about is growth mind-set and embracing change not fearing it. Not treating it in a way that should be that is instils discomfort or fear or whatever embracing it. We know it's going to happen. Let's get on with it. Let's see how that change works for us. And you do that with a growth mind-set.

If you got a fixed mind-set about that's how it's done then that's how it's always is going to be done. There is no disruption to what I do. There is no change. You cannot thrive you cannot prosper and you cannot grow too. We have constant on-the-job training.

See also answers to question, How do you lead ... and question below.

What is your biggest team challenges and what is their biggest success?

What is the biggest the biggest challenge – it is coping with the workload. Sometimes we have to turn things around with very tight deadlines for very demanding clients. But we all pull together and that's the beauty of teamwork is that we've managed to pull together to deliver that. So I think we overcome those kind of challenges.

So was the Argos case one of the team's successes?

Yes well that has gone to the Court of Appeal. We'll wait for our Court of Appeal decision* on that as well which is we've got another big one that's going for trial in October. It will be quite a landmark case as well on theft of confidential information and what constitutes company property that's being taken. And that's been very hard fought. She's been very much the David not Goliath. We are proud to serve on the side of David against Goliath. Our clients are three individuals versus literally a multibillion-dollar U.S. corporation. So that's going to be quite interesting and that has been very challenging on all sorts of levels not just technically but also personally because it's been a very bitter vendetta against our clients and that's been that's been a challenge.

(*They did win this matter at the Court of Appeal.)

Where do you see your legal practice going in the next three years?

We are expanding quite rapidly so we're growing significantly in Leeds. We're going to significantly grow in London and the next office will be in Manchester or possibly Birmingham. In the longer run and we have to do more global work. So there is currently ten of us shortly to be 12 and still growing. Therefore we are seeking a fairly significant external investment into the company. And on the back of that possibly further investment and global growth in China or America outside the EU. Yes interesting.

8. MARTIN HOLDSWORTH

Solicitor and owner of IDR Law Limited (Inheritance Dispute Resolution) www.IDRlaw.co.uk

Why practise your legal expertise as a business owner?

Short answer – I've now become unemployable.

Looking back – I've been a co-owner of law firms since 2000, so quite some time, so I've always been a business owner as such. Like most solicitors I followed the usual route of progression within a legal practice – solicitor, associate, salaried partner and then owner – always thought that when you became an owner you would find out the great secret of running a law firm – when you got to sit around the ownership table, you kind of always assumed that everybody knew what they were doing and where they were going. And then you have a moment when look left and look right and realise oh my God either they don't know what they are trying to do, or they are going in a direction that is not aligned with what you thought. Changing a firm's culture and direction is difficult in a traditional set up. Many are happy and take comfort in the structure and leaving the business to others, but for me I always became frustrated at the way things were done or not done – my experience was that growth and innovation was stifled for a number of reasons. The most common of which, in my experience, is simply fear of change or perhaps more properly, the fear of risk in change. That exists on several levels. I left a very large firm to go to a small firm and experienced the same thing albeit in different form, so it doesn't seem to be about the size of the firm that effects this. If you're not surrounded by similarly minded people, it's never going to work out for you. Change has been a constant in my life and I have learnt to embrace it and I have realised that I thrive on it – there's always going to come a point when your aspirations change – dreams grow bigger not smaller with success. You become aware that others are not on the same page and they have already reached their aspirational peak. I struggle with this as a mindset for any business owners as in my experience; it can only ever be an indicator of a slow decline to follow. I've worked with and for others since I was 19. I'm 48 now so a long time. I decided last year to stand by my own convictions and give it a go with my own law firm. Funny enough, I never doubted that it would work. I had a very clear vision and absolute belief, which was shared by my wife and family, which has always been a blessing. One thing I've had to learn to improve on is focus. Vision and belief – I am pretty good at but with a head that sees opportunity everywhere, learning to focus on the right things in the right order has been a learning curve all my life and I am still working on it. Why I practice as a business owner – short answer – because I've been blessed (or cursed) with an entrepreneurial head full of ideas and it is a lot quicker and rewarding (both personally and financially) doing it yourself and making it happen. And I genuinely love what I do. If you have found something that you love doing and surround yourself with people with similar enthusiasm and mindset, you can't fail long term. I have never been afraid changing my environment rather than hoping that change will come along one day.

What is your best and worst business habit?

I mentioned my three word mantra that I try and stick by – Vision – I never lack this and even on those days where nothing goes right, it only takes a night's sleep and the vision returns – there is always something to build, places to take your business and those of others around you – enthusiasm and passion are grossly underrated in my view. I would say that this default state for me is probably my best habit. Opportunities present themselves all the time – there's no limit as to what you can do either in law or out of law (or both)!

Focus is probably my worst habit because that needs constant work. Because I am invariably an enabler, finder, creator but always need to ensure that the ideas are followed through before moving on to the next one – or at least recruit people in to finish off the creation and launch it. I'm not the world's best administrator so I outsource and delegate as much of that as I can.

See the answer to the vision question for where it has taken Martin.

How do you manage the 'highs' and the 'lows' of being a business owner? (Stress management) and/or what are you doing to build resilience?

Business resilience is ok because we're a profitable practice that operates on a model that has proven successful for well over a decade. Every firm has cash flow pinch point and ours arise from time to time when we are investing in some of the other projects outside the practice, but we are financially resilient. I'm saying that nine months in. We'll have another conversation in two years' time.

Emotionally, it's tiring. There's no doubt about it. Gone is the real stress of trying to cajole other co-owners into a growth mindset, but that is then replaced with a different kind of stress that comes exclusively with running your own practice – everything comes across your desk in the early days – this will change as we develop but in our first year I am responsible for everything – from stationary to accounts, contracts, suppliers and so on. But once you come to terms with that it becomes controllable. How do I do it? The hours are very, very long. My wife suggested an excellent analogy for a new business – to see it as a new-born baby – it can't walk on its own for the first 12 months, needs help to walk over the years that follow, should only be left alone with someone we really trust and ultimately it will grow into an independent thing that will need less of my time. You can't leave it alone. You can't walk away from it.

Fortunately, I've got a very understanding and supportive family – we've got four kids and owning my own practice has actually enabled me to see more of them – I am based near the school they go to – I'll do the school run in the morning, I'll do the school run in an afternoon when I can and I'll have plenty time with the kids but then I'll go back to work when they're in bed, so the days are long. Business ownership in its fullest sense with a full family life has meant that I have had to give up on other pastimes that I enjoyed but I have no doubt that these will return.

Health has shown signs of being stressed at times and this is something I am actively looking at to ensure I don't become the weakest link! I think I've now reached the point at the first abbreviated financial year that cash flow is consistently good, so I'm relaxing. Cash flow pinch points always cause concern and the odd sleepless night but that is the same for any rapidly expanding company that has not sought temporary solace in private equity ownership.

Who do you turn to for support and inspiration? Who would you like to thank for their support and why?

I have a number of good friends but particular mention would go to two of them: Rev Rory Dalgliesh, a South African born Methodist minister based in York. We have shared a lot of mountaineering experiences together over the years, disappearing into the Scottish wilderness with our backpacks – we disconnect from our everyday lives and just soak it up. We both do very different jobs, but the affect is the same on us both – literally a detox for four days in the Highlands – no phone, rarely see anyone and remind ourselves how small we actually are (easier for me than Rory who stands at 6' 5"!) We try doing that twice a year when we can. It is a fantastic reboot and I am always grateful for our time together.

The second I would like to mention work in the professional sector – Andrew Brook-Dobson, a financial advisor at Brook-Dobson Brear. Andrew introduced me to some thinking that was enlightening from the outset – he introduced me to the entrepreneurs' operating system and model of running a business and he fundamentally shifted my thought pattern away from inputs to outputs. Andrew didn't just talk the talk, he lives out his commitment to outputs – enjoying a varied array of activities away from the business he runs including ski-touring, climbing in the Alps and adventure racing. A bright man that was not afraid to talk about the real issues and come at those problems in a totally unique way. He's very good at it and is quite an inspiration and always accessible.

Did or do you have a personal or business vision?

I'm a big Stephen Covey fan, so forgive me if I'm stealing some of his but we work on the basis that we want to be the best. It's not measured in terms of size and turnover. We want to be the most compassionate and well-respected inheritance dispute law firm in the country. I don't have any visions to go beyond the six lawyers –that will take us beyond the million pounds turnover from where we are now and I don't really want to go much bigger than that because I've been there before and

I've built teams up to eight and nine and the nature changes. I want us to have a personal approach to each client's problem – there is no case that comes to us where someone hasn't died already, and we want to fix it and come at it in solution orientated way. We don't litigate unless we have to, we set plans – a route map – and that starts by asking clients a simple question – "What is your goal?" (not legal jargon). And then based on that goal, we will then set out a number of phased steps and those phased steps are then broken down again to provide min/max fee estimates, so clients stay in control. We already have a volume of work coming in now that's big enough for six people so for me it's about managing client service and make sure that doesn't dip on the back of our success and the influx of work that we've had.

I also have a second company – Metrona Technologies, which is a LegalTech company I incorporated at the beginning of the year. Is not a law firm but rather an R&D company through which I am developing some ideas for products and services to feed into the probate sector. I've got four tech products and services that are in production at the moment. The first one is in September. I'm working collaboratively with another on two of those four products. I like to find areas where lawyers don't really want to tread because they know themselves, it's too expensive for them to be engaged in it but it is still quite a 'gnarly' dispute for the client.

Classic example is five beneficiaries fighting on an estate – do you have five lawyers to represent each individual? We have created a perceived fairness algorithm that solves the problem without lawyers and at less than £50. I am looking to add passive income through the LegalTech products. I do not want those inputs to increase – the people are fantastic. Hoping to have a pro bono unit.

Having Metrona Tech produce a passive income, that would be great as the aim is to get the passive income levels up to a point where I no longer need to draw any income from IDR Law. IDR Law will then use this released income to develop more services for clients and referrers alike.

I am currently engaged with a joint venture with Countrywide Tax and Trust Corporation – "The Will Clarity Statement". Another one I am working on is Frisk Reports, which is subject to a NDA so watch this space.

Did you have a business plan when you first started – if so what worked and what didn't?

My original plan was to exit from my previous firm with my incumbent team and caseload. For reasons best known to them, this changed very quickly on exit and I ended up setting up a new practice with no caseload. I turned it all around in a very intense week. With the benefit of hindsight, this was the best thing that could have happened as it enabled me to look totally afresh at my model and create an entirely paperless law firm with all my outsourced functions cloud based. My network of referrers is very loyal, and this has expanded very quickly. The business plan was adapted to reflect the new starting position and the phone hasn't stopped ringing since. The clean start allowed me to look at every function and resource in the business. I set up the EOS model plan and worked from there.

I track all my business intelligence data and this modelling demonstrated that the processes and set up would work and that has stayed true. Tracking is crucial – knowing where your business is coming from. I am continually astonished at the lack of awareness some legal business owners have about where their work actually comes from!

What are you doing differently from the organisation you have left behind and/or the competition?

Offering flexible work at competitive rates – we have a woman starting on Monday who will be doing ten hours a week from home, has everything set up and we have a hot desk for her if she wants to come in. She can choose however she wants to spread those ten hours over the week around her existing commitments. Minimum requirement is to visit the office once every three weeks. Many firms care about the input and not the output – frowned upon if you leave the office before 5pm despite doing your hours.

See also answer to the question on business plans.

What has been your greatest success to date?

Professionally, I am most proud of the creation and development of IDR Law – we remain the only law firm in the country that only deals with contentious wills and probate, competing successfully with national firms such as Irwin Mitchell.

Where do you see the threats for your legal business?

I am fortunate to have developed a practice with few natural competitors. Our positioning in the market means that we are the only practice that does not compete with their own referrers. Threats will always come from large behemoths with deep PPC pockets but the next ten years is going to see continual increase in our market, so we are perfectly placed to take advantage of this. It helps to have a firm that has a singular message about what it does.

What is your personal brand? Name your top three qualities, which enable you to run a unique legal practice.

Empathy, understanding where the client is at, knowing what they need to hear but brave enough to be yourself and give them tough advice if needed. An ability to provide clear direction – take worry and fear and create a linear path through to a goal. Beginning with the end in mind (another quote from Stephen Covey).

Why your firm's name?

I was thinking of all sorts of names – keen to not want to put my name in it – make sure people knew it was my business but without my name. I had it in mind to exist and succession – makes it easier. I wanted to make sure it did what it said – IDR = Inheritance Dispute Resolution. I was helped with this by Angus Houston at Pavilion Row who made the very helpful suggestion of using the last word 'Resolution' rather than 'Solution'.

Is there anything specific you do to manage the quality of service?

Three of the four solicitors work using our "familyflex" arrangements, which is working incredibly well. The key has been to hire very experienced solicitors who can work remotely and autonomously (with no requirement to carry out admin or business development duties).

What interpersonal skills are important to be successful with your type of clients?

See answer to the question on personal brand.

Marketing online (websites, Twitter, Facebook, Instagram, LinkedIn, YouTube or other)?

Work experience Law Undergraduate does all our blogs and case reports. Design Junkie – do our website and devising a digital strategy with them. Website is our centre point – £10 subscription after three months. There is a strategy but it is currently developing.

Offline Marketing

Building my network for the last ten years, 4,500 LinkedIn connections and developing my law tech products.

How do you lead and mange your team? Have you had any training? What would they say is your best/worst quality?

Ask any of my team – their answer is the only accurate one I suspect! I like to think I lead by inclusion, engagement, adopting a win-win philosophy (everything has to work for each of us), enthusiasm and working hard at it. Each team member has specific roles and responsibilities that plug into the whole. The fee earning engine room KPI management is run by one of the team who reports into me.

Various things over the years – wide range training, I have a condition called Aphantasia which means that I cannot see images in my mind when I close my eyes Explains why I draw a lot, talk a lot (and listen!) leadership style is collegiate. No particular formal training – learning on the job. Happy to accept fault.

How do you develop your team? Do you use the SRA Competency Framework?

Team is developed by understanding what it is that really interests them – what looks like a win-win to them and to be open to that definition changing as life moves on. There is a simple three tier structure – me – solicitors – paralegals although each works with each other. The paralegals are being supported financially and practically by the firm to become qualified solicitors. Further paralegals will then replace them.

I reflect upon the SRA competency statement – we are a niche practice. I only hire in experienced practitioners (most ACTAPS qualified or standard) and the junior members are training outside of work hours for their LPC and at work on the actual job. We manage training and knowledge sharing to ensure that updates are shared.

What are your biggest team challenges and successes?

Biggest success has undoubtedly been the paperless/familyflex operation. The challenge has been to avoid overtrading – incoming work has had to be managed in line with the human resources available to deal with it. So for example we won't make our new website live until we are confident that we have the right people in situ as the workloads arise.

Where do you see your legal practice going in the next three years?

Reduction in fee earning hours for me personally and success of online products currently being developed. Whole firm runs on trust and honesty. Paperless is the way to go – overheads are tiny.

9. NOREEN KHAN

Solicitor and owner of Kaiser Solicitors (buying and selling businesses and commercial property) www.kaisersolicitors.co.uk

Why practise your legal expertise as a business owner?

I wanted to have the ability to give back to people. I'm using my expertise and specialism that I've learnt to support business people in the process of setting up their business or new premises.

For example when I deal with buying and selling businesses for major and small companies. I quite like the entrepreneurial spirit of the people in smaller enterprises I support. I am a business owner so I understand their pressures. I think it's that it just gives me that sort of gut feel good factor at the end that you've done something for them and just sorted it out. These are ordinary people and small business owners' not major corporates. For example – A hairdresser whose got a new lease for the premises and she's purchased it from her employer/her boss. She's taken over. She's so grateful. It's just nice to see somebody achieve their business dream and grow in their journey as well as a business owner.

What is your best and worst business habit?

My best, I think if I've got a task to do I'll see it through to the end. So if I need to do something I don't leave till it's done so if that means not even eating lunch then I do it.

My worst. I can't always focus straight away, if I've got other things niggling I'll do them first and then I'll go on to the main task. But I think I should learn to do the hardest thing first rather than procrastinate.

How do you manage the 'highs' and the 'lows' of being a business owner? (Stress management) and/or what are you doing to build resilience?

I think you've got to take it as it comes. Sometimes you can have good days – sometimes you have bad days – sometimes you have quiet months – sometimes you have busy months and they just even themselves out.

What I have done and what I've taught myself is sometimes when people get short with you – situations happen. Also I think at the beginning, in it's infancy when I started a business I'd take it personally and I've realised that it's not personal its business. And I teach my staff that. When somebody might be saying something a little bit aggressive or too much on the phone and just say they're not having a go at you it's just the venting off. I think that works.

I exercise to de-stress. I think it's important just to have some outlet. I just think that you get all this energy without even realizing or where you might you might have a situation, which is very frustrating. It then snowballs so you might not even realise the client might be dragging you into it. You might be taking it away with you. So I do exercise. I'll go to the Gym – do Thai boxing – yoga. I just think that helps just focus your own mind and sort you out. And then you can go on with what you need to do.

Who do you turn to for support and inspiration? Is there anyone that you specifically like to thank for their support?

Probably my partner but also through the networks that I've built up, and I've got a friend who does the same thing we studied together – we did the LPC together. So any problems I have that I get really nervous about. He's done it all. He's got two firms. He's got a firm, which he has expanded, with three branches in Manchester. So I just think because he's done what I'm probably going through, because he's a lot bigger than me, he's good to just ask you 'what do you think?'

And equally just people that you've met like I might speak to – Jane (Winteringham) through networking. I had a challenge contacting a lady in a massive company who I'd like to get referrals from. What I was doing was not working to get their attention. Jane provided me with some advice. I just get ideas off other people sometimes if I think I can't breakthrough anything.

Who would you like to thank?

My partner, friends and my family really. They have helped me in all situations where maybe you're losing a little bit of your 'mojo'. The one I would like to single out is my dad. He has always been supportive of me in my career even helping me write and post applications for my training contract. I fell out with a partner at a place I worked as a paralegal and left, my mum thought it was a horrendous decision, but my dad said 'no you did the right thing'. Then low and behold within a month I found a training contract! He's been in business and understands the demands of meeting customer expectations but equally being hot with regulatory compliance. He always keeps me grounded and offers sound advice when I get a little bit ahead of myself.

I think that's nice to have them around even when your staff is quite good and supportive.

Did or do you have a personal or business vision?

I remember being eight years old and when a doctor asked 'what I wanted to do when I grew up. Without hesitation I replied a lawyer.' The doctor replied well you're already half way there (and my dad still recalls this conversation).

When I left and I wanted to set up, my friend kept telling me you needed to do that. My dad kept saying to me 'Why don't you do it'?

At first I thought I might like to just stick to being in employment; and then my circumstances changed, and my finances were such, that I thought maybe I should try it. And I just did it.

I went on a number of courses to expand my legal repertoire. I also plugged into other experts to boost my own knowledge and experience before I started doing this type of legal work, I love learning. I think you got to look to be a little bit brave in terms of having a go or having the confidence to do it. It is doable.

My mission is to keep clients happy by providing them with the best customer service experience because I am helping people realise their business dreams. This changes their lives and I want to help them make it happen.

Did you have a business plan when you first started? If so what worked what didn't?

I had an accountant I use so my business plan was very thorough for the SRA to agree to me setting up a regulated practice and to get the indemnity insurance too. I appreciated having a business plan because it would give me a forecast. So show me what I needed to do in order to achieve. When you actually go out and do it and you see the results it makes you want to do it more. It is great when you actually see what's written, work for you.

I managed to secure insurance. Once I got my insurance, I just rented a room in an attic in an accountant's company. Then I started contacting my friends and contacts, so I got a couple of cases that way to get me started. Afterwards I started to get inquiries from where my premises were situated. For example I was asked – 'Can you do leases or can you do this?'

Once I realised that I was going to focus on SME's business issues such as buying and selling, I then had to think about how I was going to find clients. Initially it was slow but then you find your way so then you realise if I can't do it this way you find ways to adapt. For me I thought it would be so much easier to access these clients through business transfer agents rather than finding individual clients. That would take away the pressure of me going to find an individual where I could find a company that had a bag full of those clients. So that's what I did and have a number of these business transfer agents that I work with.

I have now expanded my business development to directly target businesses and work because

What are you doing differently from the organisation you have left behind and/or the competition?

We have fixed fees on our website. We were transparent about that from the outset and whenever we give a new quote this shows the fixed fees, just so they know where they are. This shows our value of transparency is reflected on the website.

As far as my personal approach is – I think I'm focused on building relationships. I work out whom I need to speak to. I will then research that company – go on LinkedIn, use social media channels, use my contacts and people that I know through networking, to find out if they know whom I need to know and meet. The types of companies are ones supporting business transfers and sales such as brokers or banks. They want to give them money but I want to service their legal work. Also if my clients are looking for a bridging loan or some type of finance then I can put in them in touch.

What has been your greatest success to date?

The fact that I was able to set up and I've got a business that I've been running for six years successfully. And the fact that I work for myself I think that's a good achievement.

My willingness to learn new things in law or interpersonal skills. For example I used to get nervous public speaking. So I went and did public speaking grade eight and passed the exam. I did that over a couple of months. Now when I give a presentation I have a certificate and am no longer as nervous as I was. Another win.

Where do you see the threats to your legal business?

Threats – as a market changes, people might be less reluctant to use solicitors. They might want to do it themselves. Go on the Internet and work it out themselves. Although they may then come to you for guidance when they get stuck but I don't want to offer documents online at this stage. The other threats could come from other solicitors in my niche.

What is your personal brand? Name your top three qualities, which enable you to run your unique practice.

My top three qualities – straightforward personal advice and service, availability; and we have agreed fees.

We give straightforward honest advice. My blogs give clear information about some of the legal terminology and processes; and I am currently working with a cartoonist to produce some simple flowcharts. They know from the outset what they're paying and they get a personal service so they can contact me.

We are all always available so that they know that whilst it can be very stressful it's like buying houses and buying, they can rely on us. It is quite big deal to them – it's how they are going to earn their money. So obviously they want some confidence in the solicitor they deal with. If that person is not available or they're not there it can be very frustrating for that person. So even if you're able to offer that support then that support needs to be beyond what other companies are giving; and that's what your personal branding or your unique point of sale is that is recognised amongst your competitors.

My strapline is 'legal experts that work for you'. So business people can see we are here to serve them from the start.

Why your firm's name?

I chose Kaiser because that is my Dad's name and I felt it was a really strong name. I included solicitors to show from the name that we are qualified professionals here to serve businesses.

Is there anything specific you do to manage the quality of service?

Apart from the regulatory and compliance side, which is covered by externals, we work in teams and there is constant dialogue about how best to deliver our service.

We are also in the process of setting up a financial and CRM system to provide continuity of service as we grow. The Operation Manual will be also updated as we adopt and work through these new systems together.

What interpersonal skills are important to be successful with your type of clients?

You have to be able to relate to your client. You've got to listen. You've got to go the extra mile I think with some people and you work out which clients need a little bit more attention than those that don't. And when we do, we make sure that we do give them extra, so they come back to us. If the value us they will come back or recommend us. If you are in business it doesn't necessarily mean that you would stay in the business you have just purchased a commercial lease or bought a freehold property for. Or they may be they need another lease or be a serial entrepreneur. It's great when they return. This shows to us that as a firm that we've done a good job and that they're happy with us. If they weren't happy with us they won't come back. And they also do a lot of referrals to us. So I know from that we've done a good job.

Also you have to be able have a positive attitude.

Marketing online (websites, Twitter, Facebook, Instagram, LinkedIn, YouTube or other)?

Website – Yeah, I've got a lady who works for us at the moment. She's does the SEO 'stuff' and my website and other social media support. I think in this day and age it's very important as everybody Googles everything; and if you're not on Google I think it would be detrimental to business. We are concentrating I think more so on our website. In the future we want to attract clients through that channel and we are looking to continually update our website to do this.

We do a monthly article and I have found a lady (Kim) who I trust to help us on this.

We then put that on Twitter and Facebook linked to an article goes up so it does raise awareness with people that are following us. And it goes on our website.

We are currently looking at our digital strategy, as I want to ensure that we have all the virtual bases covered that we need to communicate with our clients. For example we will be shortly introducing SMS messages.

At the moment I haven't decided if a client portal is relevant. I have to make a decision about whether it's going to appeal to clients or not. I think it's slightly different where we're interpreting documents and we're giving them the feedback on a commercial lease or conveyance.

Offline marketing

The main non-digital strategy is closely working with referrers and expanding that network.

I am a member of business networks and build relationships that way too.

How do you lead and manage your team? Have you had any training? What would they say is your best/worst quality?

Approachability. I sit with them at our office and don't have a closed-door policy. I think you have to relate to your staff and that's very good for your business. You need to encourage your staff to be able to approach you with any queries that they've got no matter how ridiculous it is or how difficult it might sound. And I've I think it's important to sit with them and ask them how they're getting on or whether they have any issues?

I've got a staff development document that I give to my staff that you gave me. In a meeting I focus on three key questions. How do you think you're doing? How do you think you could improve and what you think is the worst thing about it? It just gives me a good reflection of what's going on in their mind.

I've got Lexcel. I also have a consultant mapping all my processes and systemising everything because it's helpful for the staff. So then we know we've set a precedent. This is what we're going to follow and then everybody's following the same thing. And it makes it more efficient and quicker and the clients get a consistent approach. This means we have an office manual that's been made for us. This manual has got diagrams so if the client says this, then they can go tor this manual this clause or this section. And then it tells you this is the precedent letter you need to send out. Everything is there. So now we've issued our staff with a booklet.

Qualities: I'd like to think that I'm approachable and that they can communicate with me whatever their issues are. I think that's important that each should be able to have a discussion with me. I used to work for someone who did not operate that way and I used to hate the journey to work. I just remembered I'd never want anybody to feel what I used to feel going to work for that person.

I don't think I'm very strict. I think sometimes maybe you need to be a bit more forthright maybe with this stuff, which I don't think I am.

In respect of my leadership/management training I started self-educating myself as soon as I knew I was going to set up in business and I also talked to those that had done it before. I quite like – I follow motivational speakers like Tony Robbins and John Rowan. I like the way that they think and the way that you can control your mind and it's very powerful. I now have you as my coach who helps me with all of this on a very focused and practical level to ensure that my staff and the business thrive.

How do you develop your team? Do you use the SRA Competency Framework?

Currently only I use the SRA Competency framework as a guide to develop my legal and business skills as I am the only solicitor. This will be reviewed when I expand.

I can work out what my staff's weaknesses are and what their strengths are. When you sit with them or you go through each task with them, which I do. As I sit with them, I can praise or celebrate victories and even pick up issues quickly and 'say let's do this together'.

As far as external formal training is concerned, if I think it's a good idea or if they ask me then I will send them. They can go on webinars, which are also quite helpful; particularly if it is covering an area they don't feel strong in. If its legal then they can go on the same training I go on to develop to their legal competencies.

What are your biggest team challenges and successes?

Wouldn't really know what my biggest challenge is – making sure that everybody gets on and works together to achieve the best possible outcome.

So basically in our area of work we need to get as many cases delivered to the client satisfactorily but also meeting their deadlines and meeting their expectations. In order to do that in order to achieve that it is important that everybody comes together to get where we need to get to. So it might be a case where we need to just frantically work on this one because we want to get it over the line by the end of the week. So it's just important that everybody gets on well to work together for the same objective.

On successes – Probably the completions that we have achieved together.

Where do you see your legal practice going in the next three years?

We expand our business by getting more referrers and our team to support the business growth plans I have for my business. I would like to start by increasing the value of the transactional work we do; and maybe look to opening a London to do corporate mergers.

10. PETER GIBSON

Solicitor and owner of Coles Solicitors (General Legal Services delivered in specific geographical areas) www.coles-law.co.uk

Why practise your legal expertise as a business owner?

I think at the time that I took over the business in 2006, it was fair to say that my specialism was primarily personal injury, litigation, catastrophic injury – that area of work and the practice I had acquired was doing that work and so it seemed a natural progression to move onto a firm that I was going to still be able to continue to practice my specialism as it were. What I was perhaps naive about and what I didn't perhaps appreciate; and I didn't fully grasp but have come to do so is that I was becoming a business owner and I was becoming a managing partner, I was becoming an employer, I was becoming responsible for finance and HR and marketing and all of those other things that come with business ownership of any business.

And so I took a decision, it would be around about 2010/2011 to step away from practising my specific practice area. At the time I had a number of individuals in the firm who were dealing with the same type of work, so it was a fairly easy way to dispose of my actual caseload. Now, that's not to say that I don't still see clients, I do. Many clients have come to the firm because of me, who I am in terms of my personal friendship and family relationships etc. So I see a lot of clients but I won't actually continue to carry out the work they've instructed the firm to do, so be it conveyancing, wills, probate – I will see those clients and pass it back to somebody in the team to continue the work. So why? At the time, the answer is what I was doing, there was a steady stream of work, the personal injury market has changed beyond all recognition and the marketplace is no longer what it was.

And so my career has effectively taken a new direction from being a practitioner of the law, to effectively an owner of a business that supplies legal services.

What is your best and worst business habit?

My best habit I would say is my optimism, my continual striving to achieve better, do better, continue to grow the practice, try new things, try new ways of marketing the business, trying things that perhaps others haven't done treading into territories that others have decided is not for them.

So it's very easy to be quite prejudice about a particular location and assume certain things about it. And assume that the demographics of a place are somewhat different to where we've been successful. You can't replicate your model and operate efficiently and profitably in another location. All businesses are about trial and error and some things work and some things don't. So it's a question of having the faith, having the confidence, having the will and belief to say, we're going to give this a go, we're going to try and make the best of it and actually not be ashamed to say, we did that, we tried, and it didn't work, etc.

In terms of my worst habit, if I'm being completely honest with you, is perhaps again, that optimism. It's my best habit and it's the thing that keeps me going but it can be a negative, so when you acquire a practice and you estimate how many boxes something is going to take to fill or how long it will take to assimilate staff to your procedures and office manual and how you work I woefully, woefully underestimate every time and even when I learn the lesson and say the next time I'm not going to do that, I still do it.

How do you manage the 'highs' and the 'lows' of being a business owner? (Stress management) and/or what are you doing to build resilience?

I think this is probably one piece of advice, if you can call it advice that I would offer to anybody, is make sure you've got a network around you if you are planning to set off on a journey where you are going to be solely responsible for a business. It doesn't matter how big or small that business is, be it a one-man-band making cupcakes for a farmer's market or you're growing a business that's supplying dozens and dozens of people and operating from a variety of locations, having a really good network of people that you trust and that can give you the support that you need. Having sounding boards is really useful. Being able to talk to – I don't like the word competitors particularly, but talking to people in the same industry.

I belong to a group, the Yorkshire Lawyers Leadership Group. So my membership of that over the last sort of four years has been really useful. I've been able to share ideas and share problems. It doesn't matter how big or small the law firm is. The problems and issues that we face in terms of staff recruitment, staff retention, training, management, finances, marketing, are all the same. And sharing those issues and problems with your peers and getting good feedback, and punctual feedback because the people who sit around the table, they are my competitors, but they're not my competitors in terms of them striving to put me out of business. We operate in an overlapping geography rather than an identical geography. So that's really useful. Being able to talk to family and friends who have been involved in business as well.

Who do you turn to for support or inspiration? Who would you like to thank for their support and why?

I mean I've been asked this question a number of times over the years and probably the most inspirational character in my family background from a historical perspective is my Uncle John who was born and brought up in Redcar, and he worked as a mechanic in a garage he got married to his childhood sweetheart – my aunty – and he always wanted to work for a motor manufacturer so he looked around the country and he took a job working for Vauxhall, because Vauxhall at the time had the best track record of industrial relations – no strikes, etc. So he started with Vauxhall and they went on strike didn't they. So that's the start of the story. But he was then made redundant and he received, what at the time in the very early 1980s, was a significant pay out and he started his own business he started a wedding hire business and a courier service business and he's a great character – full of positive optimism, he's a great guy and he's probably been the biggest inspiration in relation to me. But there's been lots of other people around the family as well who had their own businesses. And as well as being inspirational and motivational around 'I can achieve that; 'I can do that' and the other lesson that I've learnt from seeing people as well is the sheer level of work ethic that is absolutely required. People look at business owners and think he's driving a nice car, he's got a nice house, and life must be easy for him. And it isn't. Life can be very hard particularly as a business owner when you're responsible for other people's employment and responsible for their outgoings as well as your own outgoings. That's a real sort of ... something to really sort of hold on to that you are responsible for these people and you've got to keep working. It isn't a walk in the park. It isn't, you know, just all roses because there are times when I am in the office at four and five am, there are times when I'm in the office at 11pm. There are times when I've cancelled holidays and stayed in the office to deal with particular stuff. There are times when I've worked weekends. I like getting my hands dirty. I'm not one of these business owners that believes that you can delegate everything to everybody. I'm quite happy to get my hands dirty and I think I gain a certain degree of respect from the people that work for the firm, that Peter's prepared to put his jeans and boots on and get his hands dirty when the time's necessary.

The company motto is, lead by example but also never ask anybody to do something that you're not prepared to do yourself. And there isn't a job that I've asked anybody in this firm that I've either not done myself or helped and done myself, be it painting a wall, clearing an office, boxing-up archiving, cleaning windows, it's part of being a business owner and it doesn't matter whether that's a profession or a greengrocers or whatever it is. You know, if it's your business and you're responsible for it, you get your hands dirty and you get on with it.

Did or do you have a personal or business vision?

I wouldn't say that I started out with a vision. I knew what I wanted the firm to feel like in terms of being a supportive, cooperative culture in terms of being supportive to staff and encouraging them and helping them progress their careers. I knew I wanted my business to be part of the communities in which it operated rather than being at a distance from the community. So it was more a case of how I wanted it to feel rather than having a vision. It's easy – isn't it? In hindsight to say we have a great vision of being able to launch this practice and grow it and it hasn't happened like that. It didn't happen like that. It would be rewriting history to say that I started with the lovely grand plan about what it was finally going to look like because it is a journey and there is never a final day that you've achieved it all. Well, perhaps there is the day you sell your practice.

Before I took on the practice back in 2006, I had an old friend, He was a sole practitioner up in Tyneside and before I was planning to purchase the practice, I would have conversations with him about that. I wouldn't say he's been a mentor but he's been a voice of reason for me. He gave me this little snippet, which I sort of mentally carry around in my head, which is that: 'you don't have to be brilliant in this job. You don't have to be the best. But if you're just pleasant and helpful with people, it goes an awful long way.'

Did you have a business plan when you first started? If so what worked what didn't?

It's evolved and I think that optimism in taking opportunities that have been presented to us has helped Coles grow into what it is. And I'm not solely responsible for those opportunities having come along. Some of it's luck, some of its hard work, some of its tenacity, some of its some inspirational marketing – well all of those things.

What are you doing differently from the organisation you have left behind and/or the competition?

Ok, so we're operating in a fairly unique geography. There is no single competitor out there who covers the same geography that we do. We have rooted ourselves very much in the community in terms of participation in charity, fundraising, community support, so that's very much part of our ethos that makes us very much a part of the community.

And I think looking at it from the outside I think my competitors perhaps just do that as a box-ticking exercise whereas it's very much part of our culture and our ethos. I mean fundamentally, you know, you can go to any high street law firm and they can write a will for you or they can deal with your conveyancing. We try to be as friendly and as approachable as we can. We try to offer a welcoming environment in terms of our offices being fairly relaxed, colourful, happy places to be, as opposed to that traditional dour boo- lined, leather-clad chairs type of office.

So that's where we've tried to mark ourselves out as being different. We know even little things like putting our staff's pictures on their business cards and offering clients a tea or a coffee when they arrive. Can you believe that in this day and age that's still something that's still commented on by clients, that they've been somewhere else and were never offered a drink?

What has been your greatest success to date?

Over the last 12 years, there has been some great successes and there has been some tough times as well, You know with the recession kicking in in 2008/2009. It was a very challenging time. And I think probably we can look back and say yes, you've got all of the staff, you've got all of this office, the firm is turning over 'X' in terms of how the firm's grown and yes, somebody being very kind to me, would say that's all down to you. It isn't all down to me. It's down to a great group of people that I've built around me to do that.

I suppose yes, I'm the leader and the inspiration for that. But I would say that my greatest success would probably be building the team and that team staying with us long-term. If I look back at the firms we've acquired, we've now done eight acquisitions, the principals of the first three firms that we acquired, are still with us. We still have the support staff and solicitors from our very first acquisition working for the firm 12 years later. You know, people want to work in a happy environment, people want inspiration in an environment, people want to work in an environment that's going somewhere and be part of something. Had things not changed and progressed for those firms that we acquired, then they may not still be here.

Where do you see the threats to your legal business?

You know there are lots of these, if you look at our key work areas – the changes to the legal aid market in family work. We didn't do legal aid but that brought about a whole greater level of competition in family work.

So a lot of those legal aid lawyers then started to offer to do private family so that increased the level of competition there. You've got unbundling in family services.

I needn't repeat verbatim some of the issues that I'm sure you'll be familiar with, with regards to the personal injury market which has changed beyond all comprehension in terms of that marketplace. Probate – we're increasingly seeing more people acting for themselves. To deal with that we now offer a grant only service to clients who simply want to get that bit of paperwork out the way and what we do see is that we'll do the grant only work and then they get a little bit stuck and maybe struggle with some of the complexity of the thing, and then they'll come back to us.

So it tends to be that the practice now concentrates more on handling the large complex estates from start to finish rather than if you've got somebody who's died with only £10,000 worth of assets, and the bank is prepared to pay those monies out there's no need for to probate in the way that there once was. So that's changed.
Conveyancing market – I mean we have had home information packs,

we've seen a lot more electronic processes. That's how legal services have changed. I could go on. There's nothing more frustrating now that we're dealing with a conveyancing transactions where clients are expect to be dealt with through texts and emails and electronic portals for documents and then you're dealing with little old man one man band that still close for lunch, he's gone out to court, 'we don't do email', so whilst the marketplace and the world has moved on, there are still some lawyers out there who haven't and that can be incredibly frustrating.

In terms of the marketplace, we've seen big firms disappear. We've seen lots of small law firms disappear. So in some regards, our competition has vanished and disappeared which is an opportunity for us. And then we've seen other players in the market similar to us who are growing by way of acquisition, multi-site offices, lots of consolidation in the marketplace, and that's great because they present a much clearer identity of knowing who your competitors are and a certain level of security of service on the other side.

But whatever the threats, whatever the challenges out there – this is probably my optimism speaking through – they're an opportunity aren't they?

What is your personal brand? Name your top three qualities, which enable you to run a unique legal practice.

I would say optimism is a key to being able to successfully grow a business. Hard work, optimism and just being friendly to people. I do quite a lot of networking – breakfast networking and outdoor networking, as a way to keep growing the firm's client base, in terms of developing links and contacts and networks. We've all been to networking events where you've got new people stood in a corner, who don't talk to people, they feel intimidated, and all you've got to do is smile at these people, ask them where they've come from, how their journey was, it's not difficult. So just be friendly. It's really not rocket science.

Why your firm's name?

So the very first firm we acquired in 2006 was called David J Cole & Company Solicitors founded by David Cole in North Allerton in 1965. It had a good reputation in the town. It had been there for over 40 years. I found it a little frustrating listening to people on the phone introducing the name of the firm, which quite long but equally I wanted to respect and reflect our heritage and the history of where we came from. We're very much firmly rooted in North Allerton – that's where our head office is. That's our history and heritage and respecting David's name. David's son still works for the firm and is still part of that. We have a relationship as a firm with David's widow, so it's a matter of respecting the past but transforming the name to something a little bit more easier on the tongue, a little bit quicker to be said on the telephone and it's a little bit higher up the alphabet as well.

Is there anything specific you do to manage the quality?

So if I take you back to where we were, the firm didn't used to do client surveys, well we introduced them. Things have moved on even at the time I've been here from paper-based reply, pre-paid envelope surveys to online surveys, from the 'likes' of those reviewing solicitors on Google with people posting their reviews publicly available to others. So that's changed and that's been quite transformative. We have a range of appraisal processes for the staff.

We also have Lexcel and we have the Conveyancing Quality Scheme as measures of the way that the firm is run. We have outside consultants come in and do file reviews for us, so there are all sorts of checks and balances in our processes to ensure the quality of service that we get is good and consistent.

We have a very, very small number of complaints across the firm. You can't have a firm of this size with no complaints – it's impossible. But we work very hard to eliminate them and we try and turn a complaint if we possibly can into an improved service. We had a recent complaint from a gentleman by way of an example – he was being dealt with by two different departments in the firm, and he himself had got a little bit confused as to who was doing what, so sitting down with him, as I did and understanding what his issues were, explaining the processes that one department had to go through and the processes that the other department had to go through, to bring the two matters together, to conclude things – by me sitting down and understanding his problems, I was able to go back and do some tweaks to our internal processes but equally what I was able to do was fully explain how we'd got there and to readdress what he had instructed us to do and gave him some advice to change things so that he clearly understood where we were at and he left a very happy man.

What interpersonal skills are important to be successful with your type of clients?

Empathy, listening, but with the ability to assert authority and instil confidence and reliability.

Too many lawyers fail to engage with clients in a human way and hence individuals are "scared " of lawyers.

It is important to tackle issues head on – such as costs that will be incurred, as this is one of client's biggest fear.

Marketing online (websites, Twitter, Facebook, Instagram, LinkedIn, YouTube or other)?

I think all of these things are part of a firm's marketing strategy The website's important for people researching solicitors. We've tried a number of things in terms of online documents and self-service tools through the website. I'm not sure we will ever get there for legal services because people generally need a lawyer when they want to talk to somebody. They want somebody to listen, especially if they've got a problem they don't understand.

So I think very much the website is a brochure and I know I do it myself, if I want a telephone number I'll search on the Internet for the company. I'll go to the website and get the telephone number. I still want to talk to somebody and I think the majority of people still want to talk to people.

Yes, we use LinkedIn. There's a firm Linked In profile, I have a personal LinkedIn page as well, which is very successful. We are on Twitter. We've got several thousand followers. I believe Twitter (and Facebook) is fantastic for profile raising and raising our community voice. We've raised this for charity, we've done that for that community organisation and that helps raise the profile of our brand, about who we are, what we stand for, how we're willing to help and support the community that we generate our fees in because our staff live in our communities and serve our communities and by participating in those things it's a way of giving back.

Facebook is fantastic. We love Facebook. For two reasons. First of all we are able to tell the world, cheaply, quickly what we're doing. It's got the ability to target markets. So let's say I want to talk to females over 50 in Ripon who are contemplating getting divorced. I can do that with Facebook. There is no other media, other than social media and the Internet that is able to do that for me. So that's been really powerful. Secondly, same as for Twitter, we can show our community involvement.

We're not on Instagram. I think if we were selling a product it would be a great thing to be on but I'm not sure Instagram is necessarily for us. We do have a YouTube channel. When we've done videos before being uploaded to the website, they are on the YouTube channel. Again, they've been very much done in the format of either client reviews or a sort of brochure monologue in terms of what the firm does or what a particular area of work does. It's not something that we've concentrated on particularly but the business has been transformed by the Internet. It genuinely has.

Offline marketing

We are very much in a physical office based firm. We pride ourselves on the number of offices that we have and the towns they're located in, our accessibility in terms of being town centre offices in the main. So walk-in customers, walk-in clients, particularly for those offices that are represented with a shop front on a high street with gold lettering on the outside – are particularly good from that point of view. And having a nice clean bright indoor display area as opposed to a 25-year-old dying spider plant and blocked out windows. We've all been there, haven't we? We want to entice our clients in.

I think any PR strategy has to include digital. A recent example of the contrast between digital and paper-based marketing – the acquisition in Redcar the information that we published there online throughout our Facebook page with targeted advertising was able to reach a far greater audience for a fraction of the price in a much quicker way than designing a page, putting it in the newspaper, having the newspaper delivered.

As a business owner, the digital marketing puts you in control of who your audience is rather than a publisher saying 'this is our audience, do you want to reach them?' and a hope and a prayer that your advert is going to be seen on page 47 of that freebie magazine whereas I put a post on Facebook for over 50 year old women in Ripon, who are interested in divorce, I can do that. And I know how many times they've seen it. And I know how many times they've clicked on it. I don't know how many times someone would look at my advert in a magazine. It's changing and making business owners much more powerful and in control of how their advertising spend is used.

How do you lead and manage your team. Have you had any training about leadership and management? What would they say is your best/worst quality?

My best quality as a leader and a manager, I would say that I have faith in people and put my trust in them. I am not a micro-manager. I trust people to get on with the tasks they're given. You know you give somebody a task and you give them some objectives to achieve. I'm very relaxed about them getting on with that and doing that. I think my worst is my tolerance to lack of effort.

As somebody who is prepared to get his hands dirty, put the hours in, I'm not saying that I expect people to work way above and beyond what they're contracted to do, but I do become quite impatient and quite intolerant with people who don't share that vision and that ethos.

How do you develop your team? Do you use the SRA competency framework?

Yes, we do. I think it's still very much early stages. We've had a strategy away day with our senior management team just this week and we've talked about the appraisal processes and how we deal with that. The SRA competency framework has only been in place for about two years now and I think there's been a learning exercise on everybody's part. I think that we're going to develop this further in our appraisal process. We are looking to bring that competency framework alongside our standard appraisal process so that not only are we looking at our appraisal paperwork but we're also looking at the competency framework.

So what we're finding is that people are still doing a number of CPDs but we're finding that a number of people are not recording some of the stuff that they really should be recording. So we're re-doubling our efforts in order to make sure that that competency framework becomes an integral part of the appraisal process rather than just measuring those KPIs in our business management in the appraisal process

What are the biggest team challenges and successes?

So our biggest challenge is geography. It's a huge problem. A huge nightmare problem and we are constantly working on it. The logistics of multi-site offices offering all of the services that we do. Let me let you into a secret. We have eleven offices. We haven't got eleven employment lawyers, we haven't got eleven commercial lawyers, we haven't got eleven conveyancers, we haven't got eleven wills and probates solicitors. And unfortunately Joe Blogs when he walks through the door, he's responding to our marketing. He's walked through our little door in Guisborough or Beverley or wherever and he expects to be able to have an appointment face-to-face that day with any of those disciplines. And educating clients that yes we have the expertise, we have that knowledge, we have those skills, yes we can service you but you cannot sit down each and every time you need to deal with us in your local office with that specific individual.

And your biggest success as a team? I mean I know you said that the whole firm's success was due to you and the team, but was there any specific success you can say they did, they can own?

I think conversely to what I've just said about the geography being a challenge, I think our biggest single identifiable success is consistency. This is something that's often been commented on when we've gone through our Lexcel accreditation each year is the consistency of approach of staff, the consistency of representation of the firm at each and every location. And that takes hard work. It takes really hard work both to enforce single office manual, a single set of procedures, a single set of precedents and documents across a multi-sited organisation. That's probably our biggest single success.

Where do you see your legal practice going in the next three years?

Well, that's an interesting question. We discussed that at great length on our strategy away day. We have continued plans for growth. At this point in time, we don't have any specific geographic plans for growth so it's more a case of consolidation, in terms of growing our respective teams and growing the volume of work that we are able to handle through our infrastructure. So that's where we see the next three years of growth for us rather than acquisitions.

So that's where we see the next three years – a period of consolidation, growth in terms of perhaps lawyers, growth in terms of volume of work, growth in terms of turnover and profit. That's where we see growth, rather than growth in geography. You know, we are in some absolutely amazing locations not least one of which we're sat here in York now. There isn't a single place that people don't say 'I'd like to live there', 'I'd like to work there', 'I'd like to be there'. That's why we call our mini-brochure 'Lawyers of Locations You Love' because they are. They're locations that people do love and we're blessed with living in the most beautiful part of the world and it's a privilege to be here.

Fortunately there are days where you have incredible successes and as long as you've got more successes than you've got failures – what's Churchill's quote? **Success is not a destination; Failure is not fatal. It's the courage to carry on that's the inspiration.**

11. RACHEL ROCHE

Solicitor and owner (wills, probate, powers of attorney and related services) www.rochelegal.co.uk

Why practise your legal expertise as a business owner?

I don't think I have ever had a burning desire to set up my own business, I do not think it ever occurred to me until I spent a year abroad and got out of working in a firm. I had always thought that there is no way you can set up your own firm – too many regulations and compliance things. Having had a year away I thought let's have a look at it and I had got my professional indemnity insurance and I was away!

I think you can almost get indoctrinated working in private practice because you just think will you will never be able to do all of this – all the compliance, all the regulations. Getting away from it all and thinking about it more clearly I just thought it is actually worth having a look at it.

What is your best (and worst) business habit?

Best = try to do one thing at a time, it is easy to get distracted by emails, notifications, messages, voicemails, phone calls, etc. Far more efficient to do one thing at a time, I try to minimise distraction.

Worst = emails. I would not say it is a bad habit but...

How do you manage the 'highs' and the 'lows' of being a business owner? (Stress management) and/or what are you doing to build resilience?

I am getting better at it but I think it is a skill. Try not to take things personally if they do not go right the first time or if there are any issues. If there is an issue I think it is important to deal with it straight away and get it out of the way. Very frustrating when people don't do the work I have paid them to do because I am then trying to find someone else – a lot of this comes from tech stuff. It has been a frustrating challenge over the last few years to get the systems and technologies in place.

I try to get enough sleep.

Who do you turn to for support and inspiration? Who would you like to thank for their support and why?

Those I turn to for support, my friends I suppose, many of whom I've known since I was at school.

Other solicitors and business owners I have met on the way – I know a lot of solicitors so they understand the legal challenges. I have met a few I have just 'clicked' with and we get together ad-hoc to see what we're each up to and to have a bit of a moan about any challenges we are facing – not just legal business owners, but they could be in any industry.

Inspiration, again, other business owners who I consider to be ahead of me in terms of, say, size of their company, or what they are achieving. These are people who overcome challenges. Those I see on social media or read online about their achievements, for example, Michelle Mone.

Did or do you have a personal or business vision?

It has definitely evolved. I now have an office premises that is not my house. I always think it is difficult having a business that offers services, and not products, as you cannot see what you have produced for a client

I always knew I did not want to be a one-man band. I would like to have a few (three or four) offices. People like to have a local office to see someone if they wanted to even though it is not necessary – the personal touch is so important in the legal services in my niche. I do not want a huge practice

Did you have a business plan when you first started – if so what worked and what didn't?

I did have a business plan, I spent three or four months putting it together, I laboured over it. I needed a plan of some description to have insurance in place. I think it ran into 40 or 50 pages. Spoke about this for ages with different people. Spent a long time doing it. Everything in there we pretty much did.

What are you doing different to the organisation you have left?

I worked for a firm in the Cotswold's for a long time. A brilliant firm that taught me everything I know, but at my firm we do things completely differently because we make the most of things like e-signatures for client care. 85-90% of our work is sent out by email – minimal printing. Pretty paperless. Organisation is key.

As well as the usual I use it to review the market place and services and technology.

I use Clio, which suits my business.

What has been your greatest success to date?

Sense of achievement when I opened my office in York. I did quite enjoy writing a piece for the Parliamentary Review and going down to the Houses of Parliament. I did feel a sense of accomplishment when we launched our online will and lasting power of attorney service. Recently just signed the lease for a new office in Harrogate. There's always so much more you can do.

Where do you see the threats for your legal business?

Unregulated will writers – You will have heard of Richard Susskind's book 'End of Lawyers' – he probably does have a point, with the Internet and many other businesses being able to provide what we can, that really does put the pressure on us to up our game and to make sure we are operating as businesses in the way that the consumer expects – by being as efficient as possible. That is why I am obsessed with systems and processes in my business – in my business we have a process manual which tells you how to do absolutely anything and we update that all the time. Keeping on top of things and managing the client's expectations in a world where the client will come to you and think they know the answer already.

A challenge for me as we get bigger is keeping the standard of service the same.

What is your personal brand? Name your top three qualities, which enable you to run a unique legal practice.

Approachability – clients and professionals. Efficient. Not just legal experts but also give practical advice that is not necessarily legal i.e. emotional situations.

Our different client books offer clear advice on what to do in certain situations – more holistic than the traditional firm.

Why your firm's name?

That is my surname 'Roche' and 'legal' to make sure people know what it is from the title – important to convey we are a firm of Solicitors.

Is there anything specific you do to manage the quality of service?

Price comparisons – ringing up other firms. Feedback forms and incorporating that feedback into our practice to improve quality where appropriate.

Having really robust processes in place – explaining to staff what we expect and being consistent. All of our documentation style has to be the same. Checking work is easier if it is consistent; you know what you are looking for.

Our processes are first class and whilst I have not yet applied for Lexcel, one of my solicitors who was involved in this for her last firm, said it would not a problem to get this given our processes. I am just not sure I can be bothered with the paperwork right now and paying the fee. I don't think I am big enough to justify the fee and time and effort. The client doesn't even know what the SRA is let alone this accreditation. So that put the nail in that coffin for now.

What interpersonal skills are important to be successful with your type of clients?

Being able to listen – some people just want to get things off their chest. Communicate and get staff on board – "look after your staff and they will look after your clients" – Richard Branson.

Confidence is a skill – you are not born with it.

Patience. Learning to manage my own expectations about things – working with suppliers, consultants. It is a two-way process – it is time and experience. One thing I have learnt in business is that everything takes longer you imagine.

Marketing online (websites, Twitter, Facebook, Instagram, LinkedIn, YouTube or other)?

We use Social Media a little although I am often told it is a lot especially in networking situations. 'Oh you're the solicitor on LinkedIn' or twitter. Which is really interesting. This is good for me because it means that they've seen a post because someone has re-tweeted it or they have seen something on LinkedIn because they have seen someone liked or commented on it. So we are getting out there. I wouldn't say that using Social Media definitely leads to direct new clients but I think it is really important to raise awareness, and keeping you in the mind of your business connections, your Twitter and your Facebook followers. Yeah, we use the three platforms – LinkedIn, Twitter and Facebook.

Our website is comprehensive; there are loads of fact sheets on there. There are two books you can download as well, a glossary in there for legal terms that we never think to try and explain.

We write a blog post every month. That goes on our website and put out on social media.

I have a meeting about my website every month which produces comprehensive data and tells me how many visitors there's been, how many downloads of our various fact sheets, where the cursor has been on the page, which page people dropped off on, popularity of other pages, whether they have opted in for GDPR (I will follow that up), have they done a contact us page. Then that gives me a conversion rate. Obviously just because someone has used the website it does not mean that they will become a client.

One thing I am really a stickler about is making sure that everyone opening a file or taking down some information from a client that's rung finds out where did that person come from. I can get a bit ratty if the box is not filled out. Because it is very, very important to know where people are coming from. We can run a report on our system to work out where someone has come from – the different sources. Now I think about it, I probably don't look at it as much as I should, but something in my head tells me that is one of the most important things we can ask a client when they are new and they come to us for the first time.

Offline Marketing

I do a lot of networking. I go out and about and then I will tweet about it.

I will do seminars. Sometimes they are joint seminars with other professional service providers such as financial providers

I tried a little bit of print advertising but the last run we did was pointless. So I won't go anywhere near it again.

I do send out press releases now and again for things. I have just started working with someone for PR for the last two to three months – Chris Jones media. He typically does sports actually. He has helped with some press releases. We have had these case studies in the system but he is going to help me to write case studies of some of the work we have done over the past four years; and get those on the website as well. We want to be able to showcase what we have done for people. At the beginning they helped us create a new video for an awards entry and put together submissions for various things. So we will see if anything comes of it.

I get involved and campaign for change. The Associations I am involved with include, SFE, STEP, Alzheimer's Society and Dementia Friends, Dementia Action Alliance, The Diana Award, HM Hubbard Law Scholarship The Parliamentary Review.

How do you lead and manage your team? Have you had any training? What would they say is your best/worst quality?

Worst quality: I don't think I am that good at the HR stuff. So I now have an HR woman coming in as from next week to deal with that stuff. I think you have to get people on board who are good at what they do. Obviously I have to be involved – it is my business and that is fine.

Best quality: I have a real handle on all the figures so I think I am quite good at knowing where the work comes from – the facts and figures. I have three accountants – one that does my day-to-day accounts, another one that does my client account reconciliations for me. This is outsourced as I was sitting on some of this and I thought I don't like this so I am not doing this anymore and it takes him five minutes and it takes me half a day. The last one deals with my audits and this is done all electronically.

In terms of leading and managing, I actually don't know if I'm very good at it to be honest! I've certainly had no formal training (perhaps I could do with some at some point) and I would say that I find this part of my role as a director one of the most challenging. Perhaps when it comes to leading, that is easier than managing for me, because I feel like I have a clear vision for my business. However, managing people in situations when the other person is not being receptive, not performing, not doing what they say they are going to do or being dishonest for example is something I find very uncomfortable.

How do you develop your team? Do you use the SRA Competency Framework?

That is all mentioned in our process manual. There is a training section. The crux of it pretty much is that they are responsible for making sure they get enough CPD a year. I know it's not quite like that now and I found your SRA Competency workshop useful. There is reference to the relevant sections of the Law Society website, and there are all the forms that everyone needs to fill in.

In terms of training, we do lots of things. They are more informal things. There might be networking events that may have a training element e.g. speaker to go in and talk about various bits and bobs. If I think it is interesting or I think one of my team would find it interesting or useful, then will suggest that they go on it. There was a really good one done by the Chamber of Commerce recently about GDPR. That was excellent.

There is a lot of stuff you can do nowadays that doesn't cost a lot of money. We do plenty of webinars. We had a query on costs recently, and we had another solicitor query how we bill on a particular matter. I knew that we were right but because it is my business I wanted to make sure we were doing it right. So I actually got a Cost expert in. She did half a day with us, and we got in sandwiches and drinks. She answered all of our questions and it transpires we are doing our costing right. It was nice to actually have that. Yeah I felt reassured. Get external people in.

What are your biggest team challenges and successes?

Everyone has different skill set and qualities – making sure work gets allocated correctly to play on those strengths. Working collaboratively.

Where do you see your legal practice going in the next three years?

I would like to have three offices (maybe one in Cheltenham) and built on our online presence – have a team of three to four people to run the services we provide at a distance.

12. RICHARD CRAMER

Solicitor and co-owner with Robina Hussein of Front Row Legal (Sport, Media and Business Law) www.frontrowlegal.com

Why practise your legal expertise as a business owner?

I set it up twice actually. I left a medium-sized practice to set up my own because I felt as though I was not progressing and wanted more direct control over my destiny. I merged my then legal business in 2009 and then de-merged it in 2011.

The answer to the question is different the second time around because in 2011, I was 51 years of age and not many practices want to take a 51-year-old unless you have a huge following. My answer was well I may as well take my following and put myself in control again.

There was a debate at one stage if I do jump in with another practice as a consultant or a partner or even a firm where you are your own boss in a larger structure. I felt as though I had done it successfully once before, although I had self-doubt my wife had a lot of confidence in me. That is the reason why I am a business owner and a lawyer at the same time.

The first time around I was intrigued as to whether I could do it and the second time it was probably more out of necessity due to people not wanting to employ a 51 year old.

Met Robina in 2007 – had been a paralegal and then a trainee – shown a lot of dedication and great loyalty even after she qualified. Kept an eye out for each other. Worked out for the best.

What is your best and worst business habit?

Best = chasing the work and being proactive but that can also become a bad habit by trying to fee earn and non-fee earning work tends to go on the backburner for another week, then another week. Not sure if it is quite normal but a lot of lawyers feel their natural environment is to fee-earn and handle compliance matters, financial matters or accounts get left behind – not a great motivational feature as they are not fee earning. Perhaps I should pay more attention to that. Certain things only a senior partner can deal with.

How do you manage the 'highs' and the 'lows' of being a business owner? (Stress management) and/or what are you doing to build resilience?

Goes in spells – had a spell last year. You then come out of that then go on a high of a successful period. Don't know how I manage it. I suspect I manage it through my therapist/counsellor/wife who reminds me that we have overcome adversity in the past and that we are good at what we do. When you are on your high you are most vulnerable – comparable to football. If things are not going well, keep on working hard. Again, comparing to football, a natural complacency comes in. I read about Manchester City, I have just watched on Amazon – The Manchester City documentary and what you saw from Pep, who was a great manager, was that when they won the league with six games to go, that wasn't enough for him. He wanted to break another record. And they have come back in the summer, which is the most difficult part because you have been disheartened and you have to go again. I think he has tightened up discipline and is working even harder. That is the way to do it, keep working hard and believe in the practice. Believe in what your principles are in running the firm. If we work hard and dedicate ourselves to the practice, then the reality is that success comes.

You need a release too. This morning, there was all sorts kicking off. So I could go into my office at 6.30am or do I do my British Military fitness? I did my British Military fitness from 6.45 to 7.30am. Three quarters of an hour of being flogged in the park. But actually I feel better for it now. I have released a lot of tension and I have got rid of some aggression. Running up and down Hill 60 helps – I hate it but it helps. So I think that is important. I play golf, which is very, very important, especially in the summer time. Getting on the golf course, fresh air. Anything outdoors is very important for me. Just breathing in fresh air when you are in an office environment and cooped up in a chair, so I think just anything where you are in an outdoor environment, as opposed to being indoors.

Who do you turn to for support and inspiration? Who would you like to thank for their support and why?

I am quite secretive and try not to show emotions especially to staff. I do have self-doubts. My wife Julie is my main inspiration and support and she keeps on reminding me of my strengths and successes.

I would like to thank Robina for coming with me and working hard to make our firm a success.

Certain clients as well – just had a call from a client in Australia who was full of praise.

Did or do you have a personal or business vision?

I think so – able to draw from my previous experience. The vision and business plan changes. Always felt as a lawyer – one thing you can control is your overheads. If you are not generating cash it can be dangerous.

Did you have a business plan when you first started - if so what worked and what didn't?

I needed a facility and so I needed a plan for the bank – it acted as a discipline to keep a control of the overheads. Easy to go on a spending spree after you have had a good week. Good to manage cash – critical.

Where it has gone slightly off plan is because of the name. Front Row has almost developed into a sports media firm. A lot of existing clients have returned so it is not all sports clients, 70% are commercial clients. Nature of practice has changed and so the original plan has changed and so you adapt to the work coming in.

What are you doing differently from the organisation you have left behind and/or the competition?

Focus and my contacts from my years operating as a lawyer. We specialise in dispute resolutions and business law for the Sports industry. I am a registered lawyer with The Football Association and am an agent for Rugby League, Rugby Union and Cricket. Although we do also act for business enterprises on a range of business law.

What has been your greatest success to date?

I suppose I have just turned 58, still here and still operating. Been at it for 35 years so hopefully more years to come, although fatigue is starting to set in.

Where do you see the threats for your legal business?

A good question to answer. I think the biggest threat to me is, and I try not to worry about it too much, is the work drying out. If the work stopped coming in, and I haven't got any guarantees of work, then that would be the end of the business. So that's, whilst it's a threat, it's also a driving force. So it forces me to go out and network. It forces me to put my name out and about. It forces me to try to get good results. It then self-perpetuates itself. But that is the biggest threat, for what ever reason the work – you could have a fall out with six good clients and all of a sudden you have no work. That is probably the biggest threat for the practice.

There are other threats. I think probably the disproportionately compliance stuff we have to deal with. I understand, don't get me wrong; I am very disciplined in that way. But I sometimes think, there is an 'over-obsession' with compliance in the running of the practice. The purist will say if you were to adopt every single kind of regulation, this will give compliance a negative vibe on the back of it. And actually it can be treated as a negative impact on the practice and so I think there has to be, perhaps a greater understanding, that certainly small practices don't necessarily have the infrastructure to get it completely right. I also, don't get me wrong, if you were disobedient, it is dangerous. I understand that there are rules and regulations for a particular purpose or purposes. And I suspect that there are many practices don't even comply with, maybe, three quarters of the stuff that is out there. But those solicitors are dangerous, and those solicitors don't care, and those solicitors reduce the confidence in the profession. So not contradicting myself, I think it is a balance. And I think the SRA and the Law Society must have a list of bad practices. The Ombudsman must get a lot of complaints from certain practices. So why aren't they focusing a bit more on that? Why does it takes a terrible incident to happen when they must have a red light next to some of these practices? Because why suddenly are they closing them down? Why suddenly struck off? So I just wonder whether they have the resources allocated in the right way.

What you do see is a lot of solicitors retiring and saying 'I have had enough of this. The fun has gone out of it.'

What is your personal brand? (Name your top three qualities, which enable you to run a unique legal practice.)

Persistent, hard working and a pain in the backside sometimes – very driven.

Why your firm's name?

As you can tell I am passionate about football. Although we need a new website – idea is to rebrand it – but I have fallen behind with that task. Someone needs to do it, someone apart from me with the input from the firm.

Is there anything specific you do to manage quality of service?

What we have started to do now is to try to sift through client call to eliminate the time wasters or the ones we cannot help. So a new client came in yesterday and I addressed the issue of costs straight away. I said I am very sympathetic and I think you have had a very bad experience. She tried to buy a business and she paid a load of money before she completed. Now she can't get the money back and it's her life savings. But as much as I am sympathetic, I said to her, look you need a fighting fund just to kick it off. You are looking at a £1000 just to kick it off. And she came in yesterday with the money as her mum is prepared to support her up to a point. What I am doing is being a little bit more direct. You get your sift right and the good quality ones will filter through who you can make a difference for.

Getting rid of time wasters is tricky as it is hard to say no to a client. Become more selective in who we do work for, become more "snobby" – not in a derogatory way. We pride ourselves on being 'results-driven' and hopefully the client senses that. I always try and go beyond the duty.

What interpersonal skills are important to be successful with your type of clients?

Communication skills together with straightforward advice on the client's matters. We don't want to waste their money.

Marketing online (websites, Twitter, Facebook, Instagram, LinkedIn, YouTube or other)?

We probably have a strategy in our heads but actually doing it we're not so good at – thankfully the work we've got has been fantastic.

Offline Marketing

The client can feel the value in what we have done. Example: Client in Australia – mundane case within my experience – for the client it was the biggest thing in his life – I gathered that during the matter. I spotted the value in the client – the client was almost destroying his health. Could have invoiced him during the case but waited until the end. I may be writing off ten hours of work but he will be recommending me to other league players, as he is so well known – marketing tool.

Almost becomes too dangerous to go on a marketing campaign, as we would have too much work, which we would not be able to cope with. That would be dangerous because if you turn the tap off, you can't instantly turn it back on and get a load of work. We are addressing that because a marketing campaign or digital campaign or whatever it is, can work if you have an instant amount of work come through. You might get it in six months but what we feel here is that if we were to go on that campaign, we need more bodies. Now in the process of recruiting and recruiting quality people. Once we get to a bit of critical mass in the office, then there are two other fee earners that we want, then I think we can focus on this.

We are also working with accountants on strategy. What we are doing there, and it is as much for Robina's sake as mine, we are going through a review of our business. We are getting external advice. Part of that is going to involve, and we are about half way through, we will engage on a marketing strategy of bringing someone in; but we are not ready for that yet. No point in doing that – we need to be ready to cope with the increase in work. You do get this in July and August, the holidays, I am not as on top of my work as I should be. I don't like clients who are waiting on me for a couple of days. It feels a little bit like that at the moment but I would like to put that down to an extraordinary period with Robina's case which she dealt with – which is fantastic. We come out of that in March/April having had two years of intensive work to a lot of other work as well. I've just finished – completed on Wednesday – a big commercial transaction on the sale of a business. Which is not necessarily a fit with us but we've done it, and done it well. I reckon, across all the fee earners working on it we have probably done 350 hours potentially 400 hours. It started a year ago and finished on Wednesday. Now we've got all the mopping up to do and all the undertakings associated with it.

How do you lead and manage them? Have you had any training? What would they say is your best/worst quality?

Good question. Probably – not sure if it is the right way but I lead and manage by equating it to sport. It is called the 'captain's knock'. So I have always felt traditionally, and it might not be the right way, but it is the way that Pep manages his team. So there is a great programme to watch on how he motivates his team. He is very 'hands-on'. He talks to them all the time – show your face as much as you can. Have an open door policy as much as you can. Give them confidence, make them accountable and praise them. Remind them that they've done a good job because it costs nothing to tell them they have sent a good email – worked hard – done a good job.

So I am probably a bit traditional in that way. There are some managers, football managers who do not talk to their 'players'. Look at Mourinho at Manchester United – he seems aloof from his players. So he is probably not talking to his players. That can inspire because doubt can lead to I want to win. But I look at the way Pep talks to his players – he hugs them, he kisses them, he tells them how good they are. When you speak to the players as to his management style, they say, on interview, 'he makes me feel the best right-back in the world' or 'he makes me feel the best right-centre forward in the world'.

So I don't give praise out every minute of every day, as then it means nothing. So I try and lead by his example. For example, Robina needed me last Friday, so I stepped off the plane as it had been delayed and came straight into the office. That's leading by example. She needed support. She had a difficult lawyer sat in the other room who was putting her under extreme pressure to complete the transaction and give undertakings. I phoned her at the airport and I said to her – do not capitulate. Blame it on me.

The other way is: try not to throw people under the bus because they are sensitive creatures. I am not a political animal and if I have made a mistake – put your hands up. Human beings make mistakes all the time. That kind of approach.

Because I am 35-years qualified, when I was at law school you got no training. All you did at law school was do your degree in law, your Law Society finals but there was nothing about management style. You learnt about accounts.

So via various legal practices I have gone on courses but not as much as I should have done. I have been in groups such as the Alternative Board. I did three years on that. That was 1:1 training but it was more of a sounding board and making sure you are on the right track. Now Armstrong and Watson are filling a bit of that role although they are not my accountants – Sagars are but they don't offer that service, although John Beevers is very good. What you get with Armstrong Watson and Andy Poole is different. Went to the Lake District with other business owners and it was intensive. I found that invaluable and I should do it more. Then again, not enough hours in the day.

How do you develop your team? Do you use the SRA Competency Framework?

What I would say is that we have external compliance people who are very aware of that so I would like to think that we do the right thing and we are always on the right track. Maybe it is something that I need to deal with.

What are your biggest team challenges and successes?

I would say, and it has really happened in the last few months, we work as a team – most of the time anyway. I mean I have had some fantastic successes in my career, some lows and some highs.

We have had some fantastic results and I could talk about that forever. When I look at the way we were formed in 2011 and where we have come now, I think especially for Robina who is leading a team. Working with her on the Keystone Healthcare to achieve success, was a great result for us as a team.

Also the fact that Frances Gibbs interviewed Robina, which got published in The Times recently. Not just the case report. Although the case attracted interest from The Times and other publications. I think winning that in the face of adversity because it was a real battle. It was the toughest piece of litigation that I have ever come across against two uncooperative defendants. And to drive it forward to a trial as we did and get a judgement in our favour was a great result for the client. To me is a great success for the practice and for Robina too.

Where do you see your legal practice going in the next three years?

I would like to think we are becoming more established and more people are becoming aware of us. Development with Robina and perhaps she will take on a greater role over the upcoming years. Identifying long-term employees. Would like to see Robina take over with a succession plan in place so that I can eventually retire. I want to be able to have the choice when I am ready.

13. SAMIRA CAKALI

Solicitor and owner of SCE Solicitors (Employment and HR)
www.scesolicitors.co.uk

Why practise your legal expertise as a business owner?

That question made me go back seven years. In the end it was because I am passionate about client care – everyone is to a certain degree but I think as a lawyer or a business owner you get sucked into thinking of clients as a number for targets as opposed to an individual or a business. I wanted to look at the needs and listen to their needs regardless of the type of client.

What is your best (and worst) business habit?

Best = my Mindset – always of the Mind-set you can achieve anything as long as you put your heart and mind to it, making sure once I have seen a client I get a quote sent to them in 24–48 hours, my worst bugbear is to chase people for a quote.

Worst = not making time to work on my business – I work in it, but not on it, something I am trying to change in the next 12 months. When I am back off maternity leave I plan on looking at marketing plans and business plans. Something I am working on.

How do you manage the 'highs' and the 'lows' of being a business owner? (Stress management) and/or what are you doing to build resilience?

Again this was a difficult question – as a small business I have had a quite a few lows, one of which was the loss of my friend and senior associate last December. How I managed it was to keep going really. One of the first things I did was to get a mental health first aider certification in August.

My clients still needed me at the end of the day – there is light at the end of the tunnel. In terms of the 'highs' is to share it with the team – we try to have a quarterly night out and recently introduced end of month pizza just so that we can sit and get to talk to each other – nine times out of ten, we are in different places – in two different sites.

Who do you turn to for support and inspiration? Who would you like to thank for their support?

My friend Marie Walsh – known her for five years. I'd say she is my go to person for support when I am in a crisis. Always willing to help me and has been there for me. She's more experienced than me so she's my 'wise owl' friend. Part of the Leeds Law Society, signed up for mentoring, did not get placed with anyone, that could have potentially have been beneficial. Want to make time for more coffees and lunches with Marie.

My husband also – he was the one who suggested I should set up on my own as I was getting disheartened not doing what I had qualified to do. He said at the time, I am experienced enough to do it yet young enough to go back to a practice if I did not enjoy it. You question yourself on whether it is silly to set up on your own which sounds silly when you say it out loud. He has been a star and helped with lots. Been there a business mentor for me and is our IT specialist.

Did or do you have a personal or business vision?

Everywhere I have worked has set me up to be my own boss, lots of positive experiences. I would say one of the things that differ from my last organisation is not having the same vision – I wanted to create a law firm where people were happy to come into work – about being a team, pulling each other together and for me to be transparent with them, 'our' firm. Building that core team.

Did you have a business plan when you first started - if so what worked and what didn't?

Yes we did. In fact my husband helped me to put it together.

From the outset the website was important and again my husband was very helpful in getting that set up at the time so that was one of the things we achieved from the plan.

The main item in the business plan was we wanted from the start a specific HR services package and we did this.

On the financial side it was helpful to keep track of our goals, in particular at that time the acquisition of clients via an Excel spreadsheet.

What are you doing differently from the organisation you have left behind and/or the competition?

What I do differently is how I manage my staff and clients – trying to figure out what they want to achieve and why they want to work here and to make sure it is implemented. Two-way relationship.

Biggest thing I do differently is listening to them. If there is a trainee position available I will not look outside the firm if I have the competence inside.

Our signature package is the HR plus which is our outsourced employment and HR package, which is basically when we become our clients HR department to manage their employee relations as they are the most important aspect of a business

Goes beyond employment law, we make sure all their documents and policies are compliant e.g. bribery and GDPR. There is also a telephone line, which they can ring to their dedicated solicitor, personal and bespoke service. Sometimes grievances and disciplinary issues can take months – to save clients from constantly repeating themselves they have that continuity. Really an all-round service.

What has been your greatest success to date?

I think there are opportunities with my existing contacts and clients. The next 12 months I want to look at not driving for meeting new people but look at who we have worked for and what we could do for them – reconnecting, referrals, etc. In the past I have always chased new clients. I want to change this; we can't do the same thing and expect different results. I have tried to filter that down to the staff here as well.

Where do you see the threats for your legal business?

HR consultants – getting people to understand we are not offering the same service as them. That is the biggest challenge really. Now with Michelle's guidance and experience having done it for seven years, I now realise I do not need to sign up everyone I meet – not everyone is the right type of client for me, especially if they are looking for the cheapest service. To be honest, when I was pregnant with my first son Marvin, quite heavily pregnant, I went to see someone in Huddersfield, they had about 100 employees and he wanted something for £100 a month – I said it's just not going to happen, that is not the type of service I offer – I pointed him to Peninsula and said that maybe he needs to talk to the likes of them, but I don't even think they could afford them.

What is your personal brand? Name your top three qualities, which enable you to run a unique legal practice.

What I would say is that we are 'forward-thinking' experts. We use technology quite a bit, happy to Skype for meetings and witness statements. We are highly dedicated to clients, which is our key focus. We are affordable, accommodating, flexible, personable – lawyers with personality is our USP, people by people, we want to grow with our clients

Why your firm's name?

Whilst I am the founder member I wanted a firm that worked collegiately with others. So I chose my initials and employment as part of the name but not the whole name. Thus our name is SCE Solicitors. This allows us to expand and work with others.

Is there anything specific you do to manage the quality of service?

We get testimonials. We use vouched for ones and ask for testimonials from our clients.

We got awards for our employment services very early on. We were legal awards winners in 2013 and 2014. Then in 2015 we were global awards winner for our employment services.

What interpersonal skills are important to be successful with your type of client?

Communication especially listening. I want our clients to know that they have been heard when we are sorting out a problem. Listening to clients is so important so that we know what they want to achieve.

Being friendly and approachable as well as knowledgeable.

Marketing online (websites, Twitter, Facebook, Instagram, LinkedIn, YouTube or other)?

Historically our approach has been a scattered approach and we are trying to make that more targeted.

Do you have a digital strategy?

We have got a plan and we have to execute it. During the last few months one of the things I did while I have been off is mapped out what we were doing – and we were doing far too much. We've decided which things we are not going to be doing and we are going to see what works. So we have a plan, we just have to execute it. For example our newsletter has gotten a lot 'sexier', if I am allowed to use that word.

We are now focusing on the main three – LinkedIn, Facebook and some Twitter. Have not nailed it as such. I have a consultant I am working with, Michelle, helping me hone in with what works with my clients – work in progress. Feel like I have spent a lot of mental time trying to change that – Michelle – figuring out where our clients are.

We do have a social media policy; we're still working on that, changing things slightly

Obviously the website is another platform

Offline Marketing

We have printed brochures and we network locally as it is important to build business links within our communities.

I am a member of BNI and a local peer group to support businesses in our local area of Horsforth. I am also a member of Leeds Trinity. Other local areas we support, we are going to relevant networks there too.

How do you lead and manage them? Have you had any training? What would they say is your best/worst quality?

I lead by example and as I said I listen to their needs.

I have done both my management stage 1 and 2. Found it really helpful.

I have pulled both manuals back out – I try and read things over and over again because it is easy to forget things in a busy office. For example, I have set more targeted KPIs from reading a section. Another example is that I do yearly appraisals with my staff but decided to implement monthly ones from the notes.

I found that I was spending a lot of time with my 'high maintenance' employees and not enough with those who were doing quite well – they need that time too, it's about being loved. Employees still need to feel loved. Definitely having more of a balanced approach to employee engagement.

How do you develop your team? Do you use the SRA Competency Framework?

Training wise – we take the approach of the SRA Competency format. I don't use the SRA one as I use my own which I have tweaked along the way.

They have KPI's, targets, historically they have not been focused on the targets but we want to change that a little.

I listen to their training needs and ask questions. Do they need shadowing? Do they need to go on a course? So, that has all been learnt really, everyone has different needs. What works for one for example may not work for another?

I had a colleague that really needed everything written down, which you can't manage easily. I am also working in the business and manage the business, so I decided to use a project management software system called Trello boards. This then made it easy to collect information and delegate the tasks and there would be records that everyone could access.

What are your biggest team challenges and successes?

I think after seven years I have finally got the team I want and we will achieve great things together – it has taken a long time to get here. I think that is one of my greatest successes, is building the team who has the same vision, and mindset and works really well together. This maternity leave has been much easier than my first one where there was quite a lot of conflict and I was back at work two months later. I could feel the love between them, the respect.

Getting to grips with our new marketing plan and PR and actually actioning it. Some team members are better than others so it's making sure everyone pulls their weight equally.

Where do you see your legal practice going in the next three years?

Now that we have two offices, I would like to expand the team with another couple of qualified people. For example a newly qualified solicitor and/or Chartered Legal Executive

14. THOMAS COATES

Solicitor and co-owner with wife and two non-lawyer shareholders under an ABS (business and personal legal services dedicated to the healthcare sector) www.fta-law.com

Why practise your legal expertise as a business owner?

I am a corporate solicitor, a general one until the recession, I worked at regional firms. When the recession happened I found myself acting for dentists. Involved in lending transactions to the healthcare sector, particularly dentists remained a green light for the banks. I ended up, not by choice, specialising in that strange niche which I found myself in. As time went on I exclusively did that and moved to a firm where they had a niche specialism in that. Throughout that time you meet various people, met brokers, I headed up teams and became a partner at a regional firm at five years qualified.

One of the companies we worked with closely is called Frank Taylor & Associates who are based in Hertfordshire. We were approached by them as they had an eye on the legal sector.

I felt like I knew them better than the people I was working for at the time. There are four shareholders, 25% each, I am the only lawyer and they are all based in London. It was an opportunity too good to pass up. So that's why I ended up doing it.

What is your best and worst business habit?

I had to think about this. I struggled to pick my strengths. I can be quite critical but the one that I would say is my best business habit is that I am quite straight. I worked in firms before where there is politics. I am straight and honest with the way I deal with people; that includes staff and clients. I am upfront and above board.

Where I struggle, and I do acknowledge this, is that I am still constantly learning to be a managing director. I have managed teams and been a partner in a firm, and I was very lucky to have very good teams around me, looking back. They managed themselves, if I am quite honest.

My worst aspect, and the thing I still trying to improve on all the time, is devoting time to being a managing director rather than fee earning. I have to try very hard not to get pulled back in to the legal work.

How do you manage the 'highs' and the 'lows' of being a business owner? (Stress management) and/or what are you doing to build resilience?

I think going into it as we did, knowing that there is a financial commitment, we knew there is a risk there. And lawyers are predisposed to look at the worst-case scenario, which I did. I considered quite carefully, what if this all goes wrong – £50K out of pocket or whatever it was.

To some extent I have had to put that to the back of my mind really. You can't live everyday thinking it is all going to go wrong, otherwise we would never have done it in the first place.

Our business partners were surprised that we took them up on the offer, even to the point where we rang them one day and said: 'We've done it and handed in our notice as well'. This was way down the line when the ABS was being formed. Even they said it has taken some guts to leap out of that safety net in being in a firm with all the different departments such as IT support and the rest.

From my perspective, learning to enjoy it rather than being fearful of what happens if things go wrong.

I think I have become less emotive than I used to be, particularly when you are doing the fee earning as well. Lawyers, particularly younger lawyers, I think it can become personal. At times I have to remind them that it is only a job. I think that is my coping mechanism. I always come back to the point that even If you have had a bad week or a bad month, it is not the end of the world. We can do something else, if the worst comes to the worst. Thankfully we have had a good couple of years.

Who do you turn to for support and inspiration? Who would you like to thank for their support and why?

Unsurprisingly, the fact that my wife who works in the business, does present challenges as well. Sarah and I have always supported each other in our careers. The nice thing is that she has skills I don't and I have skills she doesn't. We do insist on a degree of separation on how we run the business. This includes where we are in the office and we have, sort of, evolved into a way of working that works for us. It does require some discipline outside of work, to not talk about work.

Sarah is the person who I primarily lean on and vice versa. Parents – emotional encouragement and financial support from an early age and through law school.

Have to give credit to my business partners who are ex-London city bankers who are older. I think one is in his mid-forties and one in his mid-fifties. They look at things in a different way to how lawyers look at things; and I use them very much as a sounding board. They don't interfere in what we are doing but they have given us some really good advice about looking at things in a non-lawyer way. This can be a breath of fresh air sometimes.

Did or do you have a personal or business vision?

Yes we did, and it has changed.

When we first started we had a business plan and our aim was to become the number one provider of legal services to the dental industry.

I think survival, of course, is the primary objective when you begin a business – we achieved this and exceeded our targets in the first year. Initially it was just Sarah and I sitting in an office on day one, having left a decent-size Yorkshire regional firm on the Friday. Trying to get the phone to ring and that kind of thing. It was a huge culture shock. So we achieved survival and all our targets in the first year; and have continued to meet our financial targets for the firm.

We have, sort of reached the stage now where the vision needs some revision. Whilst we have built a firm, which is profitable, and has 12 members of staff – a mix of solicitors and paralegals, we have identified that we have done things the other way to the main firms. They established a general practice and then added a niche on to that. Whenever we looked for a move, there was great appetite in those firms to build this type of niche as an addition to their corporate team.

We have a niche specialism on a national level but nobody knows who we are on a local level. We do not have a local presence. We rarely do anything locally as a dental niche is not really a local thing – a lot of

our clients are in London. We tend not to meet them.
So what we would like to do is to build up our reputation locally at least so people know who we are. We are starting to get some of our staff out there meeting accountants etc.

The dental industry is buoyant, but to expand locally, we would have to become non-niche in the corporate/commercial property field and we have capacity within that team. That is where we may need help on how best to achieve that.

Did you have a business plan when you first started – if so what worked and what didn't?

The one bit that didn't work was that we grew a lot faster than we expected to, therefore there was a faster need for extra staff and space. We were quite conservative in our forecast and predictions. We grew faster but that did not equate to more profit because of the overheads.

What are you doing differently from the organisation you have left behind and/or the competition?

Encountered a lot of frustrations at firms over the years. I have worked at a previous law firm where there was an autocracy and where the Managing Director made all the decisions. So we wanted to be more agile in business.

We do transactional work – 60–70% of our work is this. At other firms, this involves different departments (employment, corporate, commercial property). So you would have all those different lawyers working on their own bit of the transaction, each with their own boss and targets. You would encounter vastly different service levels and outcomes. So on the work I was bringing in, I wanted control and yet had these lawyers who were not answerable to me.

At our firm, we wanted to unify it as one team. Also 99% of our transaction work is on fixed fee, which is another reason this was necessary. That is the key thing and I think this is the thing that differentiates us from other firms. We are all working on the same file all of the time.

A 'spin-off' from that is that there is no point giving people financial targets over which they have no control. They do have a time recording target, which we monitor. We are lucky that we are a smallish firm so that we know when people are busy and when they are not. As we are growing and bringing in people with new specialisms, such as wills and probate, we are starting, because we have to measure in some way shape or form. The only way to really do that is financially. Commercial litigation is another add-on where this applies.

These are not meant to be scary and the first thing we ask our people is to set them, themselves. And if it is providing an added service to our clients, and it is not costing us a huge amount of money to have that person there, that's ok to start with and we will grow from there. Less pushy on the financial side of things.

From a managerial perspective when I was a partner at one firm I used to say to them in partner meetings 'you are so focused on financial performance' and you don't reward people for other things, that are equally if not more important.' They pay lip service to management and the ability to bring work in.

We wanted to create a place to work. You might be a great rainmaker but you might not do a lot of the legal work and thereby you don't bring a lot of the fees in. You generate the initial work for someone else to do it. So that's the sort of culture, which we wanted, its not just purely financial that leads to recognition and reward.

Another thing we do differently. We invest a lot of time in our clients without a guarantee of it turning into chargeable work. We build relationships.

What has been your greatest success to date?

Personally I was very proud to be made a partner so young in my career. It felt a real achievement at the time to become a salaried partner.

Since then, to have started FTA law in 2016 and achieving Lexcel accreditation within the first year is a success we are proud of. We have grown to 12 and are just about to move into a bigger office.

Where do you see the threats for your legal business?

I think it's the having all your eggs in one basket – my niche. We are very narrow in the work we do. I like being the managing director of my own firm so if I had to go work for someone else that might be more difficult that I first thought it might be. I enjoy what I do and I want to continue doing this.

We used to be more reliant on my type of work. Now the employment

HR services are growing; commercial litigation is starting to achieve some momentum of its own. That is self-generating and she is already covering her expenses. We are growing but the threat is that if there is a significant downturn in the transactional work we would be very different to where we are now.

We do have a doomsday scenario but I wouldn't ever want to go back to that – myself and Sarah with maybe a couple of others sat in a very small office. This would equate to a quarter of the work we are doing now. We would make, not far off, the profits we make now – strangely enough. But I don't really want to do that I want to make this more long-term covering a number of services.

What is your personal brand? (Name your top three qualities, which enable you to run a unique legal practice.)

I had to think really hard about this. I try not to think like a typical lawyer. I try to be a little more commercial. Lawyers have a distinct way of looking at things. My business partners also help me in looking at things in a different way that has been invaluable.

I am humble. I contrast that with the old attitude that the client is privileged to have that lawyer representing them. I want it to be the other way round. Approachable – people feel I am straight talking.

Why your firm name?

We debated whether to call ourselves that or not. FTA as a brand, in the dentist industry, that is quite well down. It comes from the sister companies and is well known. Do we advertise the fact that we are linked to this broker? Or do we call it something different? The view I took is that it takes a long time and money to build a brand and if there is one already there, I think we shouldn't miss out on the opportunity to have that. The 'flip-side' is that we are so closely advertising our link with them, it did mean that other brokers who we had dealt with and have previously sent me work, would turn their backs on us. We were 99% certain and that is what happened in the early stages.

We get 65% from the sister companies and the rest it is from Sarah and myself. Whilst we were initially reliant on that, it lasted six months. They don't actively send us work like they used to but by virtue of people we know we have acted in that sector for a long time, we still appear on their deals – for the buyer on the other side. We act professionally at all times so they tell their clients that we do know what we are doing.

Is there anything specific you do to manage the quality of service?

We are still a relatively small company – we all tend to follow the same processes and have Lexcel running through it. Lexcel is consistently applied.

We ask clients for feedback at the end of the transaction through a form, which has ratings from one to five, and space for any further comments that sort of thing. We then follow up on issues. We also ask for testimonials to go up on the website.

If we start acting for somebody – and it is clear it is not going to end well – it is important to manage expectations and diplomatically transfer them to another firm. It may happen once a year – it is rare.

Also if they put pressure on us to drop fees then what I tend to say 'we are not the cheapest but by no means the most expensive'. I believe that our level of service justifies our fees that we charge.' This is because I have found that the clients that haggle the hardest on fees tend to be the most difficult clients.

What interpersonal skills are important to be successful with your type of clients?

Require a lot of 'handholding'. These are academically qualified people who do not understand the legal process. When someone new joins our firm I do explain that our dentists are like residential conveyancing clients in that they do require a lot of handholding. They are on the phone very, very regularly.

What makes it more difficult is that this is not done face-to-face. A lot of it is over the phone and email. I encourage our staff to try and keep emails to a minimum because it can be misinterpreted, and use telephone conversations. Particularly if we are delivering bad news, don't use emails.

Using the right tone of voice all helps to build that relationship of trust. I encourage them to have a chat with them about their interests to build that relationship.

Marketing online (websites, Twitter, Facebook, Instagram, LinkedIn, YouTube or other)?

LinkedIn, website, twitter, Facebook

Do you have a digital strategy?

Never had a strategy as such, but quite a lot of it is dependent on Sarah using her Facebook and Twitter to build her following and reputation. She has spent a lot of time growing her reputation in the industry. She has got 1500 Twitter followers, which is not a huge amount, I know that, but it is more than most.

No formal strategy for Linked In. If we want to get to the next level we are going to have to have a strategy in place for this. It will also have to be more than Sarah and me doing this.

We have done some videos of the team working and send the hot links out via email. So if they click on the links of any member of the team it will take them to a video of them.

Offline Marketing

We do a lot in the dental press by contributing copy on a regular basis.

There is a company called Practice Plan that deals with private dentists. There are two – the other one is called Denplan.

We are in with Practice Plan who do 'roadshows' where we present to around a 100 dentists in a room all over the country. We give them video content.

We do our own seminars, which we organise; we do better in the South.

How do you lead and manage them? Have you had any training? What would they say is your best/worst quality?

I am conscious of the need for us to be fleet of foot. Want us to be agile. I've seen it before in firms where it is so difficult to get a decision made. We have regular contact with staff. We have monthly support supervision meetings with every member of staff. In a previous firm I had no conversation about my next stage of career so want to do that here. Agility is the main thing.

In respect of training, various coaches have come into various firms I have worked at. I have had training – business coaches and some management training – stage 1 and 2. I have not specifically done this for FTA law. I have also sat and listened to various types of training aimed at dentists. There is a lot of crossover.

Best = being approachable and available to staff. Worst – not rigid enough with my own time management. Setting aside that time to work within the business rather than for it.

How do you develop your team? Do you use the SRA Competency Framework?

Do not believe we do use SRA competency framework. We have the monthly support supervision meetings with all staff.

Appraisal system in place – setting objectives for the next 12 months. If it's working for them and they are happy, why would we not be happy to support our people? We have trainees, apprentices, people doing their legal exams – we are very supportive.

What are your biggest team challenges and successes?

I will call it a team challenge – staff management, making sure everyone gets on with everyone, ensuring no friction and that it is a nice place to work. We do regular socials every four months. We go out somewhere and we've done wine tasting and we always have a Christmas meal in Leeds. We let them choose where they want to go. Sarah and myself leave at a reasonable hour so that we don't see anything we don't want to. Yeah we did that one year where we should have left long before we did. So we said 'Yeah we'll learn from now'.

Yeah I'd say make it the culture because we've always tried to recruit people who think the same way as we do really – who we think get the culture. We've had we've had a couple of staff where it hasn't worked out not in terms of serious things with people being dismissed or anything like that. We had one guy who came, and he didn't like what he deemed the capitalistic nature of a commercial law firm. He was a really nice guy and he said this is not for me and I am going to do something else. Another guy we got wanted to start his own recruitment business, and to be fair to him, he said I'm not going to get an opportunity like this again, and all the rest of it. He left on good terms. He's actually back in the law now. He gave that six months and he is gone to Clarion now. It's the staff side that is the biggest challenge.

I think in terms of successes, I think what we've got now is having such a good team. I think that's the best team success we've got. Everybody takes ownership of what they're doing. And I know it's a cliché but I do believe that our staff is our greatest asset.

Where do you see the your legal practice going the next three years?

Answered above.

FOUR LEGAL BUSINESS OWNERS WITH CONSULTANTS

1. IAN MCCANN & MATT DOWELL

Solicitors and co-owners of Legal Studios (Property, Crime, Business Necessities, Workplace, Disputes) www.legalstudios.co.uk

Why practise your legal expertise as a business owner?

Matt. This will be the third business I have been involved with directly – the first one was also a legal business but I and was also employed, which had to be kept a secret. The second one was just before the financial crash to get into property development, Plan B was to go back into the law, after having made the move to being self-employed I did not want to work for another law firm in a conventional sense – had the consultancy model back in 2008/9. I did not have enormous resources to back it up, had to start off from the bottom again by working as a consultant. I recruited someone as a consultant who introduced me to Ian – the rest has been a rollercoaster ride

Ian. A lot of things made me join Matt on this rollercoaster ride. The fundamental point I had got to in my career at that stage, was that I was working for another firm setting up their commercial litigation department. I was using my talent, my expertise and my contacts and ultimately my skills for someone else's benefit – I would then be disposable if successful or not. I joined as a consultant. We believe there is a better way to deliver professional services. Attractive to me is how services should be delivered. Business model – two sets of skills – I like business development and soft skills, going out and drumming up business. Matt is less keen on that. Two sides of a coin, which can be a part of a bigger and better whole. Having a team around us to share ideas – a better way to practise law as a business than on your own.

What is your best and worst business habit?

Matt. Delegation is one of my best; happy to delegate everything, could couple that with laziness. Worst is the inability to forget about the business – inability to switch off from it.

Ian. Worst – fundamental inability to delegate anything, learning to be less awful at that, not good at it, pain for me and for others around me. I would like to make sure something is efficient as it could be. Best – Ability to recognise where we are, we are going, how to get there.

How do you manage the 'highs' and the 'lows' of being a business owner? (Stress management) and/or what are you doing to build resilience?

Matt. Recently got out of the habit of going to the gym at lunchtime. Got a dog with which I go for long walks. Get home and enjoy cooking. Do not do many sports anymore. I try to switch off

Ian. I don't know yet. Need to do more exercise.

Who do you turn to for support and inspiration? Who would you like to thank for their support and why?

Matt. I turn to Ian and family and thank them for all their support. No one springs to mind for inspiration

Ian. Matt, I do not want to do it without him. Family and anyone who has been involved in our journey – everyone has had some role to play in our development. Inspiration – nobody in the law, and I think that says an awful lot. Fundamentally the people I find interesting are business people. Simon Sinek and Steve Jobs feature in many respects but as an individual and a person, absolutely not. As someone who created an atmosphere and a culture to allow talent to flourish absolutely. So for me its people who are in the tech and management industry, they understand. And Richard Branson is another one – look after your staff and they will look after your clients. And if you look at the legal profession, I couldn't think of one.

Did or do you have a personal or business vision?

Ian. Being a consultant solicitor before doing this did not inform our vision. I already had the idea before I got back into the law as a consultant solicitor so no.

Yes insofar as that vision has become much clearer and more focused. So if you are sat in a chair doing the job, the questions is 'so what drives you mad and what do you want to do easily?' Because actually if you had a firm like ours, yes our clients are end-users because the first level of clients are us. You actually need to do that 'walking in the customer's shoes' thing, having been said customer that was quite useful. It doesn't change a lot to your vision necessarily but a lot to the implementation. This is where we want to be and that is what it looks like.

Matt. It sounds very cheesy but – my vision was of an old mill building with nice windows and columns, exposed brickwork – people would come in and work collegially. I don't think that has changed at all.

Did you have a business plan when you first started - if so what worked and what didn't?

Matt & Ian. They both laughed. We did have a business plan and it is probably where I last left it four years ago, honestly. It is essentially this – to run a margin business, add bodies, keep overheads relatively low and grow. We grow by running a place where people want to come in and work.

What are you doing differently from the organisation you have left behind and/or the competition?

Ian. I think it is two things for me. Firstly, what you are focused on; and I think as an organisation what we are focused on is enabling our team to practise law. That is ultimately what they are interested in, what they have trained to do and what they are good at.

The majority of other law firms are focused on the big target – the overhead, the turnover, the controls whatever it is – they put in the systems and controls so rigidly to achieve that and manage performance and compliance by tightening the noose and making examples of people – well certainly, that was my experience.

The flipside of that is to say that we have actually brought in people who are very good at this, they have excellent skills. You know what, lets develop those; lets create an environment where they can do that. And those other things that other firms try to increase the lawyer's skill, which by its nature will reduce their legal skills, so lets not bother with that. Lets focus on what they are good at – play to their strengths. Lets create the environment that they can flourish in.

And the second thing that we fundamentally do different at Legal Studios is that no matter what position you are – an employed paralegal, a consultant or a member of the back-office team – there is an upside here. Whether that is in terms of bonuses or a package that we have – there is a benefit. And when the firm benefits so do you.

Now other law firms just don't do that or if they do it's not worth it. I got a bonus at one of the firms I worked at and when I worked it back against my hours etc, I would have been better off having another job at minimum wage. That is not an upside, that's just another stick to beat you with.

Competitors:

Matt. In terms of perception, you could argue that we are not offering enough, at the moment. The reality is we think we are the most compelling consultancy offering in the market by a long way. We pay more; we give more support, a proper office. We have real people and we have a personality – a nurturing collegiate environment that is growing and that supports people.

However, we haven't pushed that enough in terms of our presence, largely, because we haven't got the time. We are actively looking to address that at the moment. We are better.

Some firms are virtual law firms – we are not. We are a real law firm that has a lot of consultants. Some consultants work at home, but they are the minority. The ones that do best are the ones that we see the most of. It works better for them and for us.

I think that a lot of consultants who are working from home or their bedrooms are slowly losing their edge that makes them a decent lawyer – you need colleagues or may want colleagues or need/want to split work life and home life. May want people to banter with – to bounce ideas off. So we offer that.

Ian. Concurred.

What has been your greatest success to date?

Both laugh.

Ian. We haven't gone bust.

Matt. We must be making profit as we are paying tax on it but where it is God only knows.

Ian. At one stage wanted to put a LinkedIn advert for profit and if anyone finds it, let us know!

Matt. If you look at it, it is a thing to be celebrated. If you looked at our return on capital employed it would probably be one of the highest in the world as we have very little capital employed.

We have grown from 0 to a million turnover this year – not quite exponential growth but not far off so if we continue that for the next few years I would be very happy

Ian. Another answer to that – stopping being a start up. Maturing.

Matt. Moving from start up to consolidation. We've got the resources now that we have earned enough to put the infra structures in place. Instead of having to do it ourselves, we have people to do it, which should free up our time to do other stuff.

Ian. It is really good to say we have grown the business and it has matured. We have found our market and it works. We were right after all, for me that is the biggest success that we've had.

Where do you see the threats for your legal business?

Ian: Competition from other virtual firms for me predominantly. I think other law firms will eventually catch up on the idea but it is 'turning the tanker' around problem. They have been doing the thing that they have been doing for so long that they might send the instruction but it will take 40 minutes to get to the helm. And four days later they might turn and go in a slightly different direction.

Matt. I suspect that they will just go down the acquisition route.

What is your personal brand? Name your top three qualities, which enable you to run a unique legal practice.

Matt. Ian's top three qualities – incessant optimism, resilience, and creativity

Ian. Matt's top three qualities: Stoic and resilient. Someone who has to spend the majority of their life going "Ian no that's a terrible idea, shut up". This is really important. Focus is really important and Matt's focus has been great. Fundamentally, straightforwardness – as lawyers, there are not many solicitors where you don't know where you stand.

Why your firm's name?

Matt. My wife is Italian so when you walk around Italy you see 'studio legale' everywhere and we wanted a 'studio type' feel to working here. When I first raised it as a name, I got some negative feedback but I am pleased to say I ignored them.

Had a branding workshop lately – should know this. Creativity, pragmatism and honesty with a focus on striving to be better. If we are going to be better we have to look at creative solutions – be pragmatic about what works and doesn't.

Fundamentally we're going to have to be honest with each other as a management team and everyone else about where we are and how feel. Our strapline is – where different works – in order to achieve that, we're going to have to look at things that are different. There's a better way of doing it, and if you want to do it better you are going to have to do it differently and going to have to make it work

Is there anything specific you do to manage quality of service?

Matt. We deal with any complaints that arise. Let's say that is a movable feast. That is an area we honestly need to improve upon. I think we try and recruit people who are good. We know who is good and who is not good.

What interpersonal skills are important to be successful with your type of clients?

Ian. Our clients are our consultants/our lawyers, so it's a combination of patience, positivity and influencing

Marketing online (websites, Twitter, Facebook, Instagram, LinkedIn, YouTube or other)?

Matt. Area for development – we have web designers who we know well. They are in the next office. The website is on its second iteration soon to be third. The challenge we have is one of time. It is easy enough to pay someone to make a website pretty for you, but need to keep working the content. We recognise that we have slipped a bit in terms of content generation, simply as we do not have the time.

That particularly means areas like LinkedIn and Facebook. We actually met someone earlier this week that we will probably be employing on some basis or other to come in and fill that gap – for IT generally.

I think this legal industry hasn't got going yet, in terms of going out and getting new business using these routes but I am sure it will, in areas that we probably don't know yet.

Ian. It is quite interesting as some people call it SEO but lets call it what it is – online PR. If you look at online PR and you look at tech and LegalTech specifically. I have this really annoying habit which drives people mad by saying – 'Great – fantastic but why? What are we getting out of that?'

Where do those people hang out? Our primary channel now is LinkedIn as it's where our target market i.e. lawyers hang out and are easiest to get to.

You can spend more money than you can ever earn in online PR, and in physical PR if you don't know what you are looking for and you don't know how to find the people you are looking for, it is really a bit of a waste.

Offline Marketing

Ian. Our marketing and PR is dual-purpose, it is aimed at consultants and clients.

See also previous answer above.

How do you lead and manage them? Have you had any training? What would they say is your best/worst quality?

Matt. I leave that to Ian

Ian. The style I have adopted is servant leadership – sounds a bit odd/pretentious but it is neither of those things. The thing about management for me is managing and leading people – still find the concept of being a leader a bit odd but there we are. Matt does not leave it all to me despite him saying so. I do the 'talky' bit of it but actually it's about creating the environment for people to do it themselves. That is really hard – with our model, you can't force anyone to do anything themselves, neither can Matt, neither can our office manager.

Matt. My first degree was a BSc Management Sciences (Marketing) so I have been there and read the book! I am fairly cynical about this stuff. The only book worth reading is Dale Carnegie's first book "How to Win Friends and Influence People" which basically states how to say thank you and appreciate others and be constructive in your criticism.

Ian. If you are doing a piece of work for me, the only thing you can do is get the credit for a great job, you shouldn't get the blame for a poor job. I have had several occasions where I have been thrown under the bus with a client but one time my colleague was asked his opinion on a certain matter, to which he replied 'Hasn't Ian already told you? Does he work for me? Is he in our firm? Well then he has told you and I have told you – it is the same thing.' That has stuck in my mind – a huge exception to the rule.

No we have not had any training. Our best quality is empathy but it also our worst as it makes hard-nosed commercial decisions very difficult.

How do you develop your team? Do you use the SRA Competency Framework?

Matt. We are still a small company. We are actively looking to grow them and set them on a career – not the usual box ticking. Talking to employees about future plans and asking where they want to be in five years. How can we train you to get there?

In terms of training for our consultants, no we don't. My instinct is that most would push back against this firmly.

Ian. One of the things we have talked about internally and it is certainly in the pipeline for the future as it is quite nuanced. Trying to tell consultant solicitors that they need training doesn't work. I think that saying that 'there is an opportunity here with inclusive support' is how you describe it to the consultants. Look we have, within our system the ability to look at coaching or we have a webinar or a short workshop that might be of interest to you. We have the resources here if you need them.

Having that for our people to access is an aspiration. It's a work in progress.

What are your biggest team challenges and successes?

Ian. The challenges are creating a genuine, cohesive team when you are bringing in talented driven individuals with their own workloads and priorities and of finding a way to free up understandably engrained mindsets to match ours i.e. that things can be done differently in a professional services environment. Ultimately, that's down to us and how we lead and grow this practice and in making sure our recruitment processes are robust as this type of firm and lifestyle isn't for everyone. The successes have therefore been when we've started to see real team work and cross-referrals or when the team has come to us with ideas on how we can better serve their or a client's needs.

Where do you see your legal practice going in the next three years?

Matt. Bigger and better will do – more people, more sophisticated systems.

Ian. The tech piece, if you will, could get very exciting and I do get excited about technology. We take what we want to do, that vision, that brand and this forms the basis for every decision that we make. And we go, does that fit and if it does, then we pursue it.

Everything needs to work better, faster and more intuitively. We also check with our consultants to see how they want to use IT to their advantage too. So we focus on what it is that actually makes the difference. We know tech can help but it has got to make things better. And if it doesn't, then it is just another system that people can play with.

2. JOHN BAILES

Solicitor and owner of Bailoran Solicitors (Dispute Resolution, Insolvency, Company, Commercial and Employment)
www.bailoransolicitors.com

Why practise your legal expertise as a business owner?

I'll give you a brief background. I'm really from Leeds although I studied at Northumberland University. Then working as a paralegal at McCormicks, then moved to Lee & Priestly (which was taken over by Lupton Fawcett recently). Stayed 18 months, after that worked in Blacks Solicitors for about eight years. Did a mixture of commercial litigation.

I wanted some say in my personal circumstances in relation to getting married. I suppose I've realised that we wanted to go travelling and kind of see the world before we settled down. Realising that I wanted a large family. We want four but have three at the moment.

This is the way forward now. In relation to the challenges of leaving a position at Blacks, it seemed quite scary. But I was confident with my skills and that my wife was a very good lawyer as well. And we had good relationships with people in the legal profession where we were working at Blacks; and my wife used to work at 3-volution and as such we could come back to any job, should we need it.
So an opportunity arose that I could become a consultant for a smaller firm over in Dewsbury, which has since gone sadly. I then consulted

a fee-sharing basis for about a year and that actually allowed me to test the waters so to speak as to whether or not I had sufficient client contacts and could generate work for myself. And I found that could.

I'll be honest that the firm I was at didn't necessarily have the same drive that I did from my background business. So there are certain standards that I would expect to want to provide to clients. And I thought it would be easier to do everything right, the way I wanted to do it and provide a client service; and that's why I set up as an authorised practice.

So I am a limited company and a director of that rather than a traditional partnership or LLP. It means that I effectively have control over my own destiny. In relation to that, I was not as fearful because I had tested the water and I realised that the benefits would be self-evident through the company structure. Financially you don't have to earn as much or bill as much to take home the same, purely from tax reasons – dividends rather than P.A.Y.E. I think when I was at Blacks the difference on taking home the same amount as a wage as opposed to via a company structure I was immediately £7000 better off. So that was working by myself without the rule you must bill three times bill your wage or if you're in a large firm by five times. So in relation to that it was realistic to do. Luckily I'm not particularly a material guy so therefore having a house I can't afford didn't apply.

I am always prepared to live within our means and reinvest in the business. I am a big believer in if you do what's best for the client, look after their interests and take their worries away, you can't really go wrong. Don't dabble. If it's not my area – don't take it. I don't take it for a quick fee or it undermines what you do. There are better people out there who will do it quicker and probably cheaper as well. It's just not worth it.

So lucky that I have had 50 contacts I suppose that I have built up from networking since I was – it's probably – 24 and I am 40 now. It's what you put in when you are younger in establishing relationships. I think I was always encouraged to do that. Roger Hudson was my boss at McCormicks and now the managing partner at Clarion. They went out networking and encouraged me to do so. Again when I moved to Blacks Chris Allen was a big believer in going out and meet people – go to their office – take an interest in people and its difficult to fake that.

Let's be honest litigation is transactional. So I am in the very fortunate position to get repeat work, not from clients but from their contacts by looking after them in such a way that they are happy with my best service.

What is your best and worst business habit?

I think the worst is I'm not as efficient as I should be. I think you need to be disciplined. I find that I work well under a degree of pressure you know because of the litigation. I thrive on that. But there are always things you can move forward. I enjoy the pressure; it tends to get the best out of me. Sometimes as a business owner, you realise that when it is quiet it's not the time to make life easier, although I recognise it's not as hectic and exciting. Especially as I realised this office has seven of us trying to grow it, so a lot of people need my time.

So before when I was an employee I could manage my time and it only affected me as long as the client was satisfied. Now other people want my time and the time that I lose is the time they may have to stay behind and that has a knock-on effect. So that's one of the worst things but I am trying to get better. I have been on a number of courses, read books and making myself accountable has changed my day. So trying to move on that.

Best is – I hope I am open and approachable. I'll try and help anyone whether it be in work or outside. Pick up the telephone. If you can solve their problem in five minutes – happy days. That's made my day really. The problem for you really isn't a problem for you but for them it's keeping them up at night. It's nice that you have the knowledge to do that. And they come back to you when they need you for a proper job.

What we do is actually sponsoring a local charity. It's also very fun. So we set up a 'just giving' page for the bits of 'free' advice, as it is not worth the paperwork to bill. So I ask them to give a donation instead. In the last nine months, people have donated over a thousand pounds collectively. So that's something given back on the basis of free advice and someone else has the benefit.

For me it's not necessarily about the money that comes with hard work and doing a good job. Don't be rushing to the money every time.

How do you manage the 'highs' and the 'lows' of being a business owner? (Stress management) and/or what are you doing to build resilience?

Being a dad! I think the highs; everyone can celebrate in – the staff, the clients and at home. My wife is happy that I am having a great day – kids are too young to understand.
Lows – again it is the problem solving part of the job. I think you have to not take it as personally as naturally you instinctively do. You need to step back. If something has gone wrong, then address it. Are you to blame? Then instinctively thinking I don't like this situation – where

can I lay the blame? It maybe a very natural reaction. Assess it. Get someone else to look over it. The lows can be pretty low because there is only you to deal with them and it's your problem. I think that the people I've got around me are very supportive in both situations. If you are surrounded by a proper team, they pick that up as well and they do a great job in relation to that. Luckily there have been very few lows.

Who do you turn to for support and inspiration? Who would you like to thank for their support and why?

My wife.

Because of the system I have got in my business, I have a number of consultants working here rather than employees. They come in different age ranges and experience. And as long as it was appropriate and not related to staff, I am happy to ask for support. For example, if it is about clients I talk to them and ask their opinion because you don't know everything. You might think you need to know everything but you don't.

Because I dealt with insolvency I thought I did know how to run a business on the basis that I seen and helped people save their business or recover from the loss of the business, but that was purely financial. Clearly if you don't account for you tax then you are clearly running an insolvent business, then its going to fall over.

That's very different to managing people to doing the legal work and setting up operating systems and recruiting. I do staff alignment and see what their goals are personally, rather than what's fit for me because if we grow as a business I want them to be happy rather grow apart from the firm and you never knowing. And that could be financial reasons – it could be time – the family – holidays.

So yes I will use people in the office and ask for their input. It is amazing what you get back. We have quarterly meetings and we will discuss certain things. For example the telephone system wasn't very good. Alexia is the youngest person who works for us part-time – one day a week. And she said ' Well Martin, we need a proper telephone system with integrated multiple lines'. And my immediate thoughts are how much is this going to cost. Actually it worked out to be significantly cheaper than the system we were on. It was far more professional. So listening to other people around you works.

I still have ties with other solicitor firms where I have worked. I think

it is difficult as a business owner. There are some groups that you can reach out to and get support.
Well I did some business coaching for about six months. That was useful purely because I needed to have a grassroots level management and business acumen.

Happy to ask many people even clients in different situations. If I have got a sufficiently strong relationship I will ask for their opinion. It's not legal; it is essentially how to run a business really.

Within the groups they let you get to your own answer for your own question a lot of the time; and give you the time to reflect on it. It is very obvious to the group sometimes but it's not obvious to you because you're so close.

Did or do you have a personal or business vision?

Yes. Which is to coach and help because as I said in my situation that works; and then more people join you. The difference is this is the best job you'll ever get paid for.

You're creating something that can work without you and I would like to do that. Ultimately I would like to run the business and not necessarily work for it. The idea is I want to be a niche practice. Firms are either becoming larger or niche. The small high street firms are struggling. If you do what you are doing and you do it well, then you can compete on any level no matter what size as long as you are an expert on what you do.

I would like to grow the business to around ten people, with a £1 million pound turnover, and with a 40% profit, which is quite high for a solicitors practice. I would like to be known as the 'go-to' place for commercial litigation. A lot of my clients are in difficult positions – following insolvency, the banks are pursuing them, I do not want to work for banks, I am happy going against them, I want to fight for the underdog, because I think often they are put in this position because they are good at what they do but that does not make them a fantastic businessman or director.

So you are a good builder, good plasterer and have been advised by the accountant to go limited for tax reasons but they don't understand the responsibility and implications of being a director and how they pay themselves. For example, they're still putting their holidays to Malaga through business accounts, their company fails, they're asked to pay that back but they have no idea why. So I do feel there is a degree of naivety and that they need to be protected to a degree, banks may take advantage and change the overdraft to loans,

I would like to be a firm that has a reputation for quality, for fairness and ultimately value for money because a lot of the time you charge an hourly rate, and people do not know how long a letter is. Which is a good question, as it depends on the information we need, the documentation, the amount we are talking about – is it £100 or... as long as the clients understand the value.

Did you have a business plan when you first started - if so what worked and what didn't?

Business plans – I am quite spontaneous and reactive. If I have ten ideas, I want them done now. Now what happens is that none of them are done or all of them will get done but not well. So spreading out in a way so you are not trying to sprint on all of your ideas is good. You grow it at a more organic pace and it does not detract from family life as well. The benefit of working for yourself is that you keep your own hours, same with the consultants.

What are you doing differently from the organisation you have left and/ or your competitors?

We get paid to do a job and problem-solve: and to help our client over a hurdle. Often it is quite stressful when they come to see you so you need to make that as painless as possible. And they want someone on their side – they don't want someone saying – yeah it's tough isn't it? You shouldn't have got into this situation – so I try never to be judgemental. These things happen and I wouldn't have a job otherwise. Let's not dwell on how we could have done better – let's resolve the issue and then there will be time to reflect on this. And I am there as well to help them get it better next time. Yeah, maybe depriving myself of future work but's that's the best thing for the clients and they appreciate that.

Another thing we do is that we do not take a case unless we can put the client in a better position than they were in before. If I can identify and say, I'm sorry, having reviewed this, you are in a terrible situation. You might actually go bankrupt which would be better in these circumstances then there is no point taking that client's money because it reinforces the stereotype that solicitors only bill for time and do not care about the outcome. You have to think 'if this were my money what would I do, would I be willing to part with it and what would I get for it?'

What has been your greatest success to date?

I would say building a solid team around me that allows me to spend time with family during holidays and I know that people are answering phones; cases have been progressed, although they can call me in an emergency. To be able to build a team within five years a team that I trust fully with the operation of the business; and I know that their hearts are in the right place and that they are doing the right thing. So the correct recruitment and getting the right people, that's got to be my best success rather than any financial thing.

Where do you see the threats for your legal business?

My structure is consultant based. Junior solicitors may want to be employed for the security of it and their pension, and in relation to that to get a mortgage. Having said that the consultant model for me restricts overheads, which is a good thing for me unless clients are paying. Risks are attracting potential future directors and solicitors who are potentially scared by a different reward scheme for their work. It is the traditional structure – bill three times what you earn, it works for me but may not work for everyone. Reduces the pool of available candidates. Tends to be more experienced ex-partners of other law practices.

What is your personal brand? (Name your top three qualities, which enable you to run a unique legal practice.)

I care about the client and the outcome; therefore we're in this together. I'm there to advise you the best I possibly can but I am trying to take some of the stress away.

I will get nervous with some cases when I go to court because I want to win. Not many times I get nervous in my life but going to court is one of them. Caring about the outcome so that they are able to go to bed at night not worrying have you done the right thing or have you overcharged. These are all basic principles but it seems that you should set them out more clearly – it is a very human thing. You have to put yourself in the client's position – you are being a victim. You do the extra bit – working late, I am happy to do so because that means a massive deal to them and it is not just the bill at the end of the day that motivates me, it is the outcome. Have I got their back? Has the client got a result? Actually caring. There are many solicitors out there who genuinely care in the niche practices because they appreciate the business and those personal relationships with their clients – where they can call on a Friday night if they are worried and you would take the call. That ability allows them to set up on their own. They have those connections and you are not just a number – the clients don't want to be just another number.

Why your firm's name?

I did think about that at the start – I could have chosen John Bailes & Co but it seemed 'ego-driven' but I wanted something that could potentially be transferable and not just be about me.

Is there anything specific you do to manage the quality of service?

I have got certain procedures in relation to answering the telephone to file-opening – all the operating stuff.

Clients want to be spoken to on the telephone and solicitors want to send an email – you have to work to what the client wants, even if it may take a bit longer, clients will appreciate it. Big thing for clients is costs, saying what you will do and how much it will cost and not saying 'well how long is a piece of string?' So whenever I send out things for litigation cases I will send flow charts of how it will work and an estimate of how much it will be. Then when I next see them I will tell them how much we have billed and see if it matches their expectation. It is about being transparent.

Never send a bill on a Friday, because they are then worrying about it all weekend. If you raise a bill, tell them it is coming. Half the time there may be a misunderstanding about the work. Softest skills are not necessarily legal skills – treat others how you would want to be treated.

What interpersonal skills are important to be successful with your type of clients?

Being human – putting yourself in the client's position

People realise we are providing a service; as such there is a lot of competition out there. A lot of people will go off recommendations, which is quite scary but it is about appreciating every case that comes through the door, because they could go anywhere. And why have they chosen you? Well they have chosen you because how you make them feel.

Marketing online (websites, Twitter, Facebook, Instagram, LinkedIn, YouTube or other)?

To support and endorse your credibility in the marketplace that you need to have a good website. We have just revamped ours, because the website before used to reflect me when I started up. It now reflects my team and what we want to be and what services we want to be providing. Changing that has certainly made a difference.

We are on LinkedIn and we post regularly. Rather than just talk about us I will try and give free advice or forward interesting things that will help people. Rather than saying 'I can do it, does anyone need a solicitor?' No one wants to talk to a solicitor as a general rule because its always bad news. So being in litigation it is about if you do this you won't have to see me. People will benefit from that and they know I am not doing it just for a job.

We have Twitter but I don't run that myself. I don't get clients from Twitter but it certainly makes people more aware of you.

I don't get any work from my website via enquiries or LinkedIn particularly but I think what it does is it makes people – certainly in Leeds and Yorkshire aware that we exist. Whereas before, you weren't brought to their attention. We are in a local location in Chapel Allerton not the centre of Leeds; the footfall of people who are going to see your offices is low.

Offline Marketing

Vast majority of my work comes from recommendations and meeting people face-to-face. Whilst it is old school having a chat, can you do the business? Whether they trust you means a massive amount so that will always be my personal focus.

Again the telephone – I know that isn't a strategy but it's the little things that add to the degree of professionalism that you know that you can provide which makes a difference to certain people.

Networking. Attending and meeting people at seminars is what we focus on. The other is just gloss. 'Word of mouth' recommendations and testimonials and things like that go far further.

How do you lead and mange them? Have you had any training? What would they say is your best/worst quality?

I have attended a couple of chief executives meetings but I didn't join as I think that is more for business owners discussing their problems rather than on focusing on how to solve them and management and leadership.

Reading books that I never thought I'd read. Other than that no formal training.

And working with other people – Keith the practice manager he helps me get through so much administration and everything else really, the running of the business can be delegated to him to a degree, his management of people is phenomenal really, he has been instrumental in having regular quarterly meetings and having feedback in relation to work done. Not having meetings for 'meetings' sakes. He's been good at helping me in managing staff. There is not too many of them but it is a question of their priorities and managing my time.

My best habit and my worst – I would like you to ask my staff. * My best is I try to deal with everything put before me and give my full attention to the individual. Having said that time pressures of client service mean they don't get as much of my time as I would like. My worst is, perhaps, a lack of prioritisation.

* The staff I contacted has confirmed that they have found him, very caring and willing to give his time. He encourages them to be the best that they can be, both professionally and personally. His worst is – he expects them to mind-read and they do recognise that the time pressures on him does mean they don't get as much time together as everyone would like.

How do you develop your team? Do you use the SRA Competency Framework?

I wish they hadn't changed it – it adds another level of assessing what you do and don't know. At least before with 16 hours you had to do a number of hours that were largely relevant and by osmosis you would be brought up to date.

The consultant solicitors are aware of it as these are the ones it affects. I ask them to maintain their training records, keep up to date and assess that.

The Law Society has quite a lot of videos and that sort of things. They're not too bad. It depends on what it is and where you are and what level. It is different for everyone in relation to experience and what area of law you are working in.

What are your biggest team challenges and successes?

Success – awards –you and your team have been acknowledged and satisfied the criteria for that award. It is nice to be recognised within your profession. For a small business, what you give to the clients is so big; doing applications is a great way to show what you and your team have achieved throughout the year.

Challenge – biggest challenge is getting the right candidates who want to join and are not worried by the consultancy, altering the structure doesn't affect what I have done. Being transparent.

Where do you see your legal practice going in the next three years?

I would like to get to that ten-person team – it will be difficult but as long as they are the right people, that is the most important future growth goal. I would like client and staff satisfaction to be really high – nothing below four out of five. I want good workers who want to work hard for the clients. I am not trying to be the next Walker Morris – I would like to see my children.

Anything else you would like to add?

I feel lucky and grateful for the continued support – no matter how big you go you will always remember the support. To anyone else thinking about it – just go. If you work hard for anyone else, you will work hard for yourself. It will not come immediately but it's worth it.

3. KIRSTIE PENK

Non-practising In-house Solicitor and co-owner of The Legal Director limited (supplying business-focused in-house lawyers to companies) https://www.thelegaldirector.co.uk

Why practise your legal expertise as a business owner?

I am not sure I do "practise my legal expertise" now. I certainly use the commercial expertise I learnt as a senior General Counsel, to run my business (TLD) now. I have not done any direct fee earning work for about three years but spend a lot of time working with clients and our team members to help them achieve their own commercial objectives.

What is your best and worst business habit?

Best is probably I always try and understand the urgency of what I need to do and am pretty good at managing expectations on my time.

Worst – is probably not saying "no" often enough or finding someone else to delegate stuff too?

How do you manage the 'highs' and the 'lows' of being a business owner? (Stress management) and/or what are you doing to build resilience?

As I work from home it can be quite difficult to 'switch off' from work-related things. I have definitely got better at that over the years. In fact we took a three-week holiday to New Zealand at the end of last year and I took the email app off my phone so that I couldn't check it whilst away. It was tough for the first two or three days and then it was surprisingly easy!

I also plan regular exercise into my diary. For me, that massively affects my mental well-being.

Who do you turn to for support and inspiration? Who would you like to thank for their support?

My husband and business partners (including our Chairman). I also have a mentor who I access via the peer-to-peer mentoring organisation Vistage.

I did read Michelle Obamas book over the summer and thought she was truly inspirational.

I would like to thank my parents for teaching me the importance of education and that you can achieve if you work hard. Also my husband for supporting me to do what I love doing whilst we raised our children (the two time commitments have not always been compatible).

Did or do you have a personal or business vision?

Our vision is every SME should be able to access the services of an experienced General Counsel.

We want to be recognised as the UK's leading provider of part-time general counsel services. We are the leading provider but the key bit here is to be 'recognised' as such

Did you have a business plan when you first started – if so what worked and what didn't?

We created a formal five-year business plan when we appointed our Chairman in 2015. It was at his instigation. We are about one year behind the goals we set ourselves as the plan for the three of us (the co-owners) to stop doing fee-earning work took longer than we had projected. Now the three of us don't do any fee earning work, run a team of 34 lawyers and spend all our time running and growing the TLD business.

What are you doing differently from the organisation you have left behind and/or the competition?

The last organisation I was working for was a wireless computer networking business that I was a co-owner of too. I was very much doing all the 'hands on' legal work there and spent a lot of time raising funds for the business. Although I helped set the strategy of the business I was less 'hands on' in the implementation of the strategy than I am at TLD.

No one else provides the service we provide to businesses and is a regulated law firm. There are lots of virtual law firms now (compared to when we started the business in 2009) but they do not provide the part-time sole in-house GC role that our team provide. Our lawyers only work for six or seven clients at any one time. A traditional law firm model (even a virtual one) could not support that.

What has been your greatest success to date?

Last year we grew our revenues by 44% to £3m. I'm pretty proud of that achievement.

Where do you see the threats for your legal business?

A large business, such as an accountancy practice, could decide to throw several millions of pounds at creating what we have from scratch and setting up an ABS. Having said that, we would see this as further seeding the market and helping with our sell to clients. We could also have several of our team members' leave as a group to set up a competing business – we work pretty hard at team retention and trust with our team members. In the 12 years we have been operating we have only ever lost one team member who took a large client with them.

What is your personal brand? Name your top three qualities, which enable you to run a unique legal practice.

We have four values – Supportive, Open, Enthusiastic and Decisive. For supportive, we want to help both are clients and our lawyers to achieve their goals. When I say open I mean we are equitable in everything we do and we embrace new ways of working. In respect of enthusiastic we wand to have fun doing this and have clients enjoy working with us. Lastly, on the decisive value we don't sit on the fence and we provide practical solutions.

My three qualities are:

1. Anyone I have worked with will say I am commercially focused and that is key to everything we do. I have never given 'sit on the fence' advice.
2. We are open in our dealings with our clients and team members alike.
3. We are passionate that this is the best way (in terms of value for money, efficiency and use of management time) for an SME to access legal services.

I have been shortlisted for the Forward Ladies Regional awards for 2019 in the Female Entrepreneur category.

Why your name?

Our name is ideal as it says exactly what we do – 'The Legal Director'. We did consider such things, as 'Your General Counsel' but not all business people understand what that term means. I think TLD has stood us in good stead so far.

Is there anything specific you do to manage the quality of service?

We have a very tight recruitment and induction process and only have lawyers in our team who have at least ten years PQE. We are also very good at selecting which team members will be best matched with which clients and so have had very limited issues on this front and it has usually been around personality fit or client expectations.

We have a CRM system that I have made bespoke, based upon a Microsoft Dynamic platform. We track all leads, client opportunities and candidates via this system.

What interpersonal skills are important to be successful with your type of clients?

The first one is openness both with our in-house lawyers and the clients themselves. We have full disclosure on fees charged to our clients for our lawyers. This means that we have transparency with both our clients and the in-house lawyers.

We want to enjoy working with them and the clients and so arrange social events to encourage this.

The key thing for our clients and in-house lawyers is that they are commercial. They do not 'sit on the fence' but are able to provide frank commercial advice with recommendations for the client who they are advising. This is a key difference to private practice and us, as in-house lawyers do not have the luxury of just advising and leaving the clients to choose.

Marketing online (websites, Twitter, Facebook, Instagram, LinkedIn, YouTube or other)?

We use our website, LinkedIn and YouTube to promote and sell. We have a tried and tested referrals programme using LinkedIn which gets us both new clients and new team members.

We do have a digital strategy, which we have worked on with our outsourced marketing director supplied to us via Marframe Limited.

We measure cost, opens, click throughs, BANT leads generated, conversation rates and revenue generated on a monthly basis. We also know our cost per click through and cost-per-BANT lead generated.

Offline Marketing

We hold regular meetings with all of our team members and work with them on developing a business plan to help them to mine and convert their connections we also have lead generation personnel reaching out to centrally generated opportunities. These come primarily from our website, networking events we attend and referrals from existing clients, old clients and contacts.

How do you lead and manage your team? Have you had any training? What would they say is your best/worst quality?

Our team is a tough crowd. They are all senior lawyers who have choose to work in our team usually for a variety of reasons. We know one of the things they value is the 'team' itself so we, as the leaders of the business, spend a lot of time making sure the team has as time to network and build relationships with us and the other members of the team. We do this via regular 1:2:1 meetings, regional lunches and quarterly meetings of the whole team. We communicate regularly with the team via formal and more informal methods.

We are constantly reinforcing and communicating our vision and values in everything we do with the team. These are values representing the way they can expect us to interact with them and how we all must act in dealings with TLD clients.

How do you develop your team? Do you use the SRA Competency Framework?

Our team are all self-employed senior individuals. We have one to one sessions with them each month and will look as part of those sessions at how they want to develop as individuals and as lawyers.

We subscribe to several platforms to get our lawyers a discount on seminars, webinars and distance learning for a variety of skills.

We have quarterly team meetings where we will always engage tw0 external speakers on things that will be useful for the personal development of the team or for their relationships with their clients.

E.g. we have had one on how competition law affects SMEs and another on Diversity and Inclusion training for us to flag issues to our clients. We don't use the SRA Comp framework per se – except to remind our team what the rules are.

We have used an organisation called Kiss the Fish for sales training and give such training to our team members too.

What are your biggest team challenges and successes?

Convincing some great in-house lawyers we meet to make the leap and join us is our greatest challenge given that lawyers are typically a risk-adverse group.

Our greatest success is in the number of successful women we have in our team. Women make up 50% of our team but of our top ten billers last year eight of them were female.

So although the flexible work arrangements work for women to fit around their other commitments (e.g. child care) that is not the way many women use our model – they are using the model to have a very successful (and well-remunerated) career that gives them the flexibility they want.

Where do you see your business going in the next three years?

We have plans to grow from 34 lawyers to 50 next year and then 90 the year after (by mid 2021). The challenge for us will be how we recruit another level of management whilst taking the core (very successful) team with us on the journey.

LEGAL BUSINESS OWNER - NO TEAM

1. CLAIRE MURPHY

Solicitor and sole practitioner (Commercial Property)
www.clairmurphylegal.co.uk

Why practise your legal expertise as a business owner?

It's something that evolved really. I was in the wrong place and the wrong time in the recession, ten years ago now. I had been headhunted to head up a satellite office for a Sheffield law firm while I was based in Leeds. Then when the recession hit we retrenched, and I was the most expensive salaried person in the business and so I was made redundant.

At that time, in commercial property, there weren't many opportunities to go into another partnership because work levels were reduced so I drifted into consulting for a period, in that I had a lot of clients and contacts but I needed to service them somewhere and I wasn't entirely sure I wanted to set up my own law firm. Did that for a few years and picked up some more complex work for other practices that had had pared back their commercial property expertise too much during the recession.

I always thought I'd go back into a partnership, but gradually began to realise I quite liked working independently but I didn't like working as a Consultant. Working as a consultant in my experience, I appreciate it's different for different people, it was – go out, get work, do work, bill work, collect the fees and then I was finding a lot of payment issues with law firms. In fact in a number of cases I had to issue proceedings to get paid for my work that I had brought in and done. I thought, well, I can lose that element of the process straight away. I had a decent pipeline of work; I had more than three years of decent accounts, effectively as a quasi-sole trader. So I decided to set up my own law firm and now we have been going for nearly five years. Not really looked back – not the classic entrepreneurial journey in that it wasn't always something that I wanted to do. There are pros and cons of anything but I do like the autonomy and the ownership.

What is your best and worst business habit?

Best and part of my USP is delivery really – the whole personal approach. In terms of clients I always start from the end and I ask what are you trying to achieve by when? And then I see the legal process as being helping them to get to point B, and not unnecessarily putting many other points in between the start and the end. Tailoring the service to their end goal and approach during the service. Not very original but came up with the strapline 'bespoke property solutions. This is because I do think I have a solution-driven approach. It is not commoditised; I only do the complex, messy commercial property stuff. I have a very clear business niche and that's very successful for me.

Worst – perhaps not unusual with entrepreneurial types, I am a bit of a workaholic and struggle with not being satisfied with things, which are not done to my level. I do struggle with delegation, which is not great, as a business cannot survive without a team albeit a small team.

How do you manage the 'highs' and the 'lows' of being a business owner? (Stress management) and/or what are you doing to build resilience?

I think it gets easier, in that I have got a lot of years under my belt before I set up on my own, so I already had a very strong business reputation and a strong business following. I was already quite well known in the business community. Most recently, I have been very busy and been a victim of my own success, and that has been quite an uncomfortable position.

Whilst my financial turnover for year-end, this year is going to be almost double last years, with very little extra resource. This is great on the one hand, but on the other hand that brings a lot of lows with it. I have had quite a few incidents this year where clients have said your delivery times have been pushed out, they're saying you're not delivering in the way you normally do, and asking what's going on?

I have had to have quite difficult conversations about the fact that I have had to recruit assistants but that assistance wasn't going to be there until September, that is not a very comfortable place for me to be. I am a bit of a perfectionist and I do not like having that kind of dialogue. I would always like to be above expectations rather than at or slightly below expectations – although I do accept that the expectations that clients have of me, and the reason they instruct me, may be higher than they would expect normally of the competition.

Cash flow in the early days was a very big issue but obviously not so much so as the business has become more established.

I see exercise as a stress relief and I try to manage that around what I am doing. I am a member of a 24-hour gym.

Because I am a small business, I try to not take more than a week's holiday at a time. I find if I leave it longer than that I find it difficult to manage client's expectations and even within that I end up working large chunks of it. Trying to manage proper time-out and perspective.

I do a lot of work with other lawyers who are of a similar size and a lot of specialists who are referred to me. There is a lot of peer group discussion if nothing else about management, indemnity insurance etc.

Who do you turn to for support and inspiration? Who would you like to thank for their support and why?

Other lawyers who have similar values, similar backgrounds and respect and also have a lot of clients who are small businesses so there's a commonality in understanding.

Lots of different levels really. My husband for general business matters. Mentoring level, I have two mentors. 1) A lawyer who I worked with when I first came out of London, 2) A lawyer who I worked with when I was fairly junior and learnt a lot from in terms of client management, drafting and running meetings – that kind of thing in the late 1990s.

Recently, I'd like to thank a lawyer who contacted me out of the blue through LinkedIn and referred a client to me who I have billed the biggest fee I have ever billed.

Did or do you have a personal or business vision?

Probably not as clear as it ought to be. Certainly when I started out it was I'm either going to be a partner at 30 before my contemporaries or I'm not. When I set up on my own it was very much this is what I enjoy doing so carry on and to service clients, gain more clients. Almost a victim of my success and now I am too busy. I am exploring getting other people to work with me, but having been in partnership at several firms before, I don't want to grow for the sake of growing or spend all my time managing people and holidays, sickness etc. my vision is to carry on what I'm doing, carry on making a living out of it and grow it to a level where I can get more time out of it for myself and so the business is not 100% me. That said I doubt it will be 50/50 with another or others – but it might be that it runs without me for a short amount of time, which is my goal. Ultimately, in terms of exit, to create something that someone else would want to buy so that I would have an exit, which is the longer-term plan.

Did you have a business plan when you first started – if so what worked and what didn't?

I did have one because I had to for the insurance and the SRA – I would probably be lying if I said I look at it and work to it every year – I don't. I did do it properly at the time and think it through. I probably do think in the same strategic way but to put it all on paper would take a bit of time, which is a flaw in a small business. Pretty happy with how things have worked out.

What are you doing differently from the organisation you have left behind and/or the competition?

I get my work from clients who are not happy with the service levels they are getting from competitor firms and generally I get my work on the basis that I am the partner, the director. So they are meeting me, and you either like me or you don't because what you see is what you get and it is what you will get down the line. I'm not that person you meet at first meeting and then never see or deal with again or you are passed down a pyramid of lawyers. You are buying me for the price of a junior with a competitor. I am here and I will answer and deal with things. I have the city expertise and large firm expertise. Surely a no-brainer!

The only feedback I get is that there is only one of you, we are conscious you may not be able to do all of our work at the same time as there is only one of you. That is something I am trying to address by having someone more senior come in on a part-time basis working with me, quite a lot of success with that as I get a lot of work referred to me from other lawyers as I am a safe pair of hands. But there is no personal element to it. Recently I got referred an office lease in canary wharf for £100,000 a year, that has come from another lawyer I know, as I am a safe pair of hand. That is working quite well for me.

I do realise that I am from a different era in a way. For example, when I was in a meeting trying to agree documents to exchange with this particular lawyer, he was emailing me rather than calling me or coming into the meeting room. And then when I was chasing him, he asked me 'had you not looked at your email?' and I said 'No I am in a meeting room with my client. Why would you email me?'

So I am now realising that there is a whole generation of lawyers who don't have the ability to sit in a meeting room, and hold anyone's attention or even explain their point in a way where it comes across in a less-legal technical jargon. If you like they appear less professionally sophisticated in a way people can understand. They won't deal by telephone and will only deal by email? I am increasingly finding that a big, big differentiator. I have gained clients regularly from that, from putting a plan in the middle of the table, talking about everything on that plan, and before you know it that client thinks – 'well you know your 'stuff'.'

What has been your greatest success to date?

Last year I had a poorer year than I had the previous few years because I had a client, which had gone into administration. I managed to get paid out after a lot of negotiation and manoeuvring – this client had a lot of work on a monthly bread-and-butter basis, and so any one month I would have two or three jobs for them. They would be quick in and out jobs with a quick fee. Quite a large hole there.

Having worked my contacts a lot during the earlier stages of my career and a lot during the recession when markets were depressed, I had been busy enough and I hadn't really needed to work my contacts particularly. So I thought, I'm going to work my contacts and get some work. Out of that, I managed to have four very large client wins. Any one of which on their own would have been plenty to fill this gap, that's not even including the other job that came to me out of the blue I referred to earlier

Stepping back – Gained that work because I had the contacts to make the introductions and appealed to the people in the right way. Reaping the rewards of 20 plus years of networking, hard work and delivery. My first experience of reaping it so quickly was when the market was more buoyant. That has been my greatest success – the new client wins.

Where do you see the threats for your legal business?

Anything to do with me, if anything happens to me – under the weather, incapacitated, then the business suffers because of the way it is. Other threats – if you make any noise about what you do then you are putting yourself up there for other people to target your clients, although I always think that is a threat in business.

I think there is a tendency to think that just because people know whom you act for that then they are able to get them, but I think it is far more complex than that. I think competition is always a threat but I don't see it as a massive threat to my business, in that I don't do residential. I try not to do low-level work. I'll do it if I have to do it but to turn it away would actually be damaging to the business. So for example, if I get work from the local area, from the local business people I will do it but I do not seek out the lower-level work, so therefore the whole commoditisation of legal services doesn't really affect me.

The other thing is there are threats in that any one person can move from an organisation or organisations can decide to only use legal panels and these types of things. I think where I am at right now is that I have a small share of an enormous number of pies. And so I could lose a few shares of those pies and grow the other shares without gaining any new clients. So I think at the moment, the only real threat that keeps me awake at night or causes me concern is that I am a sole director business. I haven't managed to find another person who is on enough of my wavelength. I am actively looking but haven't quite found them yet.

What is your personal brand? Name your top three qualities, which enable you to run a unique legal practice.

Personable, professional. By professional I mean I have a very high level of integrity. I am very driven and by that I mean not just driven by my business or my goals and achievements but also for my clients. They want to get somewhere by a certain time and they are not giving me what I need, in terms of instructions to get them there, then I will be reminding them of that and telling them of that. Proactivity, ownership, accountability on behalf of clients and in my own business.

Why your firm's name?

In terms of firm name and brand, these are the same. I had a strong personal 'name' as a specialist commercial property solicitor before setting up the firm and this was my brand so I decided to capitalise on this when I set up the firm.

Is there anything specific you do to manage the quality of service?

It's evolving, if I am honest. Whilst I am a perfectionist, I'm not a great person with systems. I like to, if I'm passing something to someone, empower them to make their own decisions, how they deal with it and how they run it in a bespoke way. I do struggle a bit that way if it is different from the way I operate.

The way I am doing it at the moment is that I have an open plan office – so we are working in the same office – there is a lot of dialogue as to what would you do on this or that – ad hoc. I appreciate and realise that may have to change if I grew any more than I have already. That is not necessarily something I want to do.

What interpersonal skills are important to be successful with your type of clients?

Important to be 'straight-talking' and not dress up the whole legal process with any kind of mystery.

I think managing expectation is quite important with the type of clients I have, there are a whole range – some that like to be micromanaged and be copied into every piece of correspondence, there are others which do not read correspondence or do not answer calls but still need to be engaged with. A lot of it is knowing the client and what does and doesn't work with that client – not seeing it as a 'one size fits all'. I do not have a standard way of doing things – dependent on what the client wants. Having an interactive dialogue and approach and ask 'what do you want'.

Marketing online (websites, Twitter, Facebook, Instagram, LinkedIn, YouTube or other)?

Ad hoc.

Don't go on LinkedIn every day nor do I post regularly. 'Likewise' Twitter but I have to be on Twitter so I do a lot of 'likes' – more around parenting than work now. Thinking of closing down my business Facebook page but have not gotten around to it yet.

I'm in the process of re-doing my website – need to put my new colleagues on there. It is a slow burn because it keeps on taking a backseat to work for me. So watch this space for me in the next few months.

I am very clear, I don't use any of these things as sales tools; I use them as shop windows. So my only goal is to present the right shop window and the shop window that accurately gives people a picture of what I do and what I can do for them, more particularly. It does not need to be fully up-to-date at any one time, it just needs to give them the right vibe, the right feel. The know-like-trust – and there is nothing more to it than that really. That all it has to do to match my business and clients. I don't have a digital strategy. I was a very early adopter of LinkedIn and the results were fantastic. What has worked for me, and what I did then was writing my profile in a certain way with certain buzzwords. Joining certain groups. I now use it less so, as I am constantly being approached and I accept every single invitation (to link) but I don't necessarily interact or sell to them. I sometimes respond or not depending on who it is but I am constantly told that I come up in every search for anything that I might want to do or to connect to. For example I had a really big client win from LinkedIn a couple of years ago where I literally didn't know them from Adam. I have never met them, did not have any connections in common.

Offline Marketing

In terms of PR and marketing, the majority of my business comes from existing clients and referrals so, other than having a website (still in the course of being updated) and doing the odd mailshot/ social media post and press release, all my marketing and PR is at networking functions and in one to one meetings.

How do you develop yourself? Do you use the SRA Competency Framework?

I am registered in all the right places and done all the right things over the years. I would like to say that I do everything I've got to do redevelopment over the year. I certainly start off with those aspirations, and sometimes something has to fall by the wayside.

For example, I've been on the SRA conference for two years but not for the last couple of years. Thinking of going on it again this year because I wear all these different hats and perhaps the slightly drier stuff of practice management, I need to know about but don't need to go every single year.

On the 'know-how' side I have a favourite provider that I have always liked to go on his courses. He does commercial property only.

Where do you see your legal practice going in the next three years?

I would like to be a slightly bigger team but no aspirations to double, triple or merge in particular. I have been approached by other firms to merge but at the moment, all the other firms I have spoken to would see it as a takeover. But I think – where is the benefit to me? I see myself as a small profitable team. Would be nice to have a better handle on profitability. Could expand into subletting another office.

2. GEOFF PETER

Non-Practising Solicitor and sole practitioner (Disputes with house builders) www.wingrovelaw.co.uk

Why practise your legal expertise as a business owner?

Mainly the autonomy and to be able to choose how I work and who I work for and that's not a choice you get in a commercial firm – certainly not as a junior employee.

What is your best and worst business habit?

Worst and best business habit is the same – flexibility as I spend my time on my work. I have three3 kids under five and see an awful lot of them. This makes it very easy for me rather than being an employee, and I don't have to commute to Leeds, which is where I used to work. Working from a home office means I can pitch in. At the same time you can spend more time doing work, which does not pay the bills.

How do you manage the 'highs' and the 'lows' of being a business owner? (Stress management) and/or what are you doing to build resilience?

There are different highs and lows – emotional and financial. I have been very lucky with the financials, what with the home office. All business has been mostly online. You know that I am very insulated from most financial shocks. I don't take any risk in terms of borrowings or anything like that. So the financial highs are when you finish a case and get a big payday.

Only a couple of cases haven't gone to plan but they have turned out profitable. When you work for yourself, those are the most valuable cases in a way, because they teach you how to do your business properly and avoid making the same mistake again. So you do learn from your mistakes.

In terms of emotional highs and lows, then I think again when you are concentrating on a single project which is what I do in my specialism – a very narrow niche – take a bit of comfort from the client with whom you form a close relationship with.

Who do you turn to for support and inspiration? Who would you like to thank for their support and why?

No-one living! Other people who run small businesses from my contact list. I have contacts in YSPG – speaking to other legal providers and finding out what works and what doesn't. Mainly on the administrative side more than anything.

In terms of what my natural project or plan is for my business that is a very personal thing. What I do is a combination of what I have done in the past.

Confidence comes with experience. Reflective time and making sure the admin is right, making sure the job is done right on a daily basis.

I would like to thank Rachel Roche who was very helpful at the beginning of setting up my business.

Did or do you have a personal or business vision?

Yes – very much so. Again, as I said before I arrived where I am because of what I have done in the past. A lot of it is common sense. Equally it feels right because I am using all of my skills that I have accumulated not just from the legal career but most of my life – so personal interests and non-legal skills. My education included a science degree.

Did you have a business plan when you first started – if so what worked and what didn't?

Yes.

What are you doing differently from the organisation you have left behind and/or the competition?

Choosing the work I will do and not doing the work I don't want to do. I have spent my working life working for the builders but really wanted to work for the homeowners. So now I can. These demographics don't get much access to legal advice.

What has been your greatest success to date?

Staying afloat as a business and individual successes for my clients (99%).

In terms of the business, when you do litigation you settle and then you get paid – definitive outcome for you and your client who, for example, has the defects put right.

Biggest success is that, in my particular field, is that I do know what I am doing and it is a viable service that people find valuable.

Where do you see the threats for your legal business?

Very few threats in terms of volume of work out there in the field that I specialise in. They are always going to build new homes and badly, so that the workflow is not a threat.

A major threat could be reputational. If one of the cases I am working doesn't go right – if I drop the ball, essentially that could have a direct impact on my firm, as I am very high profile in a very small field. This in turn could impact on my ability to generate work.

The other major threat is security. I am involved in the building industry, and at some stage could become a threat to the business models of some of the biggest corporations in the country. And these are not corporations that necessarily employ the most sophisticated people. So I am concerned that the business continues to grow and particularly as we reach a certain scale, about personal safety. Therefore I have taken steps to limit social media exposure for example. Also maintaining privacy and home security. So have to be a bit vigilant and use my common sense in my response and attitudes when I come up against those who may take a direct response.

Those are the concerns but not necessarily major ones in the general scheme of things.

What is your personal brand? Name your top three qualities, which enable you to run a unique legal practice.

Persistence and compassion for my clients who are often in a distressed state. I am always looking for quicker ways to achieve objectives. This did not make me popular as an employee where billing for time was important because if I could do a job in ten minutes not an hour – that works for me as I am bringing value to the client relationship.

Why your firm's name?

I called it Wingrove Law as Wingrove is my middle name.

Is there anything specific to manage the quality of service?

I practise in a very niche areas and breaking new ground so I use my unique set of complimentary skills for this area to ensure the quality is very high.

What interpersonal skills are important to be successful with your type of clients?

In addition to compassion and persistence, enthusiasm, integrity and realism.

Marketing online (websites, Twitter, Facebook, Instagram, LinkedIn, YouTube or other)?

Do have a website. Use the rest judiciously given security concerns. Don't use Facebook and I don't post pictures of my children. Twitter marketing (in the first few months only) very occasionally since then.

Offline Marketing

I don't do much advertising or marketing as there are so many people in my specific sphere of demographics and work finds me.

I know a few people who are in key positions within the industry who have property websites and a lot of traffic and pass on my details voluntarily. I don't have a professional relationship with them. Or they find my name online if they are doing a bit of research.

And I have clients who have membership of large Facebook Groups who have 1000s of homeowners and they put on my business details on that.

There is a plan to push a certain amount of marketing and advertising for my next project of up-scaling what I am currently doing. But today I have not had a huge amount of need or experience of.
Key marketing activities to date include giving evidence to a government enquiry into new build quality (seven of ten recommendations were based on my evidence). I have also made contact with other key individuals who support my pro-homeowner agenda including owners of the main property websites for new build owners, who refer work my way.

How do you develop yourself? Do you use the SRA Competency Framework?

No, no formal business training other than things like SRA Management training, which is compulsory for junior lawyers.

I read management and other books for inspiration – e.g. Amoeba Management by Kazuo Inamori; Buddhism texts; eastern philosophy;

various books with spiritual overtones or that concern spiritual practices; yoga; mindfulness. I also speak to people who run small businesses for ideas and tips etc.

Do you have a development plan?

Yes. I work on myself, like any business owner.

Where do you see your legal practice going in the next three years?

I don't tend to concern myself with the prospects of others in a similar position or the profession as a whole; my focus is on my business and how I can best serve the interests of my clients.

3. JAMES THORNTON

Solicitor and co-owner with Frank Arndt of Paradigm Family Law (Divorce and Separation, financial disputes, civil partnership breakdown, mediation, children matters)
www.paradigmfamilylaw.co.uk

Why practise your legal expertise as a business owner.

Well as a business we engage with clients in our own unique way. We can choose our approach and we can be flexible about how we service those clients

What is your best and worst business habit?

I would say our best or my best business habit is perhaps the social media site marketing strategy. It is very apt that we're speaking today. Just last night we did our monthly 'UK Business Hour' on Twitter. We were asked at the outset of setting up our business to do this. It is a coincidence really but the guys who developed our logo run this 'UK Business Hour every first Thursday on **#UKBusinessHour**, and they invited me to run this. I have done so for the last four years or so.

So it's nice that Paradigm Family Law gets its name out there to the users; and the followers of the UK business are in their tens, if not hundreds, of thousands. So when we were just setting up we have very few followers and we want to maximize the Twitter opportunities. So we've been doing that – I have been doing that religiously for the last four years every first Thursday of the month – even on holiday. I sit there wherever I might be and I engage with all these people who are tweeting their business interests and it's a very focused hour – our followers increased in a very short time. It becomes a bit addictive almost but it's quite enjoyable. My worst business habit is that it plays into that a bit – finding the boundary between work life and home life.

I have just given you an example – doing the Twitter hour when I am on holiday. And I guess being able to bring your son to work. Yes that's the good bit – one of the advantages of running our own business is that we're not going to worry about asking the boss for time off to go to our kid's sports day or for us to watch England play, whichever. But yeah that's a big plus.

How do you manage the 'highs' and the 'lows' of being a business owner? (Stress management) and/or what are you doing to build resilience?

Yeah well, I think it's been about trying to set boundaries to work life. Stress is a word that sounds negative but you can have positive stress that drives you and that which makes you feel that you want to do something and then there's negative stress. Yeah but we try and to see things in a positive light generally.

If it's the busy stress, not the negative stress then I think it helps if there is flexibility as well because if I say to myself I don't feel like doing work, generally I can do that.
I'll stop at lunchtime and maybe work a bit later in the evening. Where as in a 9–5 job you got to be there regardless. You are champing at the bit to leave by five if you can. We don't have that. So I think it's helps me to manage stress.

Who do you turn to for support and inspiration? Who would you like to thank and why?

Family friends and colleagues.

I put colleagues first depending on what it is that I'm looking for – business issues, colleagues support. If it is about a 'bad' day then family friends to sound off. I'm lucky Frank was a friend before he became a colleague so I have the best of both worlds. You know we bounce off each other depending on which of us has got issues going on.

Did or do you have a personal and/or business vision?

I think probably the same – want to create a successful legal practice that impacts on our industry. We didn't want to just be a family law practice; we want to make waves almost. We hit the fixed fee idea because nobody was doing fixed fees and we saw an opportunity and the demand from clients because it's all about clients and what they want from their lawyer. Yes the service but they want to know it's a fair price and a reasonable price and they know what the price is.

So often with lawyers it is 'how long is a piece of string?' or it is between this amount this and that amount? We thought we would stick our neck out and use our experience as know what we're doing, to come up with this formula. We apply it to all our cases and we say from the outset this is your fixed fee. Clients love it because they know what they are letting themselves in for. We want our clients to know that we're offering value at the end of the day. People value their sanity more than anything else and they say 'okay for this price I'll get my divorce sorted'. You could go buy a car for a fixed price – they buy a loaf of bread for a fixed price so why not legal services? They know what they are getting. For that you are getting your divorce, your kids, and your finances sorted out. There's nobody else committing to a fixed price to sort out the financial side

Yes it's one less thing because it's a traumatic time for them and it's one thing less to worry about. I've been on the phone ten times this week and they don't need to worry about that because they are on a fixed price.

There are some firms out there who think fixed pricing is low in the market and they put junior Staff on it – but we're not junior – 20+ years qualified. So they're getting a top level of service to buy. So it's not about a race to the lowest price. I think you can add value through the service. We can do everything online – we can access the documents remotely. All of those are actions that are necessary.

Did you have a business plan when you first started – if so what worked and what didn't work?

Mostly it seemed to work. We always knew we wanted a paperless office system. We spent a lot of time trying to find the right case management software package. It's called LEAP. It's one of the fairly random things that we found quite early on and got on-board. It's on every device we have. We can look at documents wherever we are, in court, in London, Manchester or York. The overheads are lower. We have not got enormous storage facilities because it's all in the cloud. They're extremely responsive you know if you are having any issues. We don't pay for an IT guy.

So you put on your business plan you are going to be paperless but how do achieve that? Law is not always easy because you do have paper. You know we have got judges who rely on paper – barristers too. But you can at least e-mail stuff to them and make them print it out AND physically get it from A to B. That by itself helps, as clients are not waiting for mail to arrive. It's not a case of letters in the post out tonight. Suppose then the next day he gets it – none of that. It's an email, scanned in and within a day we've done three or four actions on a file that would have taken a week without the paperless option. My clients are happy with it on a PDF and that's good enough for them.

So that was a big thing and it really works. It took us no more than a line on the business plan. It's something that helps us as it means we are faster. Some of the other lawyers you come across ways are just waiting for the snail mail to arrive. So, yeah, that's been a real plus point.

What are you doing differently from the organisation you have left behind and/or the competition?

See answers above.

Yeah, the only other thing I would mention is the team spirit we have engendered here. We were sharing a room before so we were a team in that respect but we feel much more now that we are together again.

So the idea that we're all we're all working to benefit the whole as a single entity and there is just more goodwill about the whole thing really. There isn't any kind of resentment or feelings about the hours that you work.

What has been your greatest success to date?

I think the fact that we are still here, four years on. We've grown year on year. I mean we still have grown – double year-on-year.

And we are recognised. We are really chuffed that the Law Society recognised us in October/November – that was an Excellence in Business Development recognition. They picked up on the fixed fee USP that we've got because I think the profession recognizes we are going that way. The judiciary wants fixed fees and we're ahead of the game in that respect. So it was nice that our trade body recognised that. There are lots of awards out there but this is the Law Society

Where do you see threats for your legal business?

We don't like the word threat as we see it as opportunity. We see things as being challenges and opportunities to improve things like the way we see technology.

The opportunities out there for artificial intelligence to apply to law. We see the potential for things like Alexa where people are searching for or searching for advice. They don't go online to physically type stuff in. They are speaking to Alexa or an equivalent. So we've been trying and investing in ensuring that we get found via those kinds of searches not just someone typing into Google. It is also the armchair lawyers and ones down the pub. I've got this situation and type it into Google. You get all sorts. Half the time it's American or from Europe.

So those aren't threats but people are going more online to sort their own problems out rather than take professional advice. That's an opportunity for us. That means that we should be making more of the fact that we are there for them. In fact we get so many more inquiries because of the stuff we put out in blogs. We try and write our blogs in such a way as to match the questions trying to ask you what to do. So what would someone type into Google? Therefore we put all that stuff into a blog.

Yesterday a guy from Romford read the Schedule One of the Children Act that was in a blog I wrote three years ago. He said I've got a family and I found you guys because you've got the most informative blog I have ever read on this subject. Just applies to what I am going through and I'd like you to act for me. You can't put a price on that really. We would never have got that client from any of the traditional networking or advertising unless you are nationwide but we are online nationwide.

What is your personal brand? Name your top three qualities, which enable you to run a unique practice.

Personally, my personal qualities are, I think I am tenacious. I think I am calm and collected under pressure. Yeah, I think that I have an entrepreneurial spirit. There are so many lawyers who want to be good lawyers but not be their own boss. I am both.

Why your firm name?

Paradigm Family Law. Well we hope that everybody knows that we are the fixed fee firm family lawyers. Can't say more than that – it's all over the website.

Paradigm means 'a perfect example of something'. We had not thought of the number of different ways people might try and spell it or pronounce it.

Another bizarre perspective is that a Google search on the word brings up a number of judges who use that word in judgments. – 'Paradigm shift' or' this is a paradigm?' And every time we see it – it is not always us that they are talking about. But it's that kind of word that gets used not only in the legal sphere but across the board.

The brand is the fixed fee family law. Very keen to keep 'on message' not dilute it.

Is there anything specific you do to manage the quality of service?

File and peer review – monthly meetings and daily talks.

What interpersonal skills are required to be successful with your type clients?

Empathy. Patience and determination

Every now and again stepping back from this process just to the point where you think this is something that's happened in their personal life, which changes everything.

They pay in instalments and it is a fixed fee. What we offer is a staged process through a full service to court so each stage is individually priced. It takes probably six or nine months from start to finish and we are happy to spread that cost. We don't say 'pay upfront'. We can take payment in instalments and set up a direct debit. First place I have ever worked where they are ringing me saying 'can you send me an invoice please, I want to pay you for this month's instalment.'

Marketing online (websites, Twitter, Facebook, Instagram, LinkedIn, YouTube or other)?

All of them.

We use Google Analytics to track any increases to our website following our Twitter activity. I mean when you go out to the UK population and those shows are really equipped to do it, it is worthwhile tracking this. I forgot to mention we got we got re-tweeted last night in a twitter conversation which arose from the business hour by Alex Read. We flagged up the news of the latest divorce of Katie Price and wondered what Alex Read would think. And blow me Alex Read was watching and starts likening the posts. So we now, Paradigm are on Alex's Read's feed. We don't necessarily need Alex Read as a client but the fact that it is exposing us to his list is fantastic.

Offline Marketing

It's the same.

Physically it is going to the odd lunch/breakfast/evening gatherings – business network. Well everybody is a potentially a client yes – but traditionally you'd be talking to accountants who might have lots of wealthy clients or estate agents, valuers who are instructed on things that might need us. So they will have their professional contacts that can be introduced to us.

You don't say that you are the cheapest or are the quickest or you get the best result because you can't predict that therefore you can't promise those things.

York did not have many niche family law firms. Clients would travel 20 minutes to go to somebody else that is not in Harrogate if they are known in Harrogate. We're not far away. Even Leeds comes to us!

How do you develop yourself? Do you use the SRA competency framework?

We are ticking all the boxes.

Where do you see your legal practice going in the next three years?

Other family practices behind us. They are desperate to know about our fixed fees. This is because their business models all revolve around hourly billable hours changing every hour so they are scared of fixed fees. Can't wait to go-to-go home but I have to sit here and do five billable hours. Billable hours is just wrong.

Where is the model that says what a divorce is worth? We know what our turnover is going to be more or less because we know we've got all these divorces on the books. We've quoted all these prices and we have taken all these on the books.

We know our cash flow and we are not chasing clients nor have we got lots of debt collection. So now we have done away with away with that in one stroke. There must be ones that we don't make as much money as we might have done if we had done an hourly rate. There are so many more that we have priced right.

4. JANE WINTERINGHAM

Non-practising Solicitor and owner of Adel Wills Limited (Wills and Powers of Attorney) www.adelwills.co.uk

Why practise your legal expertise as a business owner as opposed to a Solicitor?

It gives me the freedom to do what I want, allows me to work with clients in the way I want, obviously still following the legal structure and formalities, I just wanted to work for myself and give my time to my clients the way that I want to rather than feeling the clock ticking and bosses suddenly breathing down my neck for time recording.

Why did you choose not to be regulated by the SRA? I had been a solicitor for a number of years and also worked with the Crown Prosecution Service. I had taken a break from the law so was coming back into the forum. I was looking for an alternative from the S.R.A., which was not attractive to me as a sole practitioner. I investigated various professional Will Writing institutions. The one I chose was the Institute of Professional Will Writers (IPW). I came off the roll of solicitors. I re-qualified – I went and did the studying followed by a closed book written exam, an oral exam and a will drafting exercise. This involved accounting for the reasons for why I had chosen particular clauses. With other providers I could have done an open book exam but that did not sit right with me. I wanted to go back to scratch and learn it properly. With the IPW I still have a code of conduct to abide by, an insurance obligation and the bonus is that it is Trading Standards Approved.

Under the Institution of I am required to have up £2 million of insurance – public liability as well as professional. The IPW is also approved by trading standards, which is quite unusual; I don't think any solicitors firms are approved by Trading Standards. Therefore their code reflects that and is compliant with Trading Standards.

What is your best and worst business habit?

Best = building rapport and the relationships I have built with my clients. I am also a trained coach so that gives me the ability to build a deep rapport with people so they then trust me back and I can then ask them questions. I believe that has enhanced my ability to work as a lawyer.

Worst = I have a very untidy desk but I know where everything is.

How do you manage the 'highs' and the 'lows' of being a business owner? (Stress management) and/or what are you doing to build resilience?

Accepting that it is going to ebb and flow. Having been in business before, I realised there is certain life cycle to work – my life cycle to work is say between two to three weeks, from taking instructions to doing the work and then processing it. That is what I aim for depending on client's needs. In sales terms I am always looking to fill the sales funnel, with that you have to accept that there are quiet and busy times of the year, and not to get anxious. If you go quiet then you have to be business developing. So I know if I go quiet then I know I have taken my eyes off the ball as far as business development is concerned.

A lot of the stress is self-induced – I am a perfectionist. I have horses – when I am looking after my horses – that is my stress management. It's what works for you. Ying and yang – you cannot work all the time you have to switch the brain off.

I work during the day, and evening appointments, I also work some weekends if there is a real need. I do not advertise that but I will work weekends if the client requires it. I divide my day up into three – mornings, afternoons and evenings. If I am seeing clients or working in the evening then I will have part of the day off – I will not work a full day and the evening. The joy of working for yourself is you can choose what you do and when you do it. I fix the client appointments for when it suits the client and then I work around that. There will be days, which I block out and go out somewhere.

Who do you turn to for support and inspiration? Who would you like to thank for their support and why?

I have a mentor – a second pair of eyes. A gentleman called Rex Sevier. Once drafted I run my wills by him and he checks them for a small fee which includes written feedback. When I was in private practice not many people really checked my work, you could go to your principal but you were very much on your own and then you might be frightened of asking a stupid question. But I find with Rex, I can ring him up and ask him anything.

Women in Business network – Paula Gizzard who runs the network that has helped me with both peer support and business development support so she is the one person I would thank. There are too many people to mention.

Did or do you have a personal and/or business vision?

I am a quite a believer of letting my business grow organically. So what I learnt was that it was about getting traction. Have to put a lot of effort into the front end to get that traction and getting known. Letting the niche find you. To begin with I would do anything for anyone – it was about getting the business in, I would offer half price wills, to offer good deals and get the experience.

Two years on, I have realised my niche is 50-year-olds and above who are realising that they are not immortal and that they have to get organised – some people may not have children, may be estranged or the children may have gone. People have to realise they have to be self-sufficient and be organised and they want to do that – that is more my niche.

Did you have a business plan when you first started - if so what worked and what didn't?

After a year in business I actually went on your course – The Business Brilliant Blueprint – it was a very useful process to go through. It has helped add structure to my business. Structure was needed because my business had grown organically. With Ann's help I sat down and considered all aspects of what I needed to work on and looked at my competition etc. The Business Brilliance Blueprint training allowed me to really define both my offering and my business. It has really helped me to take my business to the next level and play to my strengths.

What are you doing differently from the organisation you have left behind and/or the competition?

My offering is different – I do not look at myself as competing with anybody. I am great believer that people will find you and that you attract different people. When I was a coach I was getting paranoid that there are lots of leadership trainers around but what I learnt was that you are like a tuning fork, you will resonate with certain people and others will not resonate with me. It is about finding the people that do resonate with me.

What has been your greatest success to date?

Enjoying what I am doing.

Where do you see the threats for your legal business?

Me – I am the one-man band. I have support with bookkeeping but I do everything cradle to grave. Advantage – I do not have to supervise anyone. I use a virtual assistant if I need to.

What is your personal brand? Name your top three qualities, which enable you to run a unique legal practice.

Professionalism, energy, approachability

Why your firm's name?

For my training business it took six months to decide on a name. I live in Leeds, in an area called 'West Park'. I was aware that if I wanted to go into any directory, 'A' would be at the top and my surname begins with a W so that would also be right at the bottom. Adel is the next area along from me. Would I go back and change it if I could? I probably would because I want more emphasis on lasting powers of attorney.

Is there anything specific you do to manage the quality of service?

Support from will writers and the education process I went through. The Institute of Professional Will Writers has a compliance officer and so I have been contacted to say that I will be having a compliance interview in the end of August. That is a transparent process. This is another safeguard for the general public so we have to comply.

What interpersonal skills are important to be successful with your type of clients?

Ability to get on with anyone, not to judge, have patience and the ability to listen. Having conversations to gauge the audience e.g. if it is a businessperson talk in bullet points.

Marketing online (websites, Twitter, Facebook, Instagram, LinkedIn, YouTube or other)?

LinkedIn, Facebook – I tend to lurk, do not do much with my business page; I use them both as an address book. Majority of my clients are not on those platforms.

Do you have a digital strategy?

No. I have built my business is around face-to face contact because it is a personal service. People buy from people, and people want to know me.

My website is what I would call a 'vanity website' so it is three page website. If you Google my name you will get my LinkedIn profile up first. So I have spent some time getting my profile, somewhat correct. The aim is to add a few more articles.

Also I try and add value to people, so If someone is asking for a contact or a top tip, I recommend people I know through business, and that's how I help That's how I tend to do it, professionally by recommending people or flagging up useful articles. I don't use it as an active business development tool for my clients because the majority of my clients aren't on those platforms.

Offline Marketing:

My marketing strategy is strategic networking. It's also identifying my referral partners or likely referral partners. It's also adding service and value to them.

It's about giving talks, so I have a speaking strategy to support getting the word out. If people see you answering questions interactively they see your expertise. My talks are not 'stand up and deliver' but more interactive so people know how you work.

Do you have a plan for personal development/business development?

The Institute of Professional Will Writers has the usual 'you must do so many CPDs points a year' so that is continuing professional development. They have a variety of courses and I will use that and I will source different courses to add to that. It's about keeping your knowledge fresh.

Where do you see your legal practice going in the next three years?

I see it growing – the clients I deal with like that personal approach, they do not want to go into the centre of Leeds and have parking problems or a faceless office. I do not go suited and booted – I go smart casual. It is about the rapport you have with people.

5. JILL RUCKLIDGE

Solicitor and sole practitioner of Rucklidge Family Law (Divorce, financial settlement and child arrangements)
www.rucklidges.co.uk

Why practise your legal expertise as a business owner?

I practise as a business owner and not as a consultant Solicitor because I like to control the ethics and ethos of my practice. The flexibility and autonomy that running my own business provides is also important to me.

What is your best and worst business habit?

My best business habit is organisation; I love to organise and structure my matters, accounts and compliance records.

My worst is not being able to shelve what's going on and walk away.

How do you manage the 'highs' and the 'lows' of being a business owner? (Stress management) and/or what are you doing to build resilience?

I manage the highs and lows with support from my husband, friends and family. I build resilience from taking plenty of walks with my dog!

Who do you turn to for support and inspiration? Who would you like to thank for their support and why?

I turn to my husband and friend, who has her own firm. When I bring on my new consultant solicitor, she will also be included in this group.

I would like to thank my husband for his unconditional and sound advice.

Did or do you have a personal and/or business vision?

Yes, to treat people how I would like to be treated, only take what you need and have a work/family life balance.

Did you have a business plan when you first started – if so what worked and what didn't?

I did and what didn't work were the times I was meant to work!!
What are you doing differently from the organisation you have left behind and/or the competition?

Not taking on the volume of work so that I can concentrate on quality and attention to the clients.

What has been your greatest success to date?

My greatest success is continuing to run the firm and not folding!

Where do you see the threats for your legal business?

The greatest threat to my legal practice is me and my ability to be too hard on myself and to worry too much!

What is your personal brand? Name your top three qualities, which enable you to run a unique legal practice.

I would say that my three top qualities are: that I genuinely care (and sometimes too much), to listen and identify the true problems and obstacles, to stand up where others might not. My brand is a caring and personal service.

Why your firm's name?

I chose the name of my firm because thought that using my own surname would increase credibility and familiarity with the brand when they see that I head the firm.

Is there anything specific you do to manage the quality of service?

I send out client satisfaction questionnaires to all clients at the end of a matter and invite feedback throughout to manage quality of service.

What interpersonal skills are important to be successful with your type of clients?

Active listening, compassion, communication of ideas and advice, patience and understanding.

Marketing online (websites, Twitter, Facebook, Instagram, LinkedIn, YouTube or other)?

For promotion I use the Internet, Google ads, landing pages and LinkedIn. I also do a lot of networking and I am a member of the Yorkshire Sole Practitioners Group and we pass work to each other in the group.

Offline Marketing

Google ad advertising campaigns, targeting focused service requirements that you can package into fixed fees.

Do you use the SRA Competency Framework for personal development?

I develop myself through courses offered via a variety of sources, such as your good self, the local Law Society and a professional organisation of which I am a member, Resolution.

Where do you see your type of legal practice going in the next three years?

Expanding by taking on carefully selected consultants.

6. SIMON ROBINSON

Sole Practitioner and joint owner of Robinson Ralph Limited www. Robinsonralph.com

Why practise your legal expertise as a business owner?

Sick of making money for other people – would have stuck with it if it hadn't been all the politics, back-stabbing and nastiness. I got to the point where it would make me ill.

What is your best and worst business habit?

Best – Getting back to them really quickly and not making the client feel like an inconvenience.

I probably spend a disproportionate amount of time on LinkedIn, even thought I get a lot of work from it. So I need to find a way where I can keep that profile up but not let it take up as much my day as it does currently.

How do you manage the 'highs' and the 'lows' of being a business owner? (Stress management) and/or what are you doing to build resilience?

Got to be honest, I haven't felt any lows. All been really positive. My wife is very supportive.

Who do you turn to for support and inspiration? Who would you like to thank for their support and why?

You, when we first met I did not have a clue what I was doing so those meetings were really useful in getting my thoughts organised. So that is something I would recommend that people get is a business coach because you can't think of everything yourself. It's just impossible.

I have friends who are lawyers and have set up their own practices e.g. Jeremy Rowland, of Rowland Law. He is incredibly giving of his time. Friends who are in traditional firms like Ben Daniel who was my boss at Ford & Warren and has been incredibly supportive. Also Jodie Hill who set up a few months before I did.

I would like to thank Steven Marge who did all my compliance stuff with the SRA and Gareth Milner who got my insurance sorted. Use other trusted experts in their field to do things properly. It can take up to six months for the SRA process and Steven got mine done and approved in four weeks. This included no follow up questions at all.

My mum and dad. My wife Juliet. I wouldn't be where I am today without Juliet – her support has been immense.

Did or do you have a personal and/or business vision?

Yeah, I have not formalised it yet as it is a work in progress. Generally I would like to be hiring a junior lawyer or a paralegal in the next few months but I want to see how the billing works out. Then maybe hire someone more senior either at senior associates level or partner level but if I was to turn it to a limited company or to a Limited Liability Partnership it would have to be someone I know and trust – there's very few of them.

So I would then want to get a commercial and a corporate property lawyer and turn it into an entire commercial firm. So it would never be something like Shoosmiths with 20–30 working. I am not really interested in that. It's more about having decent clients

Did you have a business plan when you first started – if so what worked and what didn't?

It is a bit too early to say. On the client side, no one who said they would come hasn't come, and clients who I wasn't expecting to come, have come.

The cost was much less than I thought it was going to be, particularly of this office. That's another tip; as well I would get an office. I found having worked at home for a year, whilst that was necessary to detox from the environment that I had been in, having an office keeps you focused. Even where you rock up at 9.30 or 10.00 you do get so much more done.

What are you doing differently from the organisation you have left behind and/or the competition?

Honestly probably not very much. I think it comes down to – people instruct people. Part of why they instruct you is that they like you. So just be yourself, and only work with people you like, if you can afford to. I am lucky that I can.

Don't take on favours for people. Don't take on work at a cheap rate. I will do favours for people if they are not trying to exploit that good will.

I do buy into people and their business. I don't just view it as a file and I go out of my way if they need something resolving quickly, I'll do it. So I think I am responsive, and I know what I am doing. Solve problems quickly. I am good at what I do and I charge a fair rate – do not over or undercharge.

So there will be people who will just like my style, and obviously people who won't

What has been your greatest success to date?

I think if you don't believe in your own product, no one else will. So I am finally sat in my own office, with my own firms name on the door, with my own clients, and not having clients saying they want to work with the big boys. Having national clients wanting to work with me – it is humbling. That has come from the effort I have made on social media and my weekly updates to show people I know what I am doing but I also not 'Lawbot 456'. I am real with a personality.

Where do you see the threats for your legal business?

Not Brexit because it does not matter what happens. Employment law is up there with death and taxes. You are always going to be hiring and firing people.

I am not particularly bothered about a Sainsbury's or Tesco kind of thing where you would fill in loads of forms online, because the type of the work I do requires human interaction.

I suppose the threat is the bigger firms, not necessarily the national ones, who can say if you give us the employment law, we have some one who does commercial – corporate etc. So because I don't do that and would have to refer out that work, it may put some clients off but I have a plan to address that going forward. Also if a client likes you, you are going to be with them through the years, it won't really matter.

What is your personal brand? Name your top three qualities, which enable you to run a unique legal practice.

Top three qualities are being responsive, taking time out to solve problems quickly and don't overcharge. I do love the social media thing and I do a lot on LinkedIn.

Why your firm's name?

The practice has just been set up and I wanted it to reflect Juliet and myself. Using both names allows us to expand. I also want the logo and colours to be bold, brash and fresh, which I think the Agency delivered on.

Is there anything specific you do to manage the quality of service?

I have been a client to other lawyers in different situations where you are ringing up to book an appointment to complain about something, it is just how you felt at the other end of it. So I say to my clients, if you don't like what I am doing – don't stew – tell me. I'd rather that than think they haven't called me in three months.

What interpersonal skills are important to be successful with your type of clients?

When I ask clients what are your current solicitors doing wrong they say they will either talk over them or be condescending. That is so not good.

Have to have a sense of humour, in the right place. You want people to feel better – one of the best compliments I get.

Second best compliment is when a client says, unprompted, we view you as an extension of the team. That is brilliant.

You have to actually care – if you don't then it comes across. You have to make time for clients. Not charging them for everything such as taking them for lunch just to get to know them.

Marketing online (websites, Twitter, Facebook, Instagram, LinkedIn, YouTube or other)?

I do put a lot of effort into social media particularly LinkedIn. You do put your head above the parapet and get it smacked occasionally. Having said that, it has paid dividends.

Do you have a digital strategy?

We have opened Facebook, LinkedIn and Twitter pages for the firm, they are there but we are trying to decide what we are going to put on them that are different to mine. Juliette is going to be in charge of those. We are meeting next week. We want our digital strategy to be different, fun and informative.

Need to discuss what our brand is going to be, what our tagline is going to be. At the moment it is one from our client 'quite simply, one of the best employment lawyers around'. I want to add something about adding value and I have a lot of clients who have given me feedback and recommendations. We want to put them on. A lot of lawyers run around looking to get into Legal 500, however I don't think clients care. No one has ever said we are not instructing you because you are not listed – some lawyers view it as an ego thing.

Offline marketing

Yet to develop a plan to support the online marketing as only just opened my office. I anticipate that this will include presentations to our target audience in due course.

Where do you see your legal practice going in the next three years?

Not online at the moment. Currently tribunal fees have gone and are coming back. The statistics show lots of postponements. We experienced, a lot of those in the bad old days. So with tribunal fees back there is a great opportunity for advocates, which I do, so that's good.

I think social media needs embracing and I am very focused on Linked In but I need to expand that.

Websites are pointless as they only show that we exist. I don't know anyone that instructs anyone on the back of a website. It is just a necessary evil, and by that I mean that you have to spend money on it: and put a bit of effort into it. Realistically, the money you earn from a website is negligible in the legal profession and I bet the statistics would show that.

The overall point of that is – you just have to keep moving forward. You always have to be getting new clients because if your HR contact within a client leaves and the new one comes in with their favourites, you are out. And you might be able to follow the other HR into their new company, which is great. This will depend on the new CEO – they want to use their own people. So you could end up with potentially having two clients or having none.

What I am really looking forward is to be in the position of saying, right we need to hire someone now, because the work is too much. That'll be great.

FIVE YORKSHIRE LEGAL STARS WHO MOVED OUT OF LAW TO RUN A NON-LEGAL BUSINESS

1. ANDREA MORRISON

Ex-Barrister and owner of a coaching business
www.andreamorrison.co.uk

Why did you decide to not practise your legal expertise and move into a different business?

I thought I would stay in the law initially when I left the Bar but I was quite ill and had chronic fatigue syndrome – burnt myself out.

Did tutoring at the University for a few years but because I was fascinated by personal development and had a real passion for that I wanted to move into this field. Also I was fascinated by how some people excelled and some people didn't and the job was the same.

I have three children facing their own issues and this is all to do with how do we make the best of our lives – the best of our potential and the opportunities that are presented there. And why do we get in our own way so much? It was not a wake up on a Monday morning and decides that I'm going to be a life coach it was a progressive draw to that nature of the business if you like.

What is your best and worst business habit?

It's the same thing. My best business habit is that I love following my intuition I love following what feels right – solutions – how can I explain this in a different way so that it resonates with them – connecting with people and coming up with a unique way of doing things. Magpie – we can do this or we can do that. Hurtling one direction after another – do have to rein it.

How do you manage the 'highs' and the 'lows' of being a business owner? (Stress management) and/or what are you doing to build resilience?

There are highs and lows – at the Bar as now – feast v famine. The way I have dealt with it is by working on my mindset. Learning about how the mind works determines my approach. So I don't let being incredibly busy affect my well-being. My well-being is constant no matter what chaos. Most of the time I achieve this. I see the 'rollercoaster' for what it is – virtual reality – can observe it without riding it. Being the observer is more than mindfulness. Understanding the nature of our thinking – how we bring our thinking to life and how we can combine that with our intuition. Fresh ideas – the light bulb moments if you like. How we combine it with that. The more we understand these principles the more we understand what's going on; and we don't get sucked in as much. Or if we do get sucked in then we notice it a bit quicker. Helps enormously with confidence and resilience.

Who do you turn to for support and inspiration? Who would you like to thank for their support and why?

I am really fortunate that I have an amazing husband about and he coaches in the same way that I do. I also have a good friend who runs a successful business, who is a similar coach to me. We are lucky in that respect in that we have a bit of a dynamic trio going on.

I also look at the leaders in my own field – George and Linda Pransky, Ali Campbell, Mike O'Neill. I look to them to what they are doing, at the direction they are taking. I hear them speak as often as I can do or if I can get the opportunity to work with them, then I do that as well.

It would have to be my husband who just puts up with a lot. He has always been so supportive even at times when I thought, right that's it, and I'm giving up. He has always had an unwavering belief in me, which has been amazing, which has provided me with stability.

Do or did you have a personal and/or business vision?

Yes I do have vision and I know what it is that I want to achieve; and it has taken a long time to get here. I have been lots of different things so now I know how my business will look.

Did you have a business plan when you first started – if so what worked and what didn't?

I remember l did have a detailed business plan for my first business and it contained everything it should have but I fell at the first hurdle due to regulatory issues as I was still at the Bar.

After that, and after my illness, I worked as a complementary therapist and ran a magazine and community project. Each has its own plan and what did not work was sticking rigidly to that plan. We are going to have this many clients and if it didn't happen we would get deflated or if we saw something that was obvious that was not in the plan then we wouldn't do it.

I do advocate goals and vision but also be aware of your surroundings to be able to take an opportunity to do something amazing. And when I did take the business in a completely different direction, amazing things have happened as a result of that. Either I have learnt something really useful, or met someone who I have kept in contact with, which would have been missed by sticking to the plan.

How are your services different from your competitors and why (with examples)?

I can work in conjunction with more traditional styles of coaches because generally speaking they put Mindset at the bottom of the list whereas it's the first and only thing that I work with. It may be they start with – lets get your ideal clients sorted out – your mission statement – your 12 months plan – five year plan etc. so they tend to focus on the outside of the business. When we work from the inside out, really understanding those belief structures, how we create our experience and what drives us. I find that my clients intuitively know what direction they need to take their business or they can tap into some fresh ideas.

So often we follow everyone else's ideas or structures because we think that they are right and it doesn't work and then we get disheartened. So it all feels hard. This then leaves it feeling hard and difficult. When we work from the inside out our minds quieten and it becomes easier.

Let's really get you connected with your creativity – you already have things you need. You are looking for it in the wrong place. Once you are there then we can talk about your business because once we talk from that place – it is so much easier. You are inspired you are happy – it just has a different feel to it.

What has been your greatest success to date?

It's not something that I necessarily reflect on in business. How do you measure success? Clients come to me and they go out in a different place. So my success is definitely the impact I have on my clients.

Without sounding too soft-hearted my biggest success is my kids and the people that they are growing into.

Where do you see the threats for your business?

Me – we are all our biggest threats to our business. I am not immune to this. I am both the failure and success of my business.

What is your personal brand? Name your top three qualities, which enable you to run a unique legal practice.

Unwavering belief in my clients – I know for a fact that they have all the tools they need. Even if they don't see it. Connectable – really important to me that I have a very good connection with my clients. Naturally positive person – nice to work with.

Why your name?

In this field you use your own name and brand.

How do you manage quality of service?

I do a lot of reflection about the impact I have on the client. For example, if I'm doing a training session I will always ask for feedback. I will always be listening to how people talk during the session. I am looking for how has this impacted on them and how have they understood it. How are they reflecting on it? Everybody is on a different journey, some may need several programmes or work intensively, and someone else may need only one session. They are all different.

What interpersonal skills are important to be successful with your type of clients?

The most important skill is connection – just be connected with this client as a coach.

Marketing online (websites, Twitter, Facebook, Instagram, LinkedIn, YouTube or other)?

Don't use YouTube yet and I want to develop a podcast.

I use LinkedIn and Facebook. My website sees a reasonable amount of traffic. It is being rehashed at the moment. I do have online products. I do a Facebook session and there are videos on my website. I often run online programmes – daily retreats – stuff like that. It's really about people where they are and if there is something that they need then I look to put that together. I am not into sales funnels.

Do you have a digital strategy?

I do but can't write it down. I want the Facebook/LinkedIn and website streamlined and aligned. Also to do a regular blog and emails out. Podcast is my favourite and fun.

People find me in different places – always have a conversation with them beforehand. Very aware that it has to be a relationship with them – understanding their business/their challenges.

Offline marketing

I do local social networking events because it is about connecting with people. In formal business ones everyone has game face and so connection is tricky. Then they avoid me because if they did speak to me then they must have a problem.

Word of mouth – people will talk about what I have done and when a colleague talks to them about a problem they say go talk to Andrea. I am the unspoken go-to-guru

Do you have a plan for personal development/business development?

Don't have a specific plan for what I am going to do over the next 12 months I have some plans for some more training in January. Three principles conference in May – I find that things will just crop up throughout the year and I will look at them, I am looking out for these. If a coach I am following has released a book or a programme then I may do that. In a traditional career you don't do this.

You put a lot of information in your head but you very rarely work on yourself. That is one of the blessings of the work that I do, is that working on yourself is professional development as well as personal development.

Where do you see your business going in the next three years?

In the next 12–18 months – a training programme for managers, leaders, coaches on the principles behind achieving your potential and life balance so they can be supportive to their colleagues and companies. They can have a greater understanding of their own capacity. I feel passionate about the fact that the more people who understand this stuff the better the world would be. I can't share this with everyone so it would be fantastic to share this with people who can change the working environment. Change the way they do business, change the way they are running their business.

The Three Principles were first articulated by Sidney Banks and are widely understood to be the principles that lie behind the human experience, I then translate them into a business context. When we understand these principles behind the infinite potential of our minds we then have enormous capacity for insight/fresh new thought and everything that we need, and then when we have that we can apply this approach within our business.

2. ANN PAGE

Non-practising Solicitor and owner of Beyond the Brief turned Author, Business Motivational Trainer and Coach trading as www.yorkshirecoursesforlawyers.co.uk

Why did you decide to not practise your legal expertise and move into a different business?

In my case, when politics drove me out of my last in-house post, I turned to my second love after the law – leadership and management training. I was passionate about these topics and creating interactive motivational learning experiences that were practical.

I was also looking for interesting work, which I could do whilst taking lots of time out with husband (who was fully retired at this stage) to travel the world. I wanted to take my own leadership and management training and experience from the corporate world into the legal profession. The first time I did this was when I was Chair of the Law Society Commerce and Industry Group. Whilst there, I initiated six firsts for the Group including Corporate Governance Guidelines for In-house lawyers. I started by freelancing for the major legal training companies. I was in fact approached to work for one of the companies to set up their leadership and management programme for lawyers, which I did.

It was not till the death of my mother and husband in the same year, that I took time out to decide what I wanted to do, given all my future plans had been totally changed. This led me to return to my home county of Yorkshire and to undertake serious training on setting and running a business including Internet business marketing. I love learning.

I explored a number of ways to set up and develop businesses both in and out of the law. I realised that actually I loved working with my profession on the teaching and coaching side. Following the business skills training I decided to add these skills to my services (e.g. The Business Brilliance Blueprint Programme) and coaching services. I did not want to be wedded to any one particular system so I offer a customised holistic approach to lawyers to address their challenges. This in turn has led me to deliver a number of mini workshops on a number of current themes. Mindfulness and Stress Management is just one example. I continue to deliver themed workshops alongside my business coaching and training.

What keeps me going – my 'Why'? It is making a difference to the lawyers that I work with or meet on my public leadership and confidence courses for MBL Seminars. It is the human interaction and the amazing feedback I receive from my training and coaching. I just love working with you. It is a real privilege to watch you grow as leaders, business owners and lawyers.'

What is your best and worst business habit?

Passion for all my business subjects and clients, I love the face-to-face training and coaching to inspire and support my clients.

Given the wide range of topics within business, I can lose focus sometimes. On a practical matter, I don't always check my diary before agreeing to do something or even insert items in my diary!

How do you manage the 'highs' and the 'lows' of being a business owner? (Stress management) and/or what are you doing to build resilience?

I practice meditation and yoga. I have a personal trainer who is planned to come to me three times a week, although it doesn't always work out that way.

I love holidays and fit in as many as I can during the year. I have a very active social life, which involves eating out, going to the cinema, theatre and ballet. I also enjoy reading fiction mainly Sci-Fi. So I love Star Wars, Star Trek and also other epics like Lord of the Rings and Harry Potter!

Who do you turn to for support and inspiration? Who would you like to thank for their support and why?

This has changed over time. I would like to thank my two sisters (Theresa and Rosemary) who have been invaluable in assisting me

in rebuilding my life since Neil's death. In particular, Rosemary's invaluable insights and support to my business life.
I would like to thank my peers from my networking groups, some of which have become good friends and my coach. My personal friends also keep me grounded.

Did you have a personal and/or business vision?

Yes, this has evolved over time.

When I moved from being a senior in-house lawyer to being a trainer and coach, I began with studying coaching with the Coaching Academy. I then studied Neuro Linguistic Programming. The NLP training was focused on how adults learn because I realised it was not enough to share my knowledge and experience. I wanted to craft motivational learning workshops and courses tailored to the lawyers needs.

I started by working as a freelancer for the major training companies. A route similar to being a consultant solicitor before becoming a legal business owner such as the route that **Jodie** and **Simon** took. I tried to learn the 'business' of training from these large companies but their whole approach to marketing and in particular pricing meant it was not a model I could or wanted to follow once I branched out. There are two reasons, I would not have the database these companies had or their marketing resources nor did I want to only compete on price as they did. Once you focus on the latter the only way is down. So even if you have had business training in your large firm, which is unlikely, it may not serve you when you spread your wings to forge your own path.

I did build my training skills and experience with the different training companies (2003-2013) on how to deliver motivational training and cope with lots of interesting things that happen in class.

In terms of my topics and content, I gained valuable insight and training of business, leadership, management and interpersonal skills during my twenty-eight years as an In-house Solicitor for several organisations and in various roles. I am also a member of the Professional Speaking Association and there have been numerous members who have inspired and informed my journey including Joy Marsden and Eilidh Milnes. These amazing ladies are sadly no longer with us. I would like to particularly thank Lee Jackson and John Howtoka from the PSA for their continual support, wisdom and guidance. I continue to read extensively and to incorporate all and any learning from delivering my services so I can continue to develop and improve.

In 2013 to 2016 I started to study all the different business skills on a yearly basis from various sources. These cover all the main topics that I teach, coach and mentor other business owners on. The decision I made following this substantive training was that I did not want to run a business outside of the legal profession. I wanted to continue to deliver motivational training and coaching using business skills translated into the legal profession.

Did you have a business plan when you first started – if so what worked and what didn't?

Over the years I have had many different types of plans some were more useful than others and it is a question of finding what works for you.

I combine my strategic and business goals in one document on a yearly basis. My strategic business plan covers my purpose and values (normally three words I am going to focus on for the next 12 months). This year's three words are: Joy, Creativity and Connection. The financial information contains potential income streams required from different services with detailed plans re marketing and course planning but no specific monthly targets.

Income goals and sales targets, on their own, don't motivate me. I understand their importance in tracking your business success. I am lucky that I am the master of my own work-life balance.

How are your services different from your competitors and why (with examples)?

When I started there were very few in-house lawyers who had moved into training and consultancy for the legal professionals. This has changed and more have taken this route.

I have always used a holistic approach in both my training, coaching and mentoring as I have a wealth of experience spanning decades! Since 2015 I have focused on business skills and Yorkshire. As far as I am aware I am the only one with my background focused on this beautiful county.

What has been your greatest success to date?

There have been many over the years but the one I often relate is: Would you believe that a girl who left school with no O-levels at sixteen would have a highly successful in-house legal career and be recognised as a Top 100 lawyer in 2003?

Where do you see the threats for your business?

The main threat is my energy levels and possible impending retirement!

What is your personal brand? Name your top three qualities, which enable you to run a unique legal practice.

Beyond the Brief was set up in 2003 as a training company aimed at lawyers in private practice. In 2013-4 I returned to my roots, the In-house lawyers section. As I had already written a book in 2007 called Managing External Legal Resources, this seemed the perfect name and brand for my website aimed at this market. What it meant was that I had to set up a new website to support the brand and keep it totally separate from Beyond the Brief which was aimed at private practice. I then wrote another book for this sector with my co-author Richard Tapp called The In-house Lawyers Toolkit.

Following an illness and two knee operations, I found I had to re-think the travelling to London to work with my in-house clients. Also my Beyond the Brief website was set up in 2003 and was not Word Press and was very old and tired. I have now taken down Beyond the Brief as a live site as now trading as Yorkshire Courses for Lawyers – a fabulous new website if I say so myself.

My top three qualities are:

1. Enthusiasm for teaching and coaching
2. Passionate about maintaining and developing my own expertise
3. Generous with my time and expertise

Why your company name?

One of the constant feedback messages I received in my in-house career was that I went beyond the brief or their expectations. This was something I wanted to carry into my work as a trainer and coach. So when I set up my non-legal business I wanted to show that I would do this for my clients from the name I was using.

Is there anything specific you do to manage the quality of service?

I take on board all the feedback I receive at the end of each training or coaching session.

From my point of view, I am a believer in continual improvements, so I reflect on what worked well or what do I want to do differently for the next course on this or other topics? I will also update the notes and slides to reflect this and any new knowledge I have come across in the interim.

On the public courses I look up the delegates on LinkedIn to get a feel for the level of attendees as well as the different background. This is so I can tailor the delivery of the material in the public workshop to their specific working lives.

What interpersonal skills are important to be successful with your type of clients?

The knowledge and desire to craft stimulating and enjoyable learning experiences on the subjects you want to teach and coach.

Ability to communicate effectively, including active listening to understand and connect with your clients.

Warmth and caring.

Marketing online (websites, Twitter, Facebook, Instagram, LinkedIn, YouTube or other)?

Whilst I have Twitter, a LinkedIn and a Facebook company page, I focus on LinkedIn, which is where my clients and professional contacts 'hang out'.

I outsource the actual posting across the three main media platforms as I currently use this as a continual profile awareness mechanism. This means that I choose to post reference to legal business-related articles that I think my clients and contacts would be interested in. In this mix I do include information about my monthly blogs and some upcoming courses. Once this book is completed I am aiming to move into posts that engage rather than just inform.

I write business based blogs for lawyers on a whole range of topics, with the assistance of my copywriter and I aim to send these out on a monthly basis to my clients and contacts via mail chimp.

Offline marketing

Networking and some public short courses. Although writing my book has meant that I have not delivered, as many as I would normally, so will be reviewing what topics I want to deliver as short public courses after the book is published.

In some years I have delivered presentations to members of law societies both paid and unpaid. I also try to attend the Small Firms Conference run by the Law Society and the Legal Sector Advisers and Suppliers Conference.

Do you have a plan for personal development/business development?

Prior to launching my business I was taught by various internal and external structure programmes during my in-house career and the results would then be tracked in my subsequent performance reviews. In fact, at the Co-operative Bank, I experienced a whole range of legal and non-legal competency frameworks when I was leading my in-house legal department. I became involved, as a Senior Manager, in the revision of the current one in 2000, and loved every minute of it.'

As I love learning I have continued to add to my knowledge and experience. I review my personal development against my strategy and goals for each 12-month period. I have a coach. On average I spend around £3000+ per year on a mix of courses, peer mentoring associations, and books. I do feel that I can't ask my clients and delegates to go on a learning journey if I am not doing this myself.

I just love psychometric testing and I am MiRo Accredited Assessor. Indeed I have an extremely large file containing all the different assessments I have done over the years working in the banking industry. According to MiRo my leadership style is Instructor style in the 'Energising' category (yellow)! So my natural style, amongst other things, is that I am an eloquent and outgoing leader. One of the struggles listed that I may encounter is holding self and others to overly high standards.

I am not a great fan of webinars and podcasts unless they are meditation ones.

Where do you see your business going in the next three years?

My main focus is to finish writing this book and get it published and launched. I will then review where I want to focus next.

I don't have a time frame for coming out of my business because I am focusing on the work that I enjoy – not building an asset to sell. That means it is a service delivered by me, and I do not plan to develop training products to sell online, even though the market is going in that direction. Having said that, I am exploring the virtual reality potential for training with a technical partner – so watch this space.

3. CATHY COCKIN

Ex-paralegal and owner of Little Miss Electrical Limited

Why did you decide to not practise your legal expertise and move into a different business?

I was a paralegal in conveyancing and had been promised a training contract with a 'to be confirmed' start date and a similar thing with the promised move to a new branch in Huddersfield.

I am quite impatient and found this frustrating. I suppose the reason I left is that I wanted to do it immediately and they didn't facilitate that. It all seemed very disorganised and got re-arranged that many times that I had booked on to an electrical training course within an hour of finding one, I that I could fit into my annual leave and as my attention had started to veer.

Also I'm not sure how much or the re-arranging was genuine and how much of it was my line manager dangling to carrot to keep me quiet. I did maintain my enthusiasm only to be called 'pushy' by HR, which didn't sit well with me.

As I'm sure you've realised I am quite an impulsive person with the shortest of patience and so the carefully planned progress that the law firm may or may not have had in mind for me was far too slow to satisfy my ambition and drive.

I got into electrics through our interest in property, which my conveyancing skills did fuel. We have a couple of properties, in which I did my first re-wires on and this was key for me getting my confidence and independence to set up on my own.

What is your best (and worst) business habit?

My best business habit is probably being willing to take on a new type of job and learn how to do it rather than be frightened of it.

My worst I think is falling soft on clients when it comes to charging them for odd jobs or odd bits here and there, they soon add up!

How do you manage the 'highs' and the 'lows' of being a business owner? (Stress management) and/or what are you doing to build resilience?

This is probably the thing I struggle the most with. It is so draining to go from getting paid a big invoice to scratching around for invoices to pay everyone on time. It can be very overwhelming but also underwhelming within such a short space of time. I just try to keep my nerve and ride it out until the next high, but it does take it out of you!

Who do you turn to for support and inspiration? Who would you like to thank for their support and why?

My big sister Rebecca Lockwood is a really good mentor and so is my partner Oliver who has been self employed for 12 years. They both have so much time for me when I'm stressing out but also confidence in me succeeding and making it work. They're my go-to people.

My customers have to be the most deserving of a thank you. All of them have supported me throughout my career change, believed in me, recommended me and used me repeatedly which has meant I have been able to build a client-base and reputation.

Did (or do) you have a personal and/or business vision?

I'd love to grow our business to have lots more female electricians all over the country. It's a big thing employing people and it's very stressful but it also makes me so proud. We get so much fantastic feedback and it makes all the hard work worth it.

Alongside this I would really like to grow our portfolio of property with my business, electrical and conveyancing skills.

Did you have a business plan when you first started - if so what worked and what didn't?

No! I just took things as they came and didn't know what to expect at what pace or how much. I've started to do a lot more planning recently which is much more sensible and manages your expectations and helps to organise things. I just kind of winged it and was lucky but I'm usually a planner and love it when plans work out.

Are these different from your competitors and why (with examples)?

'Little Miss Electrical' – female electrical contractors. We're reliable, tidy up after ourselves and we're girls!

What has been your greatest success to date?

Whilst I trained as a domestic electrician to begin with, I promoted myself to owner of the business, after about 12 months. I finally realised it was nothing to do with what I do as a job it was simply being in control of my own progression and earnings that satisfied me so starting my 'Little Miss Electrical' from scratch is my greatest success so far to date.

Also creating new jobs for female electricians in the industry. I am proud to have found really great electricians who now work for me.

Where do you see the threats for your business?

Should there be another recession this may impact our business. The construction industry is booming now but I remember when I was at high school it took a big hit when the recession hit.

What is your personal brand? Name your top three qualities, which enable you to run a unique legal practice.

I believe in great customer service and my customers find us reliable, responsive and thorough. On the business side, I like to plan the work and develop my staff.

Why your name?

I was trying to identify the fact that it was female in the title and brand name so it worked really well.

Is there anything specific you do to manage the quality of service?

I always ensure I meet with customers and take staff to the job once confirmed to run through everything, check with the customer that we understand all the details and then once the job is finished I check back in and make sure everything went well. I always ask for feedback and reviews,

What interpersonal skills are important to be successful with your type of clients?

Be honest with your customers! When I first started up I didn't know how to do most of the electrical skills I have now two years ago, but I was willing to learn and apply them as soon as a customer needed it.

People will often use me because my team and I do a good job and are reliable.

Marketing online (websites, Twitter, Facebook, Instagram, LinkedIn, YouTube or other)?

We get most of our private work from our Facebook page and also store reviews here. So this is the one I use.

Do you have a digital strategy?

Not really I keep an eye on my Facebook analytics.

Offline marketing

I do networking with WIBN and Brand Yorkshire. WIBN is amazing as everyone is so supportive and they all look after you. Whoever you need - someone there well help you.

How do you lead and mange them? Have you had any training? What would they say is your best/worst quality?

I should probably get more training on leadership and management but it's finding time! I've a never ending to do list! That's why I really appreciate your business coaching Ann.

How do you develop yourself and your team?

I develop female apprentices by on-the-job training and role-modelling my values.

We try to do as much manufacturer training as possible to get their input into how they want their products installing, which really helps.

What are your biggest team challenges and successes?

Everyone has different skills and booking them onto the right job so that they are the most suited is great. It's hard to get time to learn other skills when you're busy but we try team one up with someone else who is good at something so they can help each other learn.

Where do you see your business going in the next three years?

We'd like to cover the whole of West Yorkshire, rather than just patches. Halifax and Huddersfield have been conquered but there are always new clients in other parts of Yorkshire. I am currently expanding in Leeds – so watch this space! We would like to raise our profile across the whole of Yorkshire – that's my goal for my electrical business.

On my property portfolio I can use my legal and business skills to grow this over the next three years.

4. KATE YOUNG

Non-practising Solicitor and owner of The Safeguarding Association and Safeguarding Academy (supporting non-legal professionals working within the Family Justice Sector) https://safeguardingassociation.com

Why did you decide to not practise your legal expertise and move into a different business?

I will give you the background, use as much of it as you see fit. I was in practice for about ten years. A variety of local authorities and private practice firms. Got caught up in the first round of redundancies in the 2008 credit crunch. Can call it a recession now. Fairly newly qualified at the time, done a lot of work with firms up until this point. Went to work for the local authority and it was there that I was introduced to the idea of being a trainer, done some of it in private practice but not a lot. Headhunted out of the local authority into a medium-sized regional firm and was there for a couple of years, desperately wanted to set up a training arm, loved it, phenomenal. Then LASPO came in, which I am fairly certain will be familiar with a lot of your legal aid lawyers.

Long and the short of it – was that I was managed out. So there I was a second time redundant lawyer thinking effectively 'what on earth do I do now?' Fell into the profession, in hindsight was probably not the best route for me. I thought I should not be kicked out – this shouldn't be happening – this is meant to be a job for life.

Took the bull by its horns and became a locum. That was really to support my bigger idea to run my own training firm. Had one of those crazy motions... "everyone needs a trainer" so I'll set up my own training firm. It'll be brilliant. 18 months later – done all the whiz-bang things – brand new websites, beautiful logos...etc.

What is your best and worst business habit?

I'm still trying to figure that out.

In terms of my worst habit – I can be really lazy and I will go through a flurry of sending a lot of emails and lots of marketing and then don't follow up – or I will follow up but it will be three or four weeks later because I get caught up in 'doing the do' as it were. In a practice you generally have a team of people around you and you just say to your support team, 'just make sure that's followed-up' when its just you, you have to remember to do it yourself. I am trying my best to become better at following-up.

In terms of my best habit, whether I'd call it a habit or not – I don't know. I love the freedom having my own business gives me so I'm not afraid, or too afraid should I say, of giving things a go. So I remember when I set up my YouTube channel, the lawyer in me was going 'oh my gosh, what are you doing'? And then the other part of me went, 'why not?' You are not giving them legal advice; you are just giving them information. What's the problem with that? I'm really good at the whole 'lets just give it a go, give it a whirl, go out there and try'. I am really good at the big idea stuff, not good at the minutiae to get you from A to B, which goes back to the fact I should have never been a lawyer in the first place.

How do you manage the 'highs' and the 'lows' of being a business owner? (Stress management) and/or what are you doing to build resilience?

Having a support network – for be that has been absolutely vital. My husband has been a star. My mum and dad have been nothing but supportive – even if they do not understand what it is that I am doing. I have gone down a path, which is rather unusual, but they are there behind me, my in-laws are behind me. Within the first few months of me setting up, I found a trainer's group, did an eight-week course with them, and I am still a part of that community. For me that has been one of the biggest forms of support, although they may not do your subject, they understand the highs and lows of it. When you have had a really rough week battling with a company paying an invoice, they are really good because they have been there.

I am a part of the Female Entrepreneurs Association as well. It is now a massive organisation. It wasn't when I had joined – over 6000 women in the group. So you can go in and say this is what is happening, and I did it recently with them, we're going through a major change in our home life and I said 'who's also been through this and how do you cope with this?' They have been a huge help, like an online hug effectively – that for me has been one of the biggest things.

Also, accepting and realising that part of the reason we become our own bosses is to be able to do what we want to do – when we want to do it, and with that comes its highs and lows. Like today I was in court until 6:30 last night and just thought I am not running around today. I will give myself space otherwise stress levels just go through the roof. Once you get in touch with yourself, you know when your stress levels are rising. Having that recognition and knowing what to do to de-stress. For me, I go for a walk and reflect on my diet as that's an indicator of how things a going.

Who do you turn to for support and inspiration? Who would you like to thank for their support and why?

I was a part of the Trainer Training Company's members, and I am one of their ambassadors, one of seven. If I am really struggling, or cannot go to my husband or I know it's going to come from a place of love but I'm not going to get the answer I want, I tend to turn to them either individually or collectively and they just help me. They are fabulous at that.

Did or do you have a personal and/or business vision?

Yes I really do, in the last six months this vision has really started to crystallise. This links back to the previous question, started out thinking I just want to deliver training but there has to be a better way of delivering it. I, just like you and every other lawyer, has sat through hours and hours of CPD thinking 'please will the earth just open up and take me'. Also knew that my audience which started off as social workers were not getting the support they needed particularly around court work. So a lot of them were going in completely blind and being absolutely annihilated by very junior solicitors and counsel because they just didn't have those really basic skills they needed – so that's where it started.

Then I started to look at there has to be a better way than just flog open courses. So I realised everything was moving digitally so launched The Safeguarding Academy – which is where you and I met Ann as I was promoting that. That's worked really well as a concept. But the early part of this year I was really frustrated because I just couldn't get everything I wanted the academy to do to fit into the academy brand. It comes back down to my delightful Ambassadors and the mastermind group we had. They were just looking at me and clearly struggling to understand why I was forcing everything into the academy and thus the Safeguarding Association was born – it came out of the frustration that I was working with professionals who were unable to access the support they desperately needed.

The business I had built with the academy was not fit for purpose to take it to that next level. After having that 'aha' moment, everything has just started to fall into place. And I really am so proud of what it has done and really, really keen for it to become the biggest association of child protection professionals in the country. In fact there isn't, as far as my research has taken me. In fact I couldn't find another association collectively safeguarding professions across the sectors. Outside of local authority hubs which are purely there as contact points, there is nothing else out there, as far as I can see, that allows people to come together, to talk, to share, to get information and access the support and training they need; and to also say this is what I stand for. As members they sign up to our charter – which unknown to me at the time completely covers every facet of the new updated 'Working Together' documentation. This is the guidance document, which is relevant to anyone who is involved with children under the age of 18.

Did you have a business plan when you first started – if so what worked and what didn't?

When I started – the company was formed four and half years ago – as a part of that whole process I knew I needed to figure this out; and part of that was that I accessed as many free courses and support courses as I possibly could. The only way to access some of them was to have a business plan drawn up, which I did. But because I was very much in the learning phase and the 'I have no clue what I'm doing' phase, it was not really fit for purpose.

I am one of those people that change their mind quite quickly and because I was very much trying to figure out where I was going with it, that business plan really did not work for me. I have not drawn up a business plan in its traditional sense for the Association but it does have a number of 'markers in the sand' that I want it to achieve.

So in terms of funding you normally have to have one as that is part of the requirements. I think it is quite useful to have a 'check in' once in six months to see where you want to be and give yourself some points to measure along the way and just mark that off as you're moving through to see if you have completely gone off the kilter or if you are on the right trajectory.

How are your services different from your competitors and why (with examples)?

See answer to the question on vision.

The question I keep on being asked is 'are you accredited?' At the moment there is no requirement for any organisation to be accredited by anybody in order to delivery child protection training. When I discovered that, it was one of those, jaw hits the floor moments. One of my aims with my Association is to ultimately be seen as the premier training place for those delivering child protection training. Once they have completed the training then are certified by my Association. All my training programmes are only available to members of the Safeguarding Association because then I know they have signed up to my charter.

My closest competition to me I suppose is the NSPCC, in so far as we both share information and we both provide training. What I can say is unique about the association is that it is a support forum, as well as all the other things members get. They are:

1. Able to ask each other for support or just ask questions surrounding topic areas such as the new 'Q guidance' policy and what has everyone put in their policies.
2. Be able to speak to me at least once a week or I offer sounding boards three times a week, so if they want that face-to-face contact they can jump on the computer and have that call with me. It is not legal advice – I am very clear about that but they have someone who has 11/12 years of child protection experience able to help them navigate some of their issues. A lot of the time it is just providing them with the reassurance that what they have done is enough.

Coming back to your question, in terms of how am I different, as far as I am aware I am the first to be looking to regulate what is available to practitioners – not just limited to within the health sector, local authority of education – there is a whole raft of experts who have nowhere to go. Especially with the current drive to localise child protection again, there is a reason we went from local to regulated. Drive back to local practice. People I work with have to straddle two or three local authority areas – when they actually need one bit of advice saying their local backers may be different in terms of getting a referral through but ultimately this is where you are going.

What has been your greatest success to date?

Last year we started our annual conference, only on annual conference number two but I have had a new booking from the new Head of Childline – for me that was 'oh my God what I am doing actually matters'.

Where do you see the threats for your business?

Misinformation – there are a lot of organisations that are firmly of the belief that the only way they can access training or support is through their local Safeguarding Children's Board. This is going to be replaced by the Safeguarding Partnership soon. That is absolutely not the case but it was only once I started digging into why people were hesitant about booking that all of this started to come out.

Any major change in terms of legislation may well impact particularly if they say there has to be a level of regulation – which I thoroughly welcome but that potentially would have an impact on the business.

And one of the real issues is funding – lots of organisations desperately want the support but we are not expensive. We are definitely not rock-bottom cheap. The reality is the fact that people don't properly value the quality of training.

What is your personal brand? Name your top three qualities, which enable you to run a unique legal practice.

The biggest one for me is openness – being approachable – somebody that is seen to be knowledgeable and someone that is there and not afraid to admit when they have screwed up. Knowing when there has been a change in the wind but equally celebrating and praising yourself when you have done well. Not being someone who is not going to answer that or who is going to ignore someone for asking me a particular question. Certainly in the world of child protection, jargon, acronyms and language changes between sectors that I want people to say they don't understand and feel safe in being able to say that – if they don't say that there is every chance they are going to get it wrong. I want the community to be able to share their successes in the same way they would share their failings or challenges and being open about it.

Reliable – whether that is having a Skype call at the right time or what do you think of this? Bundled with that is being trustworthy. This ties in with my legal background.

Why your name?

The brand is very much like my qualities and me. I spoke about being open, trustworthy, and reliable.

The brand representation is very simple and straightforward it is just an S in its logo. The Association branding is pretty much the same as the Academy branding albeit the colours have changed. It is still very much a part of me.

Is there anything specific you do to manage the quality of service?

I receive feedback for any training I deliver. I am constantly reviewing how I deliver training and facilitation.

What interpersonal skills are important to be successful with your type of clients?

Very much not being someone who comes across as a know-it-all. There is a way of managing them – not being a humble brag because everyone hates those but being knowledgeable without banging on about it and having that air of understanding but not trying to preach to them.

The people I deal with are on the frontline and they are dealing with the most horrific incidents going – to some extent I am at 'arms length' from that. You have to respect your clients as they are doing serious work and knowing that they are not all going to want to work with me.

Can you actually talk to them? Are you being a good listener and hearing what they are saying? As lawyers we can be quite bad at this and hear only what we think we need to hear. We are very good at picking out the facts of the situation but we are not great at picking up the emotional cues – certainly in legal family work no one wants a crying client. At least 70% of my work was counselling, maybe 5% was law and the other bits in-between were mediation and general client management and then having to manage my partners. Very little of it is what you actually studied seven years to do.

Knowing that yes you do have a skill set and it is really valuable but actually there are areas that you probably need to improve on. I certainly had to go back to my listening skills – when you're dealing with professionals in a local authority setting, where this all started from, I realised what they were telling me was not necessarily what they needed. They were telling me what I thought I wanted to hear not the bits I needed to hear – very carefully unpicked this information so to not to tread on any egos. Being aware of how you come across and being aware of how you are perceived and being open to someone else having a different idea. I feel much more at home doing what I am doing now than I ever did – sometimes I feel as though I have a split personality.

Marketing online (websites, Twitter, Facebook, Instagram, LinkedIn, YouTube or other)?

Well I don't have an office. The website is the online shop front.

The platform I used to build the academy was Facebook which worked very well – but what I realised was that there was only a couple of types of clients on Facebook or only a couple that were willing to take you seriously through Facebook. So in terms of promotion I use Facebook, YouTube is to offer guidance.

On Twitter I run 'safeguarding hour' every Sunday night.

LinkedIn I use predominantly to do all three. Great success over the eight weeks to build my LinkedIn profile up so I could set a target of building up to a 100 connections everyday. Made sure my tag line was good. Once I got to 6,000 I stopped adding connections and now people connect with me which opens further connects. I then take 20 a day and send them a standard message about the Association – this is what I do, this is some information.

Offline marketing

I have really struggled with this because again the Association is such a new concept straddling all the sectors, so it has been difficult to figure out what the right strategy is going to be. So I am still working on that.

I was also really put off because about two years ago, maybe longer, I was in a conference aimed at child protection professionals (most in the early years sector). My research told me they are the ones that want it online and that's where I was going. I cannot tell you how many people saw my stand, with safeguarding across it, took one look at, put their heads down and shot past me. That was so disheartening on so many levels. Thankfully it's not all like that – very hit and miss though.

I try to meet face-to-face when I can – the Trainers Group we meet quarterly and we have a big trainers day, roughly about 50 people there.

I am a member of a local female entrepreneurs group for Hull.

I have just joined a co-working space – which is predominantly full of tech people – one of the things I want to do is build an app. I have been there a week and it is working fairly well.

I have to be selective with where I go to network, as I am very aware that what I do terrifies people.

Do you have a plan for personal development/business development?

The two become intrinsically linked – in terms of getting the best out of yourself you need to do a lot of self-evaluation. There is no written plan as such but I am aware of where I lack skills, I'm aware of where I need support, I look at what the business is going to be doing. For example in the Association I want it to start offering supervision – not freely available. Part of my planning is to get those skills and offer those to members. But I am very well aware that in getting those skills, that will also allow me to better understand some of my reactions to things, similar to how my mediation training did. So there is a plan but very much linked to where the business is going and what the business is or is not.

Where do you see your business going in the next three years?

Continuing to grow both the Academy and the Association. Having a more permanent team around me instead of the freelancers I am currently using is the only way that this Association is going to grow. Very much about the right information and in terms of the training I offer, the information I offer is relevant, they feel confident delivering it and that it is engaging. PowerPoint presentations have gone – very much about conversation. I used to dislike lectures as a lawyer, would have been easier to do more interactive workshops.

5. MIGUEL FLORIT

Non practising Solicitor and owner of Florit Legal (Legal Recruiter for the in-house sector) www.floritlegal.com

Why did you decide to not practise your legal expertise and move into a different business with someone and then on your own?

So, there are three parts to this question:

Part 1: In terms of moving out of the legal profession...

It's always a combination of factors.

The short answer is that I probably landed in the wrong department of the firm I trained in, but it seemed a good idea at the time, as I was not really looking to be a property lawyer, but got swayed by being offered a role by one of the best real estate practices in the UK at the time.

Originally I wanted to be an employment lawyer – owing to the people element but it was hugely popular, and my firm weren't taking anyone on below two years PQE, even though I had had an employment seat. So I am guessing I was better at property than employment! But knowing what I know now, in a very small department in a firm which then wasn't a leader in employment law, I totally sympathise with their need, to have someone just hit the ground running at 2–3 years PQE rather than having to coach and cajole me! So property it was!

Hindsight is a wonderful thing! It was not in vain – they have helped me in my recruitment career.

Part 2: Going into partnership.

We had **complementary skills** and client bases. Other business owners had told me that it can be quite lonely running a business, and I once read a really interesting and slightly 'tongue-in-cheek' book by Felix Dennis which said 'get yourself a much younger business partner' I think on the basis that they would be more energetic than you!

Part 3: In terms of my most recent career move, in setting up Florit Legal

Again it's a combination of factors, although mainly strategic. These are:

- **Offer more:** – I wanted to offer more to the clients we work for. Search and Headhunting was one of those features we hadn't previously offered. We had previously been trying to be everything to everyone – but it goes deeper than that. Example: Some of our clients have very specific requirements (in spaces such as IP, or financial services) and "search" as a solution helps with that. If we don't work for law firm clients, it means that if a client wants to target specific individuals on really specialist roles, we can do that for clients ethically, in our niche – whereas a non-niche recruiter would either struggle with conflicts of interest, or ignore them and potentially pay the price.
- **Focus:** It's important to have a niche and the time had come to focus more on our in-house legal recruitment expertise. So more of what we were already doing but in a different, and I think better way
- **Geography:** Our in-house team were being increasingly asked to work on roles in other parts of the country. By contrast, since the vast majority of lawyers work in law firms, if you do any law firm recruitment you have to be local. That can restrict your growth. So this has allowed us to do more right across the UK. Doing more of what we do best.

What is your best and worst business habit?

I have one that is both. I am a bit of a perfectionist, which means I tend to be quite analytical and weigh up the options before I make a decision on what to do – so as not to end up in trouble. It has pros and cons. Although it can hold me back, it has stopped me making mistakes by rushing in with a rash decision. However, I have learned to cope with it and realise that Rome wasn't built in a day; and done is very often better than perfection on the journey of improvement that we are continually on.

On the negative side, like many business owners who have moved from operational roles (as lawyers, recruiters or whatever) to working more strategically, I have found it hard to delegate. But I'm very lucky to have a team that know what they are doing and only need me to help with some of the bigger decisions along the way.

How do you manage the 'highs' and the 'lows' of being a business owner? (Stress management) and/or what are you doing to build resilience?

That's one I've struggled with in the past. Running a small business is all embracing. You can't put it down. Well I can't. I've not gone so far as some of the people I have worked for who used to dictate letters on the treadmill. Whilst I enjoy holidays, I now find they give me an opportunity to stop doing operational stuff and give me time to think about the business, improvements, and plan for the future.

In some ways it helps that I don't have kids. Or maybe that would have helped – I'll never know.

I used to like long runs, but now I do 10–20 minute work outs in the morning before work.

I meditate, and I visualise. In fact my former self would probably laugh heartily at me, before this err "enlightenment".

When I have time I also like DJ-ing at home in my home office with a great piece of kit my wife kindly bought for me! I used to do it professionally many years ago, but now things have moved on from vinyl, I really enjoy the creativity that digital formats provide. I am relearning what I used to do before. Not quite Fat Boy Slim, more Slim boy Fat.

Who do you turn to for support and inspiration? Who would you like to thank for their support and why?

1. My staff – for coming with me on the current leg of our joint journey, when they could very well have stayed with Florit Legal's "legacy" business and let me prove myself on my own first. I think you should employ people who are better than you and harness their excellence. We talk about things frequently.
2. My wife. I am very lucky to be married to an amazing executive coaching professional. As a former HRD in a range of businesses, Lisa has been a huge support to me in deciding what to do at various junctures in my latter career. More importantly, my wife Lisa, who just "gets me" and what I am trying to achieve.
3. I'm also a member of a global network of recruiters who help one another with everything marketing related, and received more formal coaching, from people associated with The Alternative Board.
4. My parents for not judging me when I turned my back on working as a property lawyer when it wasn't making me happy

Did or do you have a personal and/or business vision?

Yes, but I'd rather keep the business one to myself for now since it's early days and just in case I fail miserably and you do another book – entitled "Ten years on – where are they now?" Please come back in five years and if it's on track I'll happily tell you more!

As for personal – it involves keeping to a fighting weight, keeping all my own teeth and empowering others so that I can work less, and retiring to Mallorca, where 'it all started' as my parents say.

Did you have a business plan when you first started - if so what worked and what didn't?

Yes, we did. It was long. I still have it somewhere I think. We had no idea what we were doing and neither of us had ever run a business before. It was 2007 and so there was talk of recession at the time, so we partly felt that no matter what we wrote we might end up as part of the "new businesses that fail in the first three years" statistics!

So we probably didn't take it very seriously. It took us about eight years to get some external help from a business coach, who made us focus prioritise and follow through. It was mainly a list of clients we could go after and a long list of those we couldn't really touch for six months.

What worked originally?

Tony and I didn't get sued – so that's good.

- Patience and persistence: Living off savings for a while and not spending much money helped lots when the recession came – since we didn't make a fee for over six months.
- Patience AND frugality took us through a difficult year (together with a bunch of really loyal clients who paid us on time to help our cash flow. Aside from that, our first 12 months was good enough to carry us through. We had a famine on corporate finance jobs and didn't get a corporate role come through for 18 months, until around October 2009 when three of them came along like buses – were emailed in by DLA Piper and Eversheds at 5pm on a Friday when Tony was on holiday.
- Professionalism; human touch, which resulted in a lot of loyalty from our previous clients,

What's working now?

We've had an amazing start. I've completely changed the business plan. And we are way ahead of where we were in the old business. We have doubled our turnover in the first six months, and that's based on existing clients (who are still with us) but new ones seeking us out. It's really exciting.

I wanted to develop what I thought was a more sustainable business model for the next ten years. Recruitment has changed a lot in the 20 years I have been in the industry, particularly in the latter half of that. Part of me was fed up working on a contingent basis for clients. My view is that if you don't work for a client on an exclusive basis, you don't really have a client. You have a lottery and nobody gets any service.

Let me explain. It's all about 'fill rate' and the dichotomy of working on a contingent basis versus being exclusively retained and the effect those things have on service levels and client satisfaction. And ultimately the effectiveness of the recruitment project.

The first one is 'Fill Rate': In my career, I have filled virtually all the roles I have been retained on (the exceptions are those roles that got cancelled or put on ice). Retaining us means we have to fill it, because the client has paid us money before we have filled the position. They have shown us some commitment and we will do the same for them. It creates a pressure to perform, and we are totally comfortable with that. In the last seven years, we have filled every role in that category. By contrast at Florit Brooke, we filled contingent roles on a ratio of one in five. That's not a good business model, since logic states you are wasting your time for 4/5ths of the week. Who wants to feel they are wasting 80% of their time at work? That's not very motivating for anyone – clients, management, and consultants. The fill ratio is even worse in private practice. I'd say it's no better than one in ten, but some people I have spoken to would say it's lower than that.

The second is the service level: Being retained, has an added dimension for me in that it effectively replicates the solicitor-client relationship I was used to as a professional lawyer in practice. Whether you are a lawyer, or an accountant or a coach, as a professional, you expect to be retained one-on-one. Clients expect that. You wouldn't expect to be advised by multiple firms on the same aspects of the same deal. Nobody questions that. However in recruitment the level of service clients get from contingent recruiters (working concurrently) has slid low, as the fees have slid lower since they are not sure which roles they are going to fill, so they spread themselves very thinly, when the client won't commit to some form of exclusive relationship. As a result, some respected names in recruitment globally call this a race to the bottom. It's a vicious circle, clients get no service because recruiters have too much to do in trying to service too many clients, so that results in further downward pressure on fees. The service isn't valued because increasingly there is nothing to value. For mainstream roles, Talent Acquisition Managers (TAM's) are doing a very good job in filling their own roles – and why wouldn't they? It makes total sense – particularly at lower levels in law firms. Here a TAM can add considerable value when roles are relatively easy to fill. However for in-house legal role the TAMs can come up against a problem, in that those TAMs aren't engaging with lawyers on a daily basis like their counterparts in law firms. So they find it harder to recruit, with the obvious exceptions of Apple or Google, where people are falling over themselves to work for those sorts of brands. Ultimately, I didn't want to run around chasing my tail in the hope of filling one role in five, or worse. I want to do this for another ten years and I want it to be enjoyable for my clients and my consultants, and for each project to be successful for the clients.

Our business model turns traditional recruitment on its head. Our mantra is to make lasting placements, and we do everything in our power to bring this about:

- **McQuaig**: Our use of mental agility assessments helps to get the 'fit' right from the outset. That's free to clients – so they don't have to use their own, or wait until the second interview. This means they get much more information on candidates from the outset.

- **Coaching**: Once a client has appointed a lawyer, the appointee can benefit from a package of executive coaching – this helps them navigate the challenges in their first 100 days. As a former in-house lawyer yourself, Ann, you'll know that without it, not everyone takes to working in-house like a duck to water. Similarly a change of sectors, or moving up a level in a new company, it not without its challenges, and our coaching (independent) helps to embed people.
- **Guarantee**: If a client has followed our procedure, and for some rare reason (and it is rare) it does not work, we will fill the role again for free. That's a guarantee that lasts 12 months. So it's a no-brainer. Terms and conditions apply, obviously!

Are these different from your competitors and why (with examples)?

I'm not too sure what my competitors are doing to be honest. Most of the networking I do within the industry is with non-competing recruiters, sharing ideas and best practice from each of our respective industries.

In the industry there is a split between retained and non-retained work, and there's seemingly a new recruitment business born every day across the UK.

What has been your greatest success to date?

Besides my marriage, finding the courage to take the leap and start from scratch again.

Where do you see the threats for your business?

Interesting question. I think the biggest threats really come from within (things like your personal health both physical and mental, and it's important to take control of these).

Outside those, other threats are things you tend not to be able to control and very often you have to embrace the opportunities that come with them. For example, In 1999 when Bernard Howard started totallylegal.com, some people thought that was the end of legal recruitment. Fast forward half a decade and LinkedIn caused the same kind of reaction. But both have been game changers for a lot of businesses, and it's what you do with the threats that count.

Some of the biggest threats that are on the horizon, such as AI and

ML, are also game changers for everyone. The people who succeed are the ones who manage to harness the power of these machines and robots, and become early adopters.

What is your personal brand? Name your top three qualities, which enable you to run a unique legal practice.

Starting with the end in mind. See our Mission. Seeking first to understand another person, before seeking to be understood. We focus on combining the ingredients to make long-lasting placements and on the rare occasion that things go wrong within the first year, we put them right.

Is there anything specific you do to manage the quality of service?

Taking feedback.

What interpersonal skills are important to be successful with your type of Clients?

Being inquisitive. Asking open questions. Listening more than we talk. I think that's the same for any professional adviser in business.

Added to that, having a genuine interest in people, careers and developing relationships.

Marketing online (websites, Twitter, Facebook, Instagram, LinkedIn, YouTube or other)?

Some of that is 'work-in-progress'. I think that Facebook (personal) and LinkedIn (professional) have the edge among professionals.

I'm not convinced by Twitter. It's not making much money, and I find it rather shallow and distracting unless you're a celebrity.

Instagram isn't something I have really pursued yet – I think it's more consumer brand territory.

Our marketing is predominantly via LinkedIn, website and our clients, recommending other clients when we do a good job.

Do you have a digital strategy?

Yes, it's being developed. There are several strands to it which all inter-relate, and take up a lot of my time. Therefore I need to focus on just one at a time, such as in-bound leads, or life gets way too complicated. And having all my marketing being measurable in terms of ROI.

Offline marketing

I am considering when to outsource this to some people I already know, who are waiting for me to push the button. It will depend on when I expand with more people.
I have stopped doing sponsorship of events like in the past – as its not that cost effective.

How do you lead and manage your team. Have you had any training about leadership and management? What would you say is your best/worst quality?

I'm very lucky in as much as my team have worked with me for such a long time that I know they are experienced enough to be left to manage themselves on a day to day basis. They understand the long-term vision of what we want to achieve and how we want to do it, and I see them living the values we set our compass by. So, aside from some periodic checks on direction, and updates on projects, and sharing ideas, my team is relatively 'low touch', precisely because of their experience and the fact that none of us has lost sight of the mission.

In management, very little formal training. I think all business owners get a massive shock when they start a business. It's singularly the hardest thing you'll ever do, and you have to learn and prioritise as you go along, and learn from your mistakes. The need for training arises in stages, depending on your objectives. I am really receptive to learning opportunities, am surrounded by a good network of people I trust who are more than happy to dispense advice – in fact, even when I've not asked for it! I live in Yorkshire after all!

Best – empathetic, supportive, caring, understanding, loyal (has always "got your back"), also technical recruitment knowledge is the best I've worked with in 15 years – so my team tell me.

Worst – I need to be more resilient when we get knockbacks or hit roadblocks; and need to let go more and not be a perfectionist. I know that I sometimes overthink things – however, that's partly the product of being a lawyer and looking out for "what might go wrong", and trying to avoid it. Getting things wrong (which happens to us all) can make you overly cautious, but good reputations are easily lost it pays to focus on some of the finer details. I know I also need to "get out of my own way" and delegate stuff sooner. I'm working on getting that balance right. I've seen it third hand when speaking to senior in-house lawyers working for owner managed businesses – they report that the founders sometimes have trouble letting go. I guess there's a control freak in all of us to a greater or lesser extent.

Do you have a plan for personal development/business development?

Yes! It's not formal, but I'd encourage everyone to continually be looking for ways to improve themselves. It's always been something I've taken personal responsibility for – even when employed. I can probably summarise it as 'defy the odds' and 'step up' and do something every day that scares you.

What are your greatest team successes and challenges?

Aside from operational things like filling some jobs that other recruiters hadn't been able to fill and doubling our previous turnover in year 1 of the new business, I think our successes lie in our personal relationships. Both inside and outside the firm. We make an effort to understand one another, being open and supportive with each other on a daily basis, and not taking ourselves too seriously – we laugh at ourselves often. One of the team told me recently 'We all have our different styles of working and we all get on; and I don't think that can be underestimated'.

This means that we are all experienced professionals who successfully re-booted an old business model by changing the things we didn't like about it, and making improvements to our offering to clients, which, so far, has been a real success.

In terms of challenges, all businesses have 'growing pains' and we are no exception. One of the biggest challenges for us all, as individuals can be to stay resilient and positive when there are knock-backs and hurdles. The feeling was that, as a team, we generally pull together, but that we each continually need to be mindful of how we respond to challenges and the way our response affects other people.

Where do you see your business going in the next three years?

Number of options I am contemplating. But I am not sure they will happen in the next three years. My focus for the next three years is to become the go-to business for in-house legal recruitment and executive search for in-house lawyers in the UK, from GC level right down the chain.

Further options would be to:

1. Scale the existing business by going international, but staying in our niche, and/or
2. Develop a new one – either one which is allied to our existing clients (so that might be to develop other vertical markets where

our clients have recruitment challenges. So it might be compatible with things that are further down the chain of existing areas we focus on at senior level – so HR, Compliance, Risk, Company Secretaries and Governance (which is as big as the in-house legal market on its own). Or other new areas focused more on a particular economic sector: such as FinTech, or Tech generally.

APPENDIX A

RESOURCES TO ENABLE YOU TO MASTER YOUR BUSINESS SKILLS TO SERVE MORE CLIENTS PROFITABLY

INTRODUCTION

Given business skills should be life long learning this Appendix contains references to my blogs and details of my training and coaching. It is split into different parts to enable you to develop those essential skills to overcome the challenges that you face on your business or working life journey. Some of this material is covered in this book and is referenced in the box at the end of each part, and some is not.

WHERE TO START?

Do you need to take time out to create or review your business vision and strategy to turn your passion and expertise into a business?

The **Business Brilliance Blueprint © Programme** starts with a business strategy day to do just that. Yesterday's tools will not secure a prosperous future for your business. This Programme is designed for business owners to better understand the changing legal and business landscapes and to create and implement a strategy that works for them.

'Good to take time out to focus on what's important to your business, now and in the future' Jane Winteringham, Managing Director Adel Wills

The Programme's first day sets you up with practical tools and current market information specific to your business to enable you to:

- Formulate your initial vision and strategy or drive forward existing ones to meet today's challenges.
- Identify who your ideal target clients are and which to focus on to achieve your growth goals.
- Review your products and services in the light of changing client demands and the AI systems including pricing tactics for retaining the right clients.
- Maximise your personal brand in your marketplace to demonstrate your credibility, as you will have clarity about your USP.
- Review your current digital and marketing plans to achieve your objectives.

You will leave with an action Plan for the next 12 months and have the option for coaching to support your implementation of that plan. This is often delivered as a stand-alone day or as part of the programme. *'Very personal towards our company not generic at all. It was interesting considering who our existing clients are and where we want to expand geographically. Enjoyed looking at ways to put different packages together for our clients.'* Jacqui and Daniel Swift, Swift HR & Legal.

Please note this day can be taken as a stand-alone day. Therefore for full details of this Programme for those want to cover all the bases of leading and developing a business please here is a link to the brochure: http://www.yorkshirecoursesforlawyers.co.uk/wp-content/uploads/2018/05/BBB_Brochure2018.pdf

For those further a field I have deliver a three-day **mini 'MBA' on business skills** for partners. *'I found the event extremely stimulating and everyone I have spoken to has told me how enjoyable and thought-provoking they found it.'* Andreas Neocleous Managing Partner Andreas Neocleous & Co.

> The above resources support the following subjects covered by these chapters: 1.1: Why practise your legal expertise as a business? 1.4: What are your dreams for your business? (Vision and business plans - do they help?) 2.1: Your core legal service(s). 2.2: Your main legal products. 2.3: Pricing and profitability. 3.1: Who are your clients and are there enough of them. 3.2: Reaching out to your 'ideal' clients. 3.3: How does your personal brand help you in your market place? 5.2: Strategic tools to get you started and keep you on track. 5.5: Gazing into the crystal ball - what do the Stars see for their business in the next three years. 5.6: Is running a legal business for you?

WHAT ARE YOUR CURRENT BUSINESS GAPS?

Do you have a vision and business plan but are not sure how to implement these?

Do you need to polish up your business development skills?

Do you hate networking and small talk?

Do you struggle with converting enquiries into instructions?

Is your LinkedIn profile so five years ago?

The following mini-workshops and/or coaching packages will enable you to answer the questions and master these issues:

- **A diagnostic workshop** specifically on getting more clients, which includes a strategic, networking plan. *'Ann has supported* *me with sessions on business development and "getting more clients". I found them really useful, in terms of identifying where my strengths and opportunities might be. Of course, ultimately it is down to me to go out and put it all into practice, but it really helps to have someone give you that confidence and direction.'* David Sillitoe, Partner Robinson Ralph.

- **Networking with Impact** is for you where you want to maximise your time and money. *'Tailored to our needs. Ann is a fantastic speaker'* Miranda Mortlock, Partner Burnett Barker Solicitors.

- **Turning enquires into instructions**, which provides you with communication tools to fast track the 'know-like-trust' relationship with potential clients at the enquiry stage. *'Usable techniques not just theory'* Robert Crampton, Consultant Rebian Solicitors.

- **LinkedIn training** *'tailored to specific needs. Practical, sensible, logical and clear – results driven'* Bill Barton, Managing Partner Barton Legal.

To whet your appetite for these proficiencies, here are four blogs relevant to business development that address common challenges for LinkedIn and building 'know-like-trust' in networking environments:

- http://www.yorkshirecoursesforlawyers.co.uk/wenceslas-time-you-reviewed-your-linkedin/
- http://www.yorkshirecoursesforlawyers.co.uk/how-to-gain-credibility-in-your-60-second-introduction-at-networking-events/
- http://www.yorkshirecoursesforlawyers.co.uk/three-simple-words-to-create-interesting-small-talk-at-networking-events/
- http://www.yorkshirecoursesforlawyers.co.uk/a-simple-technique-for-building-your-personal-reputation-capital/

The above resources support the following subjects covered by these chapters: 2.3: Pricing and profitability. 3.1: Who are your clients and are there enough of them. 3.2: Reaching out to your clients. 3.3: How does your personal brand help you in your market place?

WHAT ARE YOUR LEADERSHIP OR MANAGEMENT NEEDS?

Are you an effective leader and/or manager?

Are you struggling in this constantly changing landscape and don't know your limits?

Do you need to lead your business through the changing landscape?

Internal or external challenges can arise at any time and business success requires agile leaders who have a variety of methods of dealing effectively with these. Leadership training can teach you the essential skills that were missing from your legal training to-date to prepare for these. Whereas coaching provides you with support and techniques for implementing your knowledge in a practical way that enables you to thrive.

Here are three options for leadership training/coaching to enable you to reduce the pressure of leading when in charge:

1. A **customised one-on-one leadership**-training package aimed at managing partners/directors in situ. As you can read from the Star's stories, most ended up in this position without any training whatsoever. This can add extra strain to an already busy role. Good leadership can provide the direction towards the right goals for your business as well as inspiring others to follow you. *'My leadership skills have soared under her tutelage. Ann is an incredible asset to my business offering me advice and help in devising and achieving my growth plans. She goes out of her way to make sure that you achieve your best results.'* Noreen Khan, Managing Director Kaiser Solicitors.

2. A public leadership workshop called **'How to lead, influence and motivate – embracing modern day challenges in the workplace'** via MBL Seminars where you can learn about how to increase your personal impact as a leader with other professionals. This includes understanding the purpose and function of leadership to enable you to lead your business into a successful future. The dates can be found here: http://www.yorkshirecoursesforlawyers.co.uk/events/ *'Ann was an excellent speaker, very enthusiastic and engaging. Course was excellent and very interactive.'* Nicole Hirst, Partner. Pini Franco.

3. A challenge is that 'being in charge' can be very lonely and it is easy to be isolated and lose track of what's important. Also

managing partners/directors are constantly being asked to deliver legal work alongside running their business. **A leadership coaching package** which is totally tailored to your circumstances enables you to focus on the art of motivating people to achieve your vision and values or could be on developing new business growth plans. A quick way to gain the power of insight into your leadership style and strengths is to take the MiRo leadership assessment. This will inform your leadership action plans going forward. Here is the link to more information on MiRo: http://www.yorkshirecoursesforlawyers.co.uk/miro/

For those at the start of their leadership journey here is a blog aimed at you:
https://www.yorkshirecoursesforlawyers.co.uk/how-do-you-lead-when-you-are-not-in-charge/

> The above resources support the following subjects covered by these chapters: 1.2: What skills and qualities do you need? 5.1. Make change your friend, 5.2 Strategic tools to get you started and keep you on track and 5.3 Why leadership is important for developing your business. 5.5: Gazing into the crystal ball - what do the Stars see for their business in the next three years.

Have you suddenly been entrusted with a team?

Do you know how to build a team?

Is your team dysfunctional?

Leading and managing partners has sometimes been described as 'herding cats'. Fellow directors and partners have different skill sets and ensuring that you bring everyone into new ways of working can be challenging. This is where the **'Partner Master Class'** series of lunchtime workshops for those based in Yorkshire, comes into its own.

There is a range of themes, which can be chosen on a pick, and mix basis to fill in any business gaps of your senior people. It is also linked to the SRA Solicitor Competencies for those organisations, which use this system. *'Straight forward, practical guidance'* Amanda Coates Partner Coates & Co. Click here for more details; https://www.yorkshirecoursesforlawyers.co.uk/sra_masterclasses/

I deliver specifically designed **team workshops to cover your departmental team's current challenges** when these are preventing a cohesive approach and performance. This can also increase employee engagement and reduce friction and staff turnover, which increase the costs to your business. The right consistent leadership or management approach can increase the productivity of your teams. Law firm culture does not have a good press and effective leadership and team training can improve culture to everyone's benefit.

Topics normally covered to overcome challenges in:

- **Building a cohesive team**, especially when it is new or there are changes to the members. Most of the Stars mentioned this as their number one challenge.
- **Productivity**. Showing your team how to play to their strengths to empower them and enable them to perform the their best.
- **Communication** such as understanding different styles and assertive techniques to promote collaborative team working and boost morale of your team.
- **Business development** including marketing and networking. *'Interactive involvement on Ann from questions raised.'* Philip Partington Director Virtuoso Legal.
- **Resilience** under stress of demanding clients and tight timetables.
- Understanding and using the change curve so you and the team can thrive in changing times. *'I enjoyed the chance to think about behaviours and managing change.'* Jane Riley, Partner Kerseys.
- Optional **MiRo team assessments** are available which will provide you and the team with insights that will enable the team to improve performance and ensure smooth communication.

One of the trials of a manager and of team effectiveness is lack of engaging team meetings. Here is my mini-series on team meetings that shows you techniques to handle a range of issues. I also enclose a link to my blog on appraising staff, as this is another area managers struggle with. Here are the links:

- http://www.yorkshirecoursesforlawyers.co.uk/what-is-the-point-of-your-team-meetings/
- http://www.yorkshirecoursesforlawyers.co.uk/make-your-team-meetings-work-for-you-planning-and-preparing
- http://www.yorkshirecoursesforlawyers.co.uk/make-your-team-meetings-work-for-you-executing-and-following-up/
- http://www.yorkshirecoursesforlawyers.co.uk/eight-difficult-behaviours-in-team-meetings-and-how-to-deal-with-them/

- http://www.yorkshirecoursesforlawyers.co.uk/eight-difficult-behaviours-in-team-meetings-and-how-to-deal-with-them/
- http://www.yorkshirecoursesforlawyers.co.uk/appraising-your-staff-appraisals-are-your-meetings-successful-or-stressful/

Chapters 5.1 Make change your friend. 5.4 Good people equals a good team - not necessarily.

WHERE ARE YOUR INTERPERSONAL SKILLS?

Are you resilient?

How good are you, and your team, at managing stress?

Do you know how mindfulness can help you?

Do you need to boost your self-confidence?

To address these areas try 'An introduction to mindfulness and stress management for lawyers'. This workshop has tips and techniques to increase your resilience to thrive as a lawyer in busy office.' *'Definitely life changing'* Alison Gray, Managing Partner Kirbys Solicitors. Click here: https://www.yorkshirecoursesforlawyers.co.uk/mindfulness-stress-management-workshop/

Self-confidence is an interesting concept. It is unusual if it is a constant, especially in a changing and challenging environment. Most lawyers starting their own businesses prefer a boost as they immediately find themselves out of their comfort or knowledge zone. This can lead to doubting their abilities to move into new endeavours.

Therefore I offer coaching and training on self-confidence to suit different learning styles:

- If you want to learn how to increase your confidence with other professionals then the workshop **'Boosting your Confidence – A guide for professionals'** via MBL seminars in Leeds and London would be perfect for you. You will learn quick and effective techniques to turn your 'inner critic' to inner cool' and communicate confidently in various different types of situations. For dates click here; http://www.yorkshirecoursesforlawyers.co.uk/events/
- If you prefer to have a personal customised solution for you I can

supply **coaching packages** on self-confidence to provide practical tools to be able to access your confidence in any situation and tame your 'inner demons'. *'I would highly recommend Ann to anyone wanting to gain confidence and take the next step in their legal career.'* Jodie Hill Managing Partner Thrive Law

Until I see you on my workshop here are three blogs on mindfulness, one on 'how to build your resilience' one on 'why lawyers feel guilty' and one 'is your desire to be perfect:

- http://www.yorkshirecoursesforlawyers.co.uk/an-introduction-to-mindfulness-for-lawyers-part-1/ This introduced the first core concept of 'being present' and my clients found that it helped them to spot when they moved from evaluating the future to being obsessed with the 'what ifs' and the impact of that on their performance.
- http://www.yorkshirecoursesforlawyers.co.uk/an-introduction-to-mindfulness-part-2/ This second blog provides insights to the concept of acknowledgement and acceptance. This puts you in a more resilient and effective Mindset.
- http://www.yorkshirecoursesforlawyers.co.uk/an-introduction-to-mindfulness-for-lawyers-part-3/ the final blog provides insights into how detachment can assist you in uncertain times.
- http://www.yorkshirecoursesforlawyers.co.uk/how-to-build-your-resilience-as-a-lawyer/
- https://www.yorkshirecoursesforlawyers.co.uk/why-do-lawyers-feel-guilty-at-work/
- http://www.yorkshirecoursesforlawyers.co.uk/is-your-desire-to-be-perfect-driving-you-into-the-impostor-syndrome/

The above resources support the following subjects covered by these chapters: 1.1. The dangers of chasing Perfection – the imposter syndrome. 1.2. What skills and qualities do I need – So I can't set up in business until I have self-confidence? 4.2. Managing the 'highs and lows'

WHAT SUPPORT DO YOU NEED?

This is a reminder because as Tom Peter's says *'the only competitive advantage you have is to learn faster than anyone else'.*

A fast track method to increase your effectiveness in business is working with a coach, who will support and challenge you in equal measure. If you are wondering if or how to engage a coach, and don't know what to expect, then these two blogs are for you. The first one explores how best to choose a coach and the second lists the benefits that lawyers have experienced from coaching:

- http://www.yorkshirecoursesforlawyers.co.uk/coaching-you-cant-read-the-label-from-inside-the-jar/
- http://www.yorkshirecoursesforlawyers.co.uk/you-cant-read-the-label-from-inside-the-jar-part-2/

'Even before I engaged Ann's services, as her student it was clear that she was eager for me to succeed in launching my new law firm, in what were challenging circumstances. As my coach we had enjoyable, thought-provoking, weekly coaching sessions. What I got out of it, most of all, was a goal-setting mentality. I commend Ann to you.' Andrew Gray, Managing Partner Truth Legal

The above resource is covered in Chapter 1.2: What skills and qualities do you need to start?

N.B. This information was correct at the time of printing and my blog posts are continually updated. For the latest see https://www.yorkshirecoursesforlawyers.co.uk/blog/

ABOUT THE AUTHOR

Ann Page is a Top 100 lawyer who enjoyed a successful 28-year career as an in-house lawyer, predominately in the banking sector. She has played an active part in various committees of the Law Society including being Chair of the Commerce and Industry Group. Since 2003 Ann has trained nearly 7000 lawyers in business, leadership, management and interpersonal skills. Ann has written two other books: 'Managing External Legal Resources' and 'The In-house lawyer's Tool Kit'. Her website is **www.yorkshirecoursesforlawyers.co.uk**

If you want to know more about Ann, her business journey can be found on page 357.